FROM TRENTON TO YORKTOWN

OSPREY
PUBLISHING

This book is respectfully dedicated to the fond memory of Charles B. Baxley (1952–2024), southern historian, tireless preservationist of Revolutionary War sites, and warm friend.

Fortiter in re, suaviter in modo

JOHN R. MAASS

FROM
TRENTON
TO
YORKTOWN

TURNING POINTS OF
THE REVOLUTIONARY WAR

OSPREY
PUBLISHING

OSPREY PUBLISHING
Bloomsbury Publishing Plc
Kemp House, Chawley Park, Cumnor Hill, Oxford OX2 9PH, UK
29 Earlsfort Terrace, Dublin 2, Ireland
1385 Broadway, 5th Floor, New York, NY 10018, USA
E-mail: info@ospreypublishing.com
www.ospreypublishing.com

OSPREY is a trademark of Osprey Publishing Ltd

First published in Great Britain in 2025

A catalog record for this book is available from the British Library.

ISBN: HB 9781472863751; eBook 9781472863737; ePDF 9781472863782; XML 9781472863775;
Audio 9781472863768

25 26 27 28 29 10 9 8 7 6 5 4 3 2 1

Maps by www.bounford.com
Index by Mark Swift

Typeset by Deanta Global Publishing Services, Chennai, India
Printed and bound in Great Britain by CPI (Group) UK Ltd, Croydon CR0 4YY

MIX
Paper | Supporting
responsible forestry
FSC® C171272

Osprey Publishing supports the Woodland Trust, the UK's leading woodland conservation charity.

To find out more about our authors and books visit www.ospreypublishing.com. Here you will find
extracts, author interviews, details of forthcoming events and the option to sign up for our newsletter.

Contents

List of Illustrations

PLATE SECTION ILLUSTRATIONS

'The Battle of Princeton,' by John Trumbull. On 1st August 1977, General George Washington surprised and defeated British forces at Princeton, New Jersey. (Getty Images)

Engraved portrait of George Washington from the original picture painted by William Dunlap. (Getty Images)

Washington and his army crossing the Delaware River on December 25, 1776, prior to the Battle of Trenton. (Getty Images)

'26th December 1776: The Battle of Trenton' by John Trumbull. (Getty Images)

Site of Washington's troops' Christmas night crossing of the Delaware from Pennsylvania to New Jersey (distant shore). (Author's collection)

Maj Gen Horatio Gates, the victorious American general at Saratoga. (Getty Images)

British Lt Gen John Burgoyne surrenders his army to Maj Gen Horatio Gates at Saratoga in 1777. (Getty Images)

British Lt Gen John Burgoyne. (Getty Images)

American Maj Gen Benedict Arnold wounded at the second Battle of Saratoga, 1777. (Getty Images)

The American position on Bemus Heights, overlooking the British line of advance towards Albany. (Author's collection)

Regulations for the Order and Discipline of the Troops of the United States, also known as von Steuben's Blue Book. (Society of the Cincinnati)

American troops march to Valley Forge, Pennsylvania, in 1777. (Getty Images)

Washington inspecting his soldiers' huts at the 1777–1778 Valley Forge encampment. (Getty Images)

Baron von Steuben, instrumental in improving the American army during the winter at Valley Forge, 1778. (Author's collection)

Recreated winter huts at Valley Forge National Historical Park. (Getty Images)

Maj Gen Nathanael Greene, American commander at the Battle of Guilford Courthourse, 1781. (Getty Images)

Engraving of the Battle of the Cowpens, South Carolina, 1781 by Thure de Thulstrup. (Getty Images)

Lt Col Banastre Tarleton, an aggressive British cavalry leader in the Southern theater. (Getty Images)

Lt Gen Charles, Lord Cornwallis, commander of the British army at the bloody Battle of Guilford Courthouse, 1781. (Getty Images)

Greene's troops crossing the Dan River in Virginia to escape Cornwallis's pursuit. (Getty Images)

Maj Gen, Gilbert du Motier, the Marquis de Lafayette, a valuable French ally and Washington's key lieutenant in the 1781 Yorktown campaign. (Getty Images)

Washington's headquarters during the siege of Yorktown, 1781. (Getty Images)

French Admiral François Joseph Paul, Comte de Grasse. (Getty Images)

'Surrender of Lord Cornwallis,' by John Trumbull, depicting the British surrender at Yorktown to American and French forces. (Getty Images)

List of Maps

Acknowledgements

An author is never the sole creator of his or her book. Many people helped me in this endeavor, offered their advice, and happily led me to avoid mistakes. I particularly thank my agent Roger S. Williams, who embraced my turning points concept from the beginning, though with a pronounced and understandable bias towards Trenton and Princeton. I'm also grateful for several folks who read and commented on chapter drafts, including William "Larry" Kidder, Mark Maloy, Mark Lender, Eric Schnitzer, Tim Arnold, David Preston, Ricardo Herrera, and Bryan Hockensmith. Others providing invaluable assistance include Kevin Weddle, John Buchanan, Lawrence Babits, Larrie Ferriero, Todd Braisted, Gary Ecelbarger, David Hogan, Bob Thompson, J. Britt McCarley, Steven Raush, Glenn Williams, Ireland Young, Charles Baxley, Christian Fearer, William Welsch, Bruce Franklin, David Silbey, Wayne Lee, Thomas Crecca, Bruce Venter, William Halligan, David and Zoe Anne Cagle, The Society of the Cincinnati, Joan Halford, Edward Lengel, Rachel Nellis. I also thank my beloved family – Molly, Eileen, and Charlie Maass – for their enthusiastic support as I spent many evenings and weekends reading, writing, and rewriting about the Revolutionary War. It is my hope that each of these fine folks enjoys this book.

Introduction: The Wildfires of History

What is meant by the concept of a "turning point" in a military campaign or a war when writing and reading military history? Similarly, what is a "decisive battle," which writers seem perpetually attracted to in their books and articles, mostly pitched to popular audiences rather than academics? Not every dramatic military event can be a turning point or decisive, yet there is no consensus definition of either term. One recent historian posits a reasonable definition of a key battle as "a period of intense, continuous or near-continuous fighting over a relatively short period in a distinct geographical area, ending usually, but not always, in a clear result – victory or defeat."[1] Add to this historical dilemma the common tendency for local enthusiasts with a vested interest in regional small-scale engagements to good-naturedly stress – or overemphasize – their importance.

Currently, making exaggerated claims of significance in book titles or subtitles is a common trend regarding prominent *and* obscure themes. There are numerous books on battles or other military events that "saved the Revolution," or the Union, or America. Other book subjects "changed American history," "doomed slavery," or "saved democracy." Many books now cover events that "changed the world forever," or "shaped the course of history." We can also read that America or the world or civilization were changed or saved by a book, Ireland, capitalism, Christianity, plumbers, Maine, the Byzantines, Winston Churchill, the 1960s, the AK-47 rifle, New York City, auto mechanics, a camping trip, a Boston bookseller, an English trading company, and Mason jars. Apparently, the Irish are not only lucky but also very influential (and busy) because they not only "saved civilization," they also "won the American Revolution." And we dare not overlook the Scots, who apparently "invented the modern world, and created our world and everything in it," all the while being "western Europe's poorest country."

Military history has many examples of these kinds of embellished titles. Some battles "defined World War II," a mission "changed the war in the Pacific," and a new fighter plane "saved the Allies" in the Second World War.

One may also read that Col John Glover's remarkable Massachusetts regiment saved Washington's army during the Revolutionary War, "shaped the country," and "formed the navy," while the 1st Maryland Regiment "changed the course of the Revolution."[2] And an innumerable number of titles are about untold or unknown stories. One author has six publications with one of those two words in his subtitles. This is not to devalue these books; many of the questionable claims were likely invented and insisted on by publishers understandably conscious of marketing needs, while other title assertions may be in part true.

Commonly seen at chain bookstores and online are oversized, discounted books detailing "decisive battles" in military history, many with lavish color illustrations and glossy maps. A typical example of these often reductive "great battles" type of coffee table books is *The Greatest Battles in History: An Encyclopedia of Classic Warfare from Megiddo to Waterloo*. Published in 2017, its short introduction does not define "greatest battles" or explain why the battles chosen were included. The book also makes odd choices of which battles to include, such as the inexplicable inclusion of the obscure battle of Paulus Hook in 1779, a small engagement in the American Revolution without significant strategic implications. It hardly merits a claim to be one of "the greatest."[3]

Another example is Charles Messenger's *Wars that Changed the World* (2019), which ambitiously attempts to examine "the defining conflicts of world history," but the author also posits that "all wars change history," so his "selection of 25 conflicts" from the 5th century BC until the current decade is quite limited for such a long time span and a broad claim. To be fair, "any selection of battles of course involves debate," as prolific military historian Jeremy Black has observed. Likewise, renowned scholar Richard Overy, in *A History of War in 100 Battles*, writes that "choosing just 100 battles from recorded history is a challenge," and that "any century of battles has to be arbitrary." One wonders then how truly decisive the battles he chose were if they were picked, as he admits, indiscriminately.[4]

British historian Edward S. Creasy was most likely to have been the first modern writer to publish a study of important engagements in *The Fifteen Decisive Battles of the World: From Marathon to Waterloo* (1851). "There are some battles," Creasy asserted, "which claim our attention, independently of the moral worth of the combatants, on account of their enduring importance." Creasy's contention suggests a more thoughtful definition of what decisive battles and crucial turning points really are. Creasy called them engagements that, if they "had come to a different termination," would not have made us "who we are." He goes on to quote the early influential English historian Henry Hallam (1777–1859), who wrote that a battle was decisive if "a contrary event would have essentially varied the drama of the world in all its subsequent scenes." Creasy, like later scholars, also made the point that "no two historical inquirers would entirely agree in their lists of the Decisive Battles of the World." His standard of what to include was quite simple: decisive battles are those "collisions" that "may give an impulse which will sway the fortunes of successive generations of mankind."[5]

One hundred years later, to give just one example, popular historian Fletcher Pratt, writing in the 1950s, offered a similar definition of a decisive or important battle. "The war in which the battle took place," he held, "must itself have decided something, must really mark one of those turning points after which things would have been a good deal different if the decision had gone in the other direction." Pratt also excluded battles and campaigns that, "although decisive, could hardly have had any other result, given the forces engaged."[6] But weren't they decisive nonetheless?

The idea of "the great battle" resulting in momentous results is not as easy to qualify or categorize as Creasy and Pratt suggested. In fact, historians over the past several decades have taken various views on how to study campaigns and engagements that were significant turning points.

Winston Churchill, deploring the tendency he saw among academics to deemphasize the importance of battles, wrote in his 1930s biography of his illustrious ancestor and brilliant general, the Duke of Marlborough, that

> Battles are the principal milestones in secular history. Modern opinion resents this uninspiring truth, and historians often treat the decisions in the field as incidents in the dramas of politics and diplomacy. But great battles, won or lost, change the entire course of events, create new standards of values, new moods, new atmospheres, in armies and in nations, to which all must conform.[7]

Professor Michael Mandelbaum of the Johns Hopkins School of Advanced International Studies makes a similar point more recently. "The concept of the decisive battle, once a familiar one, has gone out of fashion, especially in the United States," he writes. That is no doubt because, for "all the occasions on which American troops have been ordered into harm's way in recent decades, they have fought relatively few battles and no decisive ones." Nevertheless, he adds that "wars can change the course of history and great battles often decide wars." The fact that this last observation needs to be made in Mandelbaum's article tells us much about the focus of military history today.[8]

In this vein, Boston University historian Cathal Nolan writes that although "many modern historians are indifferent to military history" and "some are openly hostile ... war remains hugely important in explaining much history and wider human affairs. Indeed, it may be the most important thing." He writes that "armed conflict is too important to be reduced to bromides 'that war doesn't solve anything.'" Quite true. War in history *has*, in fact, decided many truly important things, and major wars "have altered the deep course of world history." Yet he also claims that "battles did not usually decide the major wars of the modern era that decided most everything else." Nolan holds that attrition in warfare replaced decisive battles won in an afternoon or at most a couple of days. "Exhaustion of morale and materiel, rather than finality through battles, marks the endgame of many wars. Even of most wars. Almost always of wars among the major powers in any era."[9] Any era? Nolan's overly thesis-driven argument, excluding evidence that

does not fit his thesis, quickly breaks down with numerous examples from military history. For instance, the fact that he barely mentions the American Civil War and thus ignores such battles as the clash at Antietam in a 700-page book should give every reader pause.[10]

Nolan also writes in a 2017 article that

> War is thus far more than a strung-together tale of key battles. Yet, traditional military history presented battles as fulcrum moments where empires rose or fell in a day, and most people still think that wars are won that way, in an hour or an afternoon of blood and bone. Or perhaps two or three. We must understand the deeper game, not look only to the scoring. That is hard to do because battles are so seductive.[11]

Nolan mistakenly uses a twentieth century lens to look at battles as if all of them were like the Somme, Verdun, or Stalingrad. Eighteenth-century warfare was certainly different. The scale of the battles, the size of the armies, and the politics involved in the 1700s meant that battles had significant consequences and often led to significant results. One need only consider Culloden, Poltava, Quebec, and Saratoga to counter his argument.

Not all scholars – or warriors – see battles today as did Churchill or Nolan. As British scholar Hew Strachan notes in his introduction to the recent Oxford University Press *Great Battles* series:

> For those who practice war in the 21st century, the idea of a 'great battle' can seem no more than the echo of the remote past ... contemporary military doctrine downplays the idea of victory, arguing that wars end by negotiation, not by the smashing of an enemy, army or navy. Indeed, it erodes the very division between war and peace, and with it, the aspiration to fight a culminating 'great battle.'[12]

This may be true. Other recent interpretations are not so clear. In a muddled conclusion written by the UK's National Army Museum, we read that the 1690 battle of the Boyne in County Meath, Ireland, was both "militarily indecisive" and "a turning point with far-reaching consequences," a battle that "has taken on a great historical and cultural significance."[13] Could it be both?

Battles, it seems, have gone out of fashion in some historical circles as meaningful events. "Until a few decades ago," writes Professor Yuval Noah Harari, "battles were the historical events *par excellence*, and 'decisive battles' served as axes around which many histories of the world revolved." Not so today. Harari finds that "among the vast majority of world historians, battles are decidedly out of favor. It is extremely unfashionable today to ascribe global or even regional historical developments to the outcome of this or that battle." He then notes that "at least some battles were indeed capable of changing the course of history. However, under close scrutiny it transpires that only few battles really deserve the appellation 'decisive.'"[14] This conclusion applies to the American War of Independence. Similarly, Cathal Nolan correctly concludes that "a war is usually deemed to have been decisive when some important strategic and political goal was achieved in arms, gaining a lasting advantage that secured one side's key values and hard interests." He writes that "if the term 'decisive battle' is to illuminate rather than obscure military history, it must be used more narrowly, to mean singular victories, or defeats that created lasting strategic change, leading directly or ultimately to the decision in the war that frames them." This, too, applies to America's Revolutionary War, in which few military events can be said to be decisive turning points that lead to victory.[15]

Harari's definition of decisive battle is how I approach the key turning points of the long destructive war for American independence. In this book, turning points refer to battles, campaigns, sieges and other military events that are decisive *and* result in significant change that alters the trajectory of the conflict toward the war's outcome. Nolan's conclusion that "we are drawn to celebrate battles because they seem to deliver a *decision*" is true. In the case of the Revolutionary War, I identify and explore five military turning points that were the most significant events that led to American victory and independence in 1783. These five are the battles of Trenton and Princeton; the sprawling Saratoga campaign in the New York wilderness; the suffering Continental army's 1777–78 winter encampment at Valley Forge; the events leading up to and including the bloody battle of Guilford Courthouse; and the culminating Yorktown campaign (including the naval actions off the Virginia Capes). A concluding chapter will discuss why many of the war's most famous battles, while important, were not the key turning points that, in Churchill's words, "change[d] the entire course of events." Those wanting more elaboration on this last point before reading about the war's turning points may wish to read my concluding chapter first.

To be sure, many battles in world military history had important outcomes, but one must ask if they acted as catalysts for significant changes in the course of a conflict that led to victory. For example, the South African battle of Rorke's Drift in 1879 during the Anglo-Zulu War is widely known among military history students and scholars (and film buffs). About 150 British hard-pressed soldiers bravely fought off repeated attacks by thousands of charging Zulu warriors for a dozen hours. Although the heroic British victory was a morale boost to the public, the fighting had little strategic importance.

In a larger example, the battle of Agincourt, fought in 1415 during the Hundred Years' War, was a bloody English victory over French forces in the countryside south of Calais. Though quite well known today, in part due to Shakespeare's play *Henry V*, and potentially the only medieval battle (some) Americans could name, it was not a turning point in the war, as historian Anne Curry has recently written. "Agincourt has not been seen as a decisive battle, [and] rightly so," she concludes. "Since the [French] king and Dauphine were not present at the battle, government continued as before ... Whilst prisoners had been taken, none were so significant that they would force the French crown to rush to negotiate and pay ransoms." In hindsight modern historians see that "Agincourt was a moral but not a strategic triumph," and the clash "had not brought [Henry] advantage save in terms of military damage to and demoralization of the French."[16] Thus, Agincourt was not a turning point in that it had little lasting effect.

Some historians, including Alan Forrest, make a similar assessment of the Battle of Waterloo. He writes that the famous 1815 battle "finally brought peace to Europe ... ended Napoleon's dreams of hegemony, and [that] went on to form a central plank in Britain's military identity during the Victorian era." The French defeat "led to Napoleon's second abdication, and established the Duke of Wellington's reputation as one of the greatest British military commanders of the modern era." But was it "a great battle from a military perspective?"[17] More than a few modern historians, as well as Napoleon's enemies at the time, would answer "no." Forrest states that Waterloo "was, of course, a decisive victory, the battle that inflicted Napoleon's final defeat ... [and] brought an end to a generation of war, in which millions of soldiers lost their lives, civil society had been undermined, and agriculture and industry across Europe have been disrupted to serve the war economy." But he also notes that "across Europe Waterloo's status was more uncertain." A huge number of German-speaking soldiers fought beside Wellington's British regiments at Waterloo on the left flank, but Forrest says "in German eyes, [the 1814 battle of] Leipzig was the really significant encounter, the moment which signaled Napoleon's defeat ... Leipzig, not Waterloo, would remain the vital battle for Germany, and for Europe." Many in France would have said the turning point of the Napoleonic Wars "had come earlier, in the Peninsular War, or during the 1812 Russian Campaign, at Borodino," or, indeed, at Leipzig. Forrest points out that "the war was already lost with the 1814 campaign and the surrender of Paris; Napoleon had abdicated, and been exiled to Elba; the Bourbons returned to the throne; and the European order had been restored at the Congress of Vienna" through June 1815.[18]

By the time of the Battle of Waterloo, the Allied forces "so heavily outnumbered Napoleon's army as to make the outcome of the campaign a foregone conclusion." Waterloo "was not in itself critical to the outcome of the war," Forrest asserts, and the "odds that faced the French in 1815 were overwhelming. If not at Waterloo, the defeat would've happened elsewhere."[19] Thus, many argue that the great battle was not a turning point, but a bloody coda on a war that had already been decided.

Another example exists in a 17th-century battle fought near York, England. Oliver Cromwell's famous victory at Marston Moor on July 2, 1644, during the English Civil War was the largest battle of that conflict; Cromwell called it a great victory for the Parliamentary forces over the Royalists, and it was. But while some historians have argued that the battle was a major blow to the Royalists in the north of England as it significantly increased the reputation of Cromwell (who was the cavalry commander that day for Parliament's cause) and secured their control of the region, others disagree. Some modern scholars do not regard the battle as a turning point, as Parliamentary victory was not assured afterwards, particularly since two defeats at Lostwithiel and the Second Battle of Newbury soon afterwards were major setbacks to their cause.

One may also turn to the American Civil War to see that many of its large-scale battles were indecisive, even if they seemed to have important immediate results. President Abraham Lincoln was often frustrated by Union army defeats but also by northern victories not followed by aggressive pursuit of the southern enemy to annihilate them, such as after Antietam and Gettysburg. Confederate leaders, too, bemoaned "empty" victories that did not result in destroying defeated enemies during or immediately after a battle. Gen Robert E. Lee's Confederate army soundly defeated Union forces in 1863 at Chancellorsville, Virginia, which is often called his tactical masterpiece and greatest victory, but his subordinate generals could not maneuver their exhausted troops effectively to crush the defeated Yankees against the Rapidan and Rappahannock rivers behind them and allowed them to escape. The Confederacy simply could not afford to suffer 12,000 casualties in a three-day battle and not destroy the enemy. Therefore, while costly for the defeated Union army in terms of casualties, Lee's daring victory was hollow and indecisive. Likewise, the furious battle of Chickamauga fought in Georgia later that year was another bloody slugging match that, although an unquestionable tactical triumph for the Confederates, did not bring the war any closer to a southern victory in its aftermath.

These three examples are not to imply that there are few battles or campaigns that *were* turning points in other conflicts. Wolfe's triumph at Quebec in 1759 made British victory over France in the Seven Years' War assured, with lasting worldwide consequences, including the French removal from Canada, Britain's financial crisis, and the coming of the American Revolution in 1775. Japan's crushing victory at the sea battle of Tsushima in 1905 "brought about the end of the Russo-Japanese War and affected dramatically the two belligerents' geopolitical vision and naval outlook for decades."[20] The grinding attritional warfare amidst the smoke and rubble at Stalingrad was the crucial turning point of the bitter Soviet–German War that began in 1942 – if not of World War II in Europe. This brutal months-long urban slugfest repulsed the

German offensive to crush the Soviet Union and obtain Hitler's key goal of *Lebensraum*. It also dealt a fatal blow to Nazi Germany's hopes for military victory in the East. Many more examples could of course be suggested.

Classicist and military historian Victor Davis Hanson has written much about the importance of battles in history. "Battles really are the wildfires of history," he observes in *Ripples of Battle* (2003), "out of which the survivors float like embers and then land to burn far beyond the original conflagration." He urges his readers to "go back to the past to see precisely how such calamities affected now lost worlds – and yet still influence us today." Hanson adds that "battles ... alter history for centuries in a way other events cannot."[21] In this vein, this book attempts to show which events of the Revolutionary War were crucial to achieving American independence and altered history for going on two and a half centuries.

As Creasy noted, not every writer or reader will have the same turning points on their lists, and I expect some readers will disagree with a few of my selections and even how many I have made. It is my intention to show in five chapters why I consider the military events I have suggested to be turning points in the Revolutionary War, as I defined this term earlier. My concept for this book is to provoke debate and discussion among those interested in the young country's founding conflict. But as discussion and debate may ensue, I hope too that no matter how readers react to and engage with my argument, we never forget, in British military historian Hew Strachan's words, that "however rich and splendid the cultural legacy of a great battle, it was won and lost by fighting, by killing and being killed."[22]

Ten Crucial Days: The Battles of Trenton and Princeton, 1776–77

The decisive winter battles of Trenton and Princeton in 1776 and 1777 have many iconic moments of the Revolutionary War associated with them in public memory. The miserable, muddy trudge across northern New Jersey by rebel soldiers after the American defeats around New York City; George Washington and his troops crossing the icy Delaware River on Christmas night; the surging Americans' surprise morning victory over the hired German troops at Trenton; the daring, midnight march away from Trenton by Washington's soldiers that fooled the redcoats; and Washington's bold attack and heroic charge that rallied the troops at the bloody battle of Princeton not only encouraged Patriots at the time but continue to impress and enthrall Americans today. They contributed to the first decisive turning point of the revolutionary struggle that kept the depleted Continental Army in the field and the flickering cause of independence alive.

The origins of these important victories that kept the American cause alive go back to the military operations several months earlier around New York City in the spring and summer of 1776. After the British forces under Maj Gen William Howe evacuated Boston in March 1776, besieged by the rebellious Americans' amateur army, General and commander in chief George Washington shifted his newly formed Continental Army south to New York and its environs. Both Howe and Washington quickly turned their attention to the city

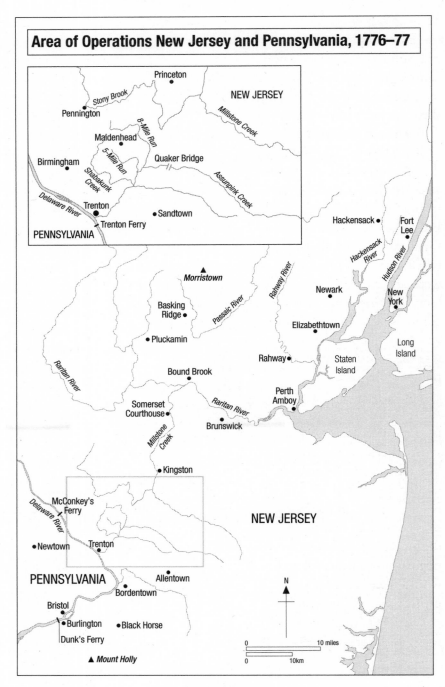

Area of Operations New Jersey and Pennsylvania, 1776–77

MAP I

on Manhattan Island, a strategic port with a fine sheltered harbor. For the British, the city would be a base for future operations, while the Hudson (North) River would provide an excellent avenue for northern campaigns deep into New York's wilderness interior. It was also home to numerous supportive Loyalists. No wonder it became the focus of their operations.

Born into an aristocratic family in 1729 and an illegitimate uncle of King George III, William Howe had seen extensive military service during the French and Indian War (1754–83) in America. Just a month after the War of Independence broke out in the colonies Howe arrived in Boston in May 1775 (along with generals Henry Clinton and John Burgoyne), then commanded the bloody assaults against the colonists' fortifications on Breed's (Bunker) Hill on June 17.* Although the rebels retreated in confusion from the grassy knoll, Howe's casualties were shockingly heavy, especially among the British officers. When Gen Thomas Gage, the British commander in chief in the seaboard colonies, returned to London in October, Howe superseded him and was subsequently formally appointed to the top role in April 1776. He was the "most formidable enemy America has," Washington wrote late the previous year.[1]

The general's older brother also served in America, the heralded Adm Lord Richard Howe, who commanded the Royal Navy in colonial waters starting in July 1776. Both brothers were sympathetic to the colonies' plight and served in America dutifully, but reluctantly. Moreover, in May 1776, at their request, they were dually appointed by the British Crown as peace commissioners to reach some kind of reunion with the king's American subjects, short of recognizing complete independence. As it turned out, the limited diplomatic parameters stipulated by the king's ministers as a basis for negotiating a peaceful reconciliation were those the American leaders would never accept, especially after independence had been declared on July 4 in Philadelphia.

Once Washington was certain that New York would be the primary focus of the enemy's campaign that year, he began to send his regiments

*The battle was fought at Breed's Hill, but was later named for nearby Bunker Hill.

on March 14 to prepare defenses there. He set out for the city on April 4, worried about the chances the Continental Congress could support New York's defenses logistically and his amateur army's capacity to resist the expected British attack. The anxious general wrote in late April that inadequate efforts to defend the strategic city would have "fatal and alarming consequences" for the American cause.[2]

In the summer of 1776, George Washington was still inexperienced in commanding a large army, although he began his military career two decades earlier on the colonial frontier. As a 22-year-old, he had assumed command of Virginia's provincial forces in 1754 when the French and Indian War ignited in the remote Ohio country. During this wilderness conflict young Washington struggled to raise troops, supply and equip them, and drill them to fight. He was largely unsuccessful. In his first campaign, he had to surrender the primitive Fort Necessity in western Pennsylvania to the French on July 4, 1754. The next year he unwisely provoked a testy relationship with Virginia's much older lieutenant governor, Robert Dinwiddie, and resigned his commission in frustration over rank in early 1755. He then served capably and bravely in Maj Gen Edward Braddock's disastrous campaign against Fort Duquesne (modern Pittsburgh) that summer, narrowly escaping death in disorienting combat in the smoky forest battle that wiped out most of the British force. Then in 1758 he made a name for himself during Brig Gen John Forbes's grueling wilderness march that finally captured Fort Duquesne before he left military service. In these five years of trying backwoods fighting, young Washington never led large numbers of troops as he would beginning in 1775, and was only an overall campaign commander in 1754, when he had to ignominiously surrender Fort Necessity. All told, the war had been a conflict of mixed experiences for the Virginia colonel from Mount Vernon on the Potomac.

To defend New York in 1776, Washington eventually concentrated about 20,000 troops there, who were "much dispersed" at several posts separated by water on Manhattan, western Long Island, and in New Jersey.[3] All of these indifferently armed and equipped soldiers were vulnerable to enemy warships and amphibious landings by veteran British forces. Spreading out his inexperienced troops to defend

24

multiple locations was an unwise move, especially for untested soldiers, as Washington would soon come to see.

As American leaders anticipated, the Howe brothers sailed to New York from Halifax, Canada, on June 10, and landed their seasick troops on Staten Island on July 2. After a period of refitting in their camps, the army of 24,000 redcoats and Hessians – German hired troops shipped to America as reinforcements – then came ashore unopposed on western Long Island on August 22. Five days later Gen Howe launched a strong attack on the American defensive positions south of Brooklyn. His troops soundly defeated rebel forces with a devastating flank attack on August 27. It was, however, an incomplete victory. Howe's failure to aggressively follow up this success allowed Washington to withdraw his despondent soldiers from their defenses at Brooklyn to Manhattan by a stealthy nighttime evacuation on the foggy night of the 29th with collected boats rowed by Col John Glover's Massachusetts regiment of Marblehead seafarers and fisherman. When the British advanced against the American lines the next day, the surprised skirmishers found the trenches empty. This would not be the last time in 1776 Glover's experience that New England boatmen played a key role in Washington's operations.

Washington's bitter defeat on Long Island was only the beginning of a string of disheartening setbacks in the field for his poorly armed and equipped army, led by inexperienced officers. After Washington evacuated his troops from Brooklyn, Howe began an inexplicably slow-paced pursuit of the harried American forces, who took advantage of his lackadaisical chase. The British routed Patriot defenders with an amphibious assault at Kip's Bay on Manhattan's east side on September 15. The next day, elements of both armies fought at Harlem Heights near the north end of Manhattan, where the American army won a small victory against British forces that momentarily lifted the rebels' morale. But the lethargic Howe moved too slowly to cut off Washington's troops hurrying north to escape Manhattan Island.

The British now occupied New York City, while Washington had to keep moving his fatigued men farther north to avoid Howe's sluggish pursuit. His plan was to march his troops to the hilly Hudson Highlands, which would be easier to defend, but he had to hold off the enemy long enough to remove provisions and supplies from the village of White Plains, across King's Bridge in Westchester County. Seemingly every day troops began leaving the American army as their enlistments were up, or they simply deserted. Writing on September 25 from Harlem Heights to John Hancock, then President of the Continental Congress, Washington reported disconsolately that "we are now as it were, upon the eve of another dissolution of our Army," and warned his correspondent that "our cause will be lost."[4]

On October 17, Washington again withdrew his troops to avoid being flanked or encircled at Harlem Heights by British forces. At White Plains, the general made a stand on fortified high ground along the Bronx River to buy time to move the army's supplies to safety, but on October 28 a strong British frontal assault there forced the Americans to fall back before Howe could make another attack. By early November Washington decided to disperse his forces. He dispatched over 3,000 troops to Peekskill on the Hudson, about 25 miles to the north, under Brig Gen William Heath; 7,000 men under the eccentric Maj Gen Charles Lee ten miles northeast to North Castle; and sent 3,600 men led by Maj Gen Israel Putnam across the Hudson to Hackensack, New Jersey near Fort Lee. The British army then turned back to the south to New York's Fort George without further pressing Washington's army, once the American troops left their front.

The next two weeks would see two disasters for American arms due to the indecision and inexperience of their leaders. Earlier in the year, army engineers built a pair of large forts on the Hudson to prevent British warships from sailing up the river and getting in the rear of Manhattan's lower defenses. One post was Fort Washington, perched on high ground on the northwest side of the island. On the cliffs opposite this bastion was Fort Lee in New Jersey. Fort Washington was the last position occupied on Manhattan by American troops after the army left the island following the engagement at Harlem Heights. The fort was vulnerable to attack despite being situated on a high ridge and was difficult to support from Fort Lee. Moreover, Washington did not seem to have a sound reason for keeping an isolated post so close to the enemy. Against his better judgment, Washington kept the 2,800-man garrison in position upon assurances from Maj Gen Nathanael Greene, one of his principal lieutenants, that the fort could be held against an enemy assault. Greene was wrong. On November 16, a mixed force of British and Hessian troops stormed and captured the fort along with its defenders (many of whom would die miserably aboard prison ships in New York Harbor) and guns. It was a serious blow to the rebels' already desperate fortunes.

One of the most conspicuous Hessian officers that day was Col Johann Gottlieb Rall, a veteran brigade commander, whose men assaulted the fort from its steep northern approaches and accepted its surrender. Though no one could then have known it, Rall would figure prominently in six weeks as the commander at Trenton, which his troops garrisoned at the time.

Howe quickly followed the capture of Fort Washington by ordering an attack on Fort Lee led by Lt Gen Charles, Lord Cornwallis, whose 5,000 redcoats crossed the tidal river early on November 20. Washington had wisely ordered the vulnerable fort abandoned after the surrender of Fort Washington – he was not going to allow thousands of troops to be captured defending an outpost this time. Although most of the garrison managed to escape west to Hackensack led by the commander in chief, an enormous amount of invaluable supplies, arms, tents, artillery, ammunition, equipment, and 2,000 cattle were left behind in the frantic withdrawal, along with some 200 drunken American soldiers. It was yet another dispiriting American reverse, and this time it sent Washington's army of 3,000 discouraged men on a grueling autumn retreat across northern and central New Jersey.

On the following day, the troops resumed the march southwest, many having thrown away their equipment to lighten their load. During the cold evening of November 22, the column arrived at Newark, halting to take a defensive position on the far bank of the Passaic River. The Americans were followed by Cornwallis's redcoats who left Hackensack on the 26th, in an unhurried pursuit delayed by four days. As the enemy marched, they "spread desolation wherever they go," noted Greene, the "British and Hessian troops plunder without distinction."[5]

Howe had ordered Cornwallis to take charge of the troops chasing Washington's dwindling ranks for good reason. Just 37 years old, Cornwallis was already a seasoned officer, having served in the Seven

Years' War in Europe. As a Member of Parliament, he was a favorite of King George III, and had earned a promotion to major general in 1775. Arriving in America with the new rank of lieutenant general at Cape Fear on North Carolina's coast with reinforcements in February 1776, he and his troops later supported Howe's Long Island operations in August. Cornwallis was known as an officer attentive to the needs of his troops, and willing to share the hardships of active campaigning. Howe knew, of course, that Cornwallis was an aggressive leader – the perfect general to go after Washington's retreating columns.

The British force quickly made up for lost time so that on November 28, when Washington's harried column left Newark, Cornwallis's troops arrived there later the same day. On the following morning, Washington's weary soldiers stumbled in to Brunswick on the Raritan River and assumed defensive positions on the river's right bank. "We arrived ... broken down and fatigued – some without shoes, some had no shirts," wrote a Delaware officer. A Continental sergeant wrote that "the sufferings we endured is [sic] beyond description – no tent to cover us at night – exposed to cold and rain day and night – no food of any kind but a little raw flour."[6] For the Americans the situation looked bleak. On that day Washington wrote that "the situation of our Affairs [was] truly alarming." The general could only continue the retreat. He reported that his force was "by no means sufficient to make a stand against the Enemy, much superior in number, with the least probability of success."[7] One day later he advised John Hancock in Congress that "without a sufficient number of Men & Arms, [the British] progress can not be checked; At present our force is totally inadequate to any attempt."[8]

Not until December 1 did Cornwallis resume his pursuit of the disconsolate rebels from Newark to Brunswick in rain and high winds over muddy roads. By this time only about 2,000 men remained in Washington's camps due to desertion and the expiring enlistments of 2,000 American soldiers, who refused additional service; about 40 percent of his army left the ranks, although several hundred of these troops were New Jersey militiamen who continued to serve in the state during the campaign. "The loss of these troops at this critical time reduced [Washington] to the necessity [to] order retreat again," wrote

Greene a few days later. Hard-pressed, Washington's remaining soldiers disputed the attempts of Cornwallis's redcoats to force a crossing of the Raritan. Still, after sundown the Continental commander ordered his forces to continue their dolorous retreat toward Trenton. Washington wrote to Congress that he expected to fall back to the Delaware River and cross into Pennsylvania, as he was unable to stop the enemy's steady advance with his weakened, shrinking army. Many congressmen were alarmed, as Brunswick was the last adequately defensible position for Washington's troops to halt the enemy on the road to the Delaware. The general had stopped at several towns during the retreat – Hackensack, Newark, Rahway – each of which offered a water barrier as an obstacle to slow Cornwallis. But between the Raritan and the Delaware at Trenton – dangerously close to Philadelphia where Congress had been meeting – there were no significant rivers behind which the Continental Army could attempt to slow or halt the enemy's pursuit.[9]

Regardless of how his retreat alarmed Congress and the citizenry of Philadelphia, Washington and his troops had no choice but to continue their flight southwest to elude the much larger enemy army chasing them. The American column left Brunswick after damaging the bridge there and headed toward Princeton about 16 miles away. The redcoats marched into Brunswick on a rainy December 2. There the British pursuit stopped, as Howe had previously ordered Cornwallis to limit his advance to the Raritan River, so as not to move too far from supporting troops and supplies on the road back to New York. This halt allowed Washington's tired and hungry troops to reach Princeton unharried that morning, where they remained for several days.

At Brunswick Cornwallis halted his command for four days. Although his worn-out foot soldiers and dragoons (to say nothing of their mounts) surely welcomed the days of rest after their long trek of over 40 miles from Hackensack, this pause of the British pursuit has been criticized by historians, as well as British and Hessian officers on the spot, ever since. Cornwallis was often just hours behind Washington's troops on their retreat, and by December 2 the British outnumbered the Americans by about four to one. Should Cornwallis have ignored Howe's orders and pressed on to destroy what was left of Washington's weak command, which Greene called "a very pitiful Army"?[10] Routing or capturing

Washington's small army would likely have broken the back of the rebellion and forced Congress to scatter, especially with the string of defeats American forces had endured since the August battle on Long Island. It was a golden opportunity to crush the tired rebel soldiers on the run. Cornwallis would later ignore orders in the Carolinas to seize unanticipated opportunities to attack American forces in situations similar to that in which he now found himself. But here Cornwallis elected to stay put, allowing Washington – and likely the cause of independence – to escape destruction.

Perhaps the contradictory dual nature of the Howe brothers' tenure in America as both warriors and aspiring peacemakers contributed to the hesitancy of recently knighted Sir William Howe to push the pursuit aggressively. For each attempt the brothers made at leniency in 1776 to return rebels to the Crown's authority, the general and the admiral also launched attacks on American forces, whose homes and towns were then pillaged and burned. In the words of historian Andrew Jackson O'Shaughnessy, this was a "mixed system of war and conciliation."[11] At the very least this incongruous approach sent mixed signals to those Americans considering taking loyalty oaths, although hundreds of New Jersey men did sign the oaths hoping to avoid penalties and enemy plundering.

Howe, Cornwallis, and other Crown officers may also have pulled punches to avoid heavy casualties in battle. Well trained and equipped veteran troops were difficult to replace if killed, wounded, or captured. Howe later testified that he did "not wantonly commit his majesty's troops, where the object was inadequate" in the New Jersey campaign. His reluctance to finish off a beaten foe and his cautious advances when a prompt attack would have crushed the enemy became his *modus operandi* in late 1776. He delayed attacking Washington repeatedly from Brooklyn to White Plains. "I would not risk the loss that might have been sustained in the assault," Howe wrote. Then, after the fall of Fort Lee, as we have seen, he limited Cornwallis's pursuit of the rebels to reaching Brunswick.[12] Perhaps Howe's reluctance to deliver a knockout blow resulted from witnessing the horrific casualties the British suffered at the 1775 battle of Bunker Hill, where he commanded the redcoats' three bloody frontal assaults on the Patriots' breastworks. Howe himself concluded that "the success is too dearly bought" that June day. Heavy losses at Boston may have led him to avoid head on attacks and aggressive pursuits of the rebels thereafter, in what has been dubbed the "Bunker Hill effect."[13] More than one junior officer in the British army, especially among the Hessians, were surprised by the slow pace of the "chase" of Washington's column in New Jersey, and what appeared to be a reluctance to close with the enemy. A recent historian of Howe's service in the American war also finds that the general's conduct of the 1776 New York campaign and the "painfully deliberate" pursuit of Washington into New Jersey "had repeatedly given Washington time to digest unpalatable truths and take the necessary decisions to extricate his men from danger."[14]

During their cautious advance, the British were also concerned that a rumored Patriot force of several thousand men under Maj Gen Charles Lee was maneuvering to attack Cornwallis's column from the rear or on the flank. Lee's threat was regarded with great concern by Howe's senior lieutenants, who had some difficulty determining the Americans' precise location. Thus, perhaps to Howe the British army's pause at the Raritan River seemed prudent, even though local Loyalists urged Cornwallis to continue to chase Washington's outnumbered, ragged soldiers on the run and destroy them.

The aggressive Cornwallis quickly grew impatient with his limiting orders to halt his advance at Brunswick, so he sent a mounted courier racing to New York with an urgent plea for Howe to rescind the restrictions against more rapid operations. Howe rode from New York to meet with Cornwallis and arrived at the British camp on December 6. Almost immediately Howe ordered the pursuit to resume. Now less than a day's hard marching from bagging the fleeing enemy, British and Hessian troops quickly moved along the Princeton Road starting at 4pm. The brief respite for the soldiers of both armies was suddenly over.

Washington pushed his army to the ferry landing on the banks of the Delaware at Trenton, and on December 7 the general ordered the last of his troops to cross the river into Pennsylvania, a process that had begun as early as the 3rd. Several days beforehand Washington had ordered the English-born former British officer Col Richard Humpton of the 11th Pennsylvania Regiment to gather "through purchase, hiring, and confiscation" all boats and ferry barges he could find along the river and quickly move them to Trenton.[15] Once the soldiers, horses, and guns had crossed the river by the 8th, these boats were held upstream on the river's right bank to keep them away from the enemy. Now there were no means left for the British to chase what was left of the rebel forces when the redcoats arrived at Trenton that afternoon, just minutes after the American troops had cleared the town. The timing was so close that when advance elements of Howe's vanguard rushed into Trenton, they encountered anxious Loyalists who urged them to hurry and catch the last of the Americans pushing off in their boats. But Sir William could not be pressed into action. "Howe had let slip a major opportunity to win the war," a British historian concludes. More colorfully, a witty Virginia officer on the scene wrote that "General Howe had a mortgage on the rebel army for some time but had not yet foreclosed it." Nor would he.[16]

Looking back, Thomas Paine, still a soldier with the hard-pressed American forces in New Jersey, brilliantly summed up the army's plight up to this time in *The American Crisis*.

> With a handful of men, we sustained an orderly retreat for near 100 miles, brought off our ammunition, all of our field pieces, the greatest part of our stores, and had four rivers to pass. None can say that our retreat was precipitate, for we were near three weeks in performing it, that the country might have time to come in ... The sign of fear was not seen in our camp ... Once more we were again collected and collecting ... by perseverance and fortitude, we have the prospect of a glorious issue.[17]

To Howe it was obvious that Washington had evaded him at Trenton, at least for the time being, so the campaign was now over, in his mind. He and Cornwallis had chased Washington far beyond his original intent, Brunswick, and were no longer within a safe or effective distance to receive reinforcements and supplies from the New York area. Howe learned from Loyalist spies of the Americans' desperate condition, and naturally assumed he would wipe them out in the spring, or even sooner when the wide river froze over. Accordingly, the British commander in chief declared that his army would go into winter quarters on the 13th and began his long, cold ride back to New York two days later.

After Washington's fatigued soldiers finished crossing the Delaware to Pennsylvania on the 8th, he moved most of them to bleak camps away from the river for protection, around the village of Newtown, nine miles west of Trenton. "Two hours afterwards the British appeared on the opposite bank and cannonaded us," wrote a Delaware officer, "this was the crisis of American danger." A modern scholar of the British high command during the war concurs and calls the predicament "the lowest ebb of the Revolutionary cause."[18]

Near their Spartan encampments, American pickets closely watched the river crossings and ferry landings along 25 miles of the Delaware for two weeks, to guard against threatening enemy movements. Washington set up sectors along the riverfront to be guarded by several elements of his command – and stretched them too thin. From Yardley Ferry, six miles upstream from Trenton, four brigades of 2,400 Continentals secured the riverbank upstream to Coryell's Ferry, a span of about 11 miles. Guarding the Delaware opposite Trenton and Bordentown were 1,500 Pennsylvania militiamen under Brig Gen James Ewing, an experienced soldier and early advocate for independence from Great Britain. They were augmented by a small New Jersey militia force led by Brig Gen Philemon Dickinson, whose elegant home was at Trenton. Their orders from Washington were "to give every possible opposition to the Enemy, particularly at crossing the River" and to "give the earliest and most spirited opposition." Additionally, Washington, who had by this time developed an excellent widespread intelligence network of his own, urged Ewing to "spare no pains, nor cost, to gain information of the Enemys movements, and designs – whatever sums you pay to obtain this end I will chearfully refund."[19] Finally, in the southern riverside section Washington had the support of about 1,500 volunteer militiamen called the Philadelphia Associators, and 900 Continental soldiers positioned to defend a ten mile stretch of the river, all commanded by wealthy and well-educated Col John Cadwalader, a prominent local merchant and early advocate for independence whom Washington regarded as a military genius.

By December 12, Congress and many Philadelphians had fled the city, fearful of the looming British approach. They knew, as did Washington, that once the Delaware froze hard the British would be able to move troops across it against the American forces and the city. For weeks Washington had been repeatedly calling on several of his recalcitrant commanders to bring their troops south from New York and reinforce him and protect Philadelphia, but without success. Maj Gen Horatio Gates, a former British officer and veteran of the Seven Years' War, had about 9,000 men far to the north at Fort Ticonderoga on Lake Champlain, and Gen Lee and Brig Gen William Heath commanded 11,000 troops between them at North Castle and Peekskill, respectively.

The crisis Washington faced after the fall of Fort Lee brought to light an awkward command situation involving Gen Lee, the American army's second in command. The English-born Lee was an eccentric officer, but due to his early successes in Virginia and South Carolina in 1776, and his extensive previous service as a British officer, many American leaders were impressed by him, including a deferential George Washington. Born in 1732, Lee entered military service at age 14. Described by a contemporary as "plain in his person even to ugliness," Lee lived an unconventional lifestyle incompatible with polite society. He was difficult to get along with and had a penchant for biting sarcasm. Politically he came to side with the Whigs, grew increasingly more radical, and moved permanently to America in 1773. He offered his military services to Congress in 1775, was an early advocate of American independence, and was enthusiastically welcomed by the army.[20]

Once Washington had marched out of the American camps north of Manhattan back on November 12 with 4,000 to 5,000 troops bound for Fort Lee, Gen Lee was left in command of North Castle with about 7,000 men. When Fort Lee fell and the garrison fled south, Washington sent urgent requests to Lee to bring his men south to join him. Washington's pleas started a frantic three-week period during which Lee insubordinately evaded his superior's calls for help – not orders – with coy maneuvering and stalling. He came to think of his command as a separate army, not strictly beholden to Washington's authority. Although he finally crossed his battalions over the Hudson River on December 2, he still would not commit to joining Washington; rather, he suggested operating independently in the British rear as a guerilla force. This was the detachment that British intelligence had trouble locating and assessing the strength of, which, as noted above, contributed to their slow pursuit in New Jersey of the Americans to the Delaware.

Meanwhile Lee, rarely one to hold his opinions to himself, corresponded secretly with Washington's trusted adjutant general Lt Col Joseph Reed, a smart New Jersey native and graduate of the college later called Princeton University and London's Middle Temple for legal training. In their private letters both men criticized the commander in chief for indecision when holding Fort Washington and taking advice from the amateur soldier Nathanael Greene. "An indecisive mind is one of the greatest misfortunes that can befall an army," Reed wrote critically to Lee about his chief. Washington inadvertently learned of this surreptitious criticism but kept his temper in check. He repeatedly sought to have Lee and his regiments join him, but curiously did not order him to do so directly until December 14. By then, events had transpired to rid an exasperated Washington of Lee's recalcitrance. On December 13, Lee was captured by British dragoons at Basking Ridge, New Jersey, at a house imprudently too far from his army's camps, just after he dispatched a letter to Gates deploring Washington as "damnably deficient." Immediately after Lee's capture his successor, Maj Gen John Sullivan, promptly brought Lee's 2,000 remaining soldiers to Washington's camps by December 22. At the same time, Gates arrived with only 600 men left from the 2,000 weary soldiers that had started their long march south from Fort Ticonderoga on the New York frontier. Feigning illness, Gates went off to visit Congress at Baltimore, refusing a command to serve with Washington. Gates soon made known his displeasure with Washington as commander of the army to several sympathetic congressmen (as he would do again later in the war).[21]

While Washington concentrated all the troops he could near Trenton, British forces in late December showed few signs of active offensive operations against the American army and the Patriot militia in Pennsylvania. Once Howe suspended the chase of the rebel army across the Delaware in mid-December, he ordered thousands of his troops to occupy a line of New Jersey villages along the main road from Hackensack to Trenton. While some of his regiments remained at New York, others encamped at Newark, Brunswick, Elizabethtown, Princeton, Trenton, Bordentown, and several other New Jersey towns, all under the command of Maj Gen James Grant whose headquarters were at Brunswick. Howe adopted this plan to enable the scattered battalions and brigades to live off the countryside rather than overburden his limited supplies at New York.

There was also the question of New Jersey's civilians. Thousands of them were disheartened by the American army's reverses beginning on Long Island and decided to take advantage of an amnesty offer valid for 60 days, proclaimed on November 30 by Gen Howe in his role as peace commissioner. These people had to be protected from the rebels; placing garrisons across the northern part of the state would do that and encourage others to swear allegiance to King George III as well. This volatile situation also meant that there were fewer men answering the Patriots' call to militia service to fight the British invaders.

Howe's plan to deploy troops in cantonments across New Jersey was risky, however, as even he admitted at the time. "The chain [of outposts], I own, is rather too extensive," but he added that logistical necessity and winter weather forced him to adopt this measure. His men were now spread apart in villages across 95 miles, so that each detachment was vulnerable to attacks and raids by militia forces or Washington's army. Moreover, having these separated garrisons live off the towns and countryside quickly turned into an unofficial license for marauding redcoats and Hessians to plunder the local population without bothering to distinguish between New Jersey Patriots and Loyalists. Howe also failed to recognize that he did not have enough soldiers to adequately guard the string of posts *and* New York. Part of the troop shortage stemmed from his plan to capture Rhode Island for use as a naval base. He sent an ill-timed expedition under Sir Henry Clinton for this purpose on December 1 with 6,000 troops, which then deprived him of a significant part of his army at a crucial moment with New Jersey largely occupied and Washington hard pressed. Prior to embarking on the seaborne expedition, the ever nettlesome Clinton,

Sentiment at a stand and ready to run thro different Channels; the People refusing to supply the Army under various pretenses, but evidently from a disaffection to the Cause and the [depreciated] Currency are combined evils calculated to pave the way for General Howe's advances.[29]

The army was in a deplorable condition, which worsened all month. A Delaware officer remembered that "we lay amongst the leaves without tents or blankets, laying down with our feet to the fire ... it was very cold. We had meat but no bread. We had nothing to cook with but our ramrods."[30] No wonder there were so many deserters and soldiers on the sick rolls.

Even Washington at some points in the somber weeks of December seemed doubtful of the future success of American arms. To his younger brother Samuel in far off Virginia, Washington confided "between you and me I think our Affairs are in a very bad way not so much from the Apprehension of Genl Howes Army as from the defection of New York, New Jersey, and Pennsylvania" from the cause. In the same letter he also wrote "if every nerve is not straind to recruit the New Army with all possible Expedition I think the game is pretty near up."[31]

Yet for all these dark doubts, the continental commander could not suppress optimism for a victorious campaign or battle against the enemy. He apparently started contemplating striking the British before his troops had crossed the Delaware into Pennsylvania. At least by December 14, even before he was reinforced by the long missing troops of Lee and Gates, he wrote optimistically that "if we can collect our forces speedily, I should hope we may effect something of importance."[32] This seed of an idea for a bold strike on the enemy led to what two prominent historians of the war call "one of the most spectacular military adventures in American history."[33] Perhaps it was also, argues eminent scholar Don Higginbotham, "his only really brilliant stroke of the war."[34] It was crucially needed as December came to an end.

And Washington knew he *had* to win a victory soon. Always in the general's mind was that many of his soldiers' enlistments expired at midnight on December 31, when they would be entitled to leave the army at once. Of course, this meant that if he were going to strike the enemy in New Jersey, he had to do so quickly while he still had an army. Moreover, a victory – maybe even just a successful raid on an enemy outpost – might prevent more discouraged civilians from taking loyalty oaths offered by the Howes and switching their allegiances, and get the militia to muster in support of the Continentals. "In short the conduct of the Jerseys, has been most Infamous," Washington bitterly observed. "Instead of turning out to defend their Country and affording aid to our Army they are making their Submissions as fast as they can … the few Militia that were in Arms disbanded themselves or slunk off in such a manner upon the approach of danger as to leave us quite unsupported, & to make the best shift we could without them."[35]

There was also a more personal concern for Washington that drove him to contemplate a bold stoke before the year ended: his own reputation had to be salvaged. From his service of five years as a young Virginia provincial officer on the frontier in the French and Indian War, Washington demonstrated a petulant, prickly sense of honor and a strict adherence to military decorum that he observed as Continental commander as well. He was a vigilant guardian of his professional reputation. The esteem in which other leaders held him was of inestimable importance to him. Now he looked for an opportunity to redeem the defeats around New York City and his humiliating retreat from Fort Lee to the Delaware River. He knew of grumblings in Congress about his string of setbacks, and that some of his own officers – Reed, Gates, and Lee among others – and the rank and file criticized him in secret. For example, army physician Benjamin Rush observed that "a distrust has crept in among the troops of the abilities of some of our general officers high in command," doubtlessly including Washington.[36]

None of these difficulties stopped the Virginia general from trying a throw of the dice in cold, late December. After the beleaguered American army moved into Pennsylvania, Washington developed a plan to take the war to the enemy in a daring surprise attack, encouraged by his officers including Joseph Reed and militia leaders Samuel Griffin (a Virginia Continental officer) and John Cadwalader. "We are all of the opinion my dear General," Reed wrote to his chief, "that something must be attempted to revive our expiring credit" and that "some

Enterprize must be undertaken in our present Circumstances or we must give up the Cause." In other words, the people, Congress, and its financial creditors wanted to see the army do *something* to fight back.[37]

Washington and his senior officers recognized that nearby Trenton was a promising target. It was close to the American positions, was not within easy supporting distance of enemy encampments at Princeton and Bordentown, and much of the surrounding populace had become alienated by the Hessian garrison's destructive looting and confiscation of supplies. No doubt his thinking was based in part on his intelligence network in New Jersey, but simply put it was his best opportunity to win a critical victory his army and the new country desperately needed.

Given what modern readers know of the winter operation's successful outcome, it may be difficult to appreciate what a bold and risky venture this was ... or even desperate. Washington's small army was poorly armed and equipped, suffering from illnesses, and many of his ragged men lacked winter clothing and shoes. They had been beaten in the field, forced to trudge across New Jersey, and had barely escaped destruction by the British army. And now with so many troops set to go home on January 1, he would not have enough men in the ranks afterwards to even contemplate an attack. Would there even be an army on New Year's Day? As the general wrote to Col Reed on December 23, "necessity, dire necessity will – nay must justify any [Attempt]."[38]

Once generals Sullivan and Gates finally brought their footsore troops to the Newtown area camps joined by Pennsylvania militia companies, Washington's force grew to about 6,000 hungry men by December 22. Over the next few days at councils of war, Washington and his lieutenants developed an audacious plan to strike at Trenton. Washington decided that "Christmas day at Night, one hour before day [on the 26th] is the time fixed upon for our Attempt on Trenton." Already thinking ahead, he added that he "orderd our Men to be provided with three days Provisions ready Cook'd; with which, and their Blankets they are to March, for if we are successful which heaven grant & other Circumstances favour we may push on" and even make an additional attack, likely at Princeton.[39]

By Christmas Eve, a confident Washington and his officers decided to attack Trenton early on the morning of December 26, approaching the town from several directions. With the main force, on the 25th Washington would move the army of about 2,400 troops, including its artillery, across the Delaware River at McConkey's Ferry, nine miles upstream from Trenton. Once in New Jersey, the strike force would divide into two columns. One column under Gen Sullivan would march south on the River Road to approach Trenton from the west. This detachment included the brigades of Col John Glover, Col Paul Dudley Sargent, and Brigadier Gen Arthur St Clair, a Scotsman with previous service in the British army, including the siege of Quebec in 1759. Gen Greene's column, consisting of the brigades of generals Adam Stephen, Lord Stirling, Hugh Mercer, and Matthias Alexis Roche de Fermoy, a French volunteer officer, would veer off to the east and take up a parallel line of march to arrive at Trenton from the north. Simultaneously Ewing was to cross the river opposite Trenton with New Jersey and Pennsylvania militia to take up a blocking position just south of the town along Assunpink Creek, to prevent any fleeing Hessians from escaping the town. Finally, farther south Cadwalader's 1,500 Philadelphia Associators and 800 New England Continentals commanded by the sickly Col Daniel Hitchcock would cross into New Jersey from Bristol to distract the Hessian forces located at Bordentown and Mount Holly. They would "create a diversion" so that Col von Donop would not send relief to Trenton. Washington's plan was highly ambitious, required careful coordination in foul weather, and was subject to unpredictable changes, delays, and circumstances. The audacious operation called for multiple columns of American troops to act in sync with each other without modern communications over miles of ground held by enemy forces. It was certainly daring if not unrealistic. Coordinating the movements of several elements to arrive simultaneously at the objective is a difficult task for professional soldiers in any era. But "these are the times that try men's souls," wrote volunteer Thomas Paine in an essay called *The American Crisis*, published and widely read at this time. "The summer soldier and the sunshine patriot will, in this crisis, shrink from the service of his country; but he that stands it now deserves the love and thanks of man and woman." Washington and his officers were surely hoping they had winter soldiers in their cold and hungry ranks.[40]

In preparation for the movement toward Trenton, Washington issued his final orders. Late on Christmas Day, he wrote to Cadwalader "I am determined, as the night is favourable, to cross the River, & make the attack upon Trenton in the Morning. If you can do nothing real, at least create as great a diversion as possible."[41] In Washington's mind, this was it.

On the afternoon of Christmas Day, the American forces began to move steadily to the river crossings as a clear day gradually turned into a bitter evening storm of snow, rain, and ice for hours to come. It was "one of the severest Hails and rain storms I ever saw," declared Nathanael Greene.[42] Washington was with the main force crossing at McConkey's Ferry, where the river was about 1,000 feet wide. The challenging effort to get tired soldiers, skittish mounts, and indispensable field artillery pieces over the river at night was planned and directed by the young Henry Knox. "Floating ice in the river made the labor almost incredible," Knox later recalled. Previously, Washington had ordered boats to be collected and hidden upriver; now they were ordered down to the ferry landing for the army to cross. These included about 16 sturdy flat-bottomed craft, 30 to 65 feet in length and three feet deep, called Durham boats, muscled across the river by a crew using long poles and used for heavy cargo on the river. Glover's Marblehead Regiment of Massachusetts seamen, which had saved the army from disaster at Brooklyn that summer, the 27th Continental Regiment, and other men from other units manned the boats that wet, freezing night.[43]

Washington and his struggling soldiers crossing the frozen Delaware has become an iconic American image, evoking the enormous risk and effort needed to succeed. "Perseverance accomplished what at first seemed impossible," Knox later concluded.[44] Another American officer described the harrowing scene: "Troops began to cross about sunset, but the force of the current, the sharpness of the frost, the darkness of the night, the ice, which made during the operation, and a high wind, rendered the passage of the river extremely difficult," James Wilkinson wrote. A young Massachusetts fifer also described the daunting conditions: "after a while it rained, hailed, snowed, and froze, and at the same time blew a perfect hurricane."[45]

The fire-lit river crossing was indeed a success as Washington stoically watched the progress from the New Jersey side – but the relentless storm put the operation behind schedule. It was early in the new day before the troops and cannons set out toward Trenton in the bitter cold, about four hours distant. "The quantity of Ice, made that Night, impeded the passage of Boats so much, that it was three OClock before the Artillery could all be got over, and near four, before the Troops took up their line of march," the general later reported.[46] Washington would have to launch his assault in the pale light of the blustery winter day, but there was no turning back. "I determined to push on at all Events," he reported. Some soldiers marched without shoes, while two men froze to death during pauses in the advance. Not only was the plan off schedule, but Washington could not know that the two lower river crossings he had ordered were unsuccessful due to ice jams along the far riverbank that impeded landing the troops and guns. Although Ewing had been sending small "hit and run" patrols across the river for days to harass the Hessians around Trenton, on the morning of December 26, he was not able to land any of his militia close to town to block an enemy escape.

South of the objective, Cadwalader attempted to cross the river from his camps at Bristol, but this column was only able to land part of the force, and without artillery, due to the ice in the river and along the far bank. His hopeful plan to strike and distract the Hessians at Mount Holly was dashed.

But the main force pushed on. Around 6am at the crossroads called Birmingham, Washington's command split into the two columns under generals Sullivan and Greene to approach Trenton as planned in what one soldier called "a secret expedition." Washington accompanied the latter as snow and ice continued to fall and be blown by high winds. At about 7:30am, Greene's vanguard encountered a small party of Virginia troops coming from the direction of Trenton, where they had attacked an enemy outpost only hours beforehand. Although Washington was furious for fear that Rall's garrison was alerted to danger, the episode would soon work in his favor, as the Hessians now thought a rumored attack was already over.[47]

The German garrison quartered in the riverside town had not been idle despite the bad weather. Much of what has been written about the battle of Trenton has depicted Col Rall as a gregarious drunkard who gambled and imbibed too much on Christmas night, ignored intelligence about a looming attack by the Americans, and whose brigade was unprepared to fight on the 26th. While Rall did hold the American army in low regard, called them "nothing but a lot of farmers," and had contemptuously refused to erect earthworks at key places around the town, the Hessian colonel was not idle that snowy day. He did in fact drink and play cards on Christmas night, but Rall was a long-serving professional soldier who had his men frequently patrol the area around Trenton for days on end looking for enemy threats. He frequently alerted his superiors to his regiments' perilously exposed position, but von Donop and Grant refused to heed his warnings or reinforce him. Many nights he ordered his soldiers to sleep in their uniforms and accoutrements, with their muskets nearby so they would be ready to quickly form up and resist a sudden attack. The exhausted Hessians, writes a close student of the campaign, "felt they were still on campaign, not standing down in winter quarters." Constant patrolling, long nights, and two weeks of harassment by militia, combined with the harsh storm, affected Hessian readiness that night much more than any holiday celebrations.[48]

At about 8am, Greene's brigades marching on the Pennington Road arrived at the enemy picket posts just north of town and quickly deployed in line. A few minutes later Washington and his troops could hear the booming of artillery from the direction of the River Road off to their right. "General Washington's face lighted up instantly" when he heard the guns. Even he must have been delightfully surprised that after a grueling nine-mile night march in a lashing winter storm on bad roads, his two attack columns had reached their objectives simultaneously as planned. Greene and Sullivan "exhibited the greatest proof of generalship by getting to their respective posts within 5 minutes of each other, tho' they had parted 4 miles from the Town, and took different Routes," wrote an impressed Virginia officer on the snowy march. "The difficulty of [the troops] passing the River in a very severe Night, and their March thro' a violent Storm of Snow and Hail, did not in the least abate their Ardour," Washington proudly noted. He described the operation two days later to John Hancock. "As the Divisions had nearly the same distance to march," he reported, "I ordered each of them, immediately upon forcing out the [Hessian] Guards, to push directly into the Town, that they might charge the Enemy before they had time to form." Washington wrote that the advance German sentinels "behaved very well, keeping up a constant retreating fire from behind Houses," but were pushed back into Trenton's streets by the charging American battalions. A few hundred Hessian soldiers from the town managed to cross the bridge over Assunpink Creek and escape south before Sullivan rushed forward two of his brigades to capture the crossing. Washington had also wisely sent troops on the north side of town to block a potential escape route on the Princeton Road. Trenton was now surrounded.[49]

Perhaps the key to the American army's triumphant morning was the prompt seizure by Greene's troops of high ground on the north side of Trenton, at the heads of Queen and King Streets, where Washington posted himself. There newly promoted Henry Knox placed nine cannons to fire down the cobblestone streets. The young Bostonian understatedly wrote that the blasts of the American "cannons and howitzers ... in the twinkling of an eye, cleared the streets." Although the Hessians made two brave counterattacks against the Continentals, they were trapped. Rall suffered a mortal wound, and within an hour all three of his regiments surrendered. The Germans had 22 men killed, 83 wounded, and lost about 900 prisoners. Only four men in Washington's command were wounded, including the commanding general's young second cousin, Capt William Washington, and the plucky 18-year-old Lt James Monroe of Virginia (the future US president) who marched with one of the advance elements.[50]

Washington was elated. "This is a glorious day for our country," he was heard to say.[51] He would soon issue general orders in which he thanked "the Officers and soldiers for their spirited and gallant behavior at Trenton ... It is with inexpressible pleasure that he can declare, that he did not see a single instance of bad behavior in either officers or privates; and that if any fault could be found, it proceeded from a too great eagerness to push forward upon the Enemy."[52] Those who had crossed the river in the operation were to receive "a proportionate distribution" of the value of "all the Field pieces, the Arms, Accoutrements, Horses and everything else which was taken yesterday" as a reward. He proudly noted in a letter of the same day that "one thousand stand of arms, four standards & six pieces of brass artillery" had been captured, all quite valuable to the American army.[53]

Washington and his generals quickly decided after the enemy prisoners were secured and hustled across the icy river that the army could not remain at Trenton, since some of the Hessian escapees likely had already warned von Donop of the American victory. Greene urged Washington to pursue the Germans who had fled southward and to attack the enemy posts at Burlington and Bordentown. But Washington did not want to risk too much. He cited "the distressed situation of my Troops ... who had experienced the greatest fatigue in breaking a passage through the ice and all the Severities of rain, & Storm." Moreover, many of his jubilant soldiers were now quite drunk from consuming rum from enemy supplies captured in the town.[54]

Nevertheless, success often breeds dreams of further victories. Once back in Pennsylvania the general in chief wasted no time planning his next move. "I have called a meeting of the General Officers to consult of what measures shall be next pursued," he wrote on the 27th, "we will try to concert a Plan & upon such principles as shall appear to promise success."[55] Washington concluded that he had to follow up the victory of the 26th with another offensive, lest the battle be taken as merely a sudden raid on an isolated enemy outpost. Moreover, hundreds of Continental Army soldiers would leave their dreary camps in just four days, so he had to act quickly. He also learned that day that Col Cadwalader had finally managed to cross his 1,500 militiamen over the ice-choked river into New Jersey, thinking that the main American army was still at Trenton. Since the Hessians had by then abandoned their posts at Burlington and Bordentown, an emboldened Cadwalader now urged Washington to move immediately back into New Jersey. "A pursuit would keep up the Panic," the anxious young colonel wrote to his chief, "if we can drive them from West Jersey, the Success will raise an Army by next Spring, & establish the Credit of the Continental Money, to support it."[56] Washington instantly saw the logic of this suggestion, his council of senior officers became convinced, and the troops began moving again toward the Delaware River to return to New Jersey starting on December 29.

Washington began to concentrate a force at Trenton including militia reinforcements under Cadwalader and from Brig Gen Thomas Mifflin, a Philadelphian and former quartermaster general of the Continental Army of dubious integrity, who was now leading 1,800 Continentals and Philadelphia Associators at Bristol. It took three days for Washington's own men to cross the river; some units did not arrive in town until the 31st. Amidst a scarcity of provisions, he now had gathered about 7,000 troops by January 1, 1777.

Washington was worried about the British as he concentrated his soldiers at Trenton. Fleeing Hessians had abandoned their isolated outposts and spread the panicked word about the American victory as they hurried north. Once Howe learned about Rall's debacle at Trenton, he placed Lord Cornwallis in command of marching troops to destroy the rebel army and restore order as far as Trenton. Gathering additional regiments as he pressed on toward the college town of Princeton, Cornwallis had assembled about 10,000 redcoats and Hessians there by sundown on New Year's Day.

Meanwhile, Washington and his generals faced a grave danger on December 31 with the expiring enlistments of thousands of veteran Continental soldiers that day. The commander in chief, Knox, Mifflin, and other officers paraded the regiments set to leave, and appealed to their honor, patriotism, and the recent victory to remain with the army just six more weeks. To wealthy Philadelphian Robert Morris, a leading delegate to the Second Continental Congress, Washington begged for help.

Tomorrow the Continental Troops are all at Liberty – I wish to push our Success to keep up the Pannick & in order to get their Assistance have promised them a Bounty of 10 Dollars if they will continue for one Month – But here again a new Difficulty presents itself we have not Money to pay the Bounty, & we have exhausted our Credit by such frequent Promises that it has not the Weight we could wish. If it be possible, Sir, to give us Assistance do it – borrow Money where it can be done we are doing it upon our private Credit – every Man of Interest & every Lover of his Country must strain his Credit upon such an Occasi[o]n.[57]

Fortunately, about half of those soldiers eligible to depart the next day chose to remain in camp, having been promised a $10 bounty in hard money ("a most extravagant price," Washington admitted, as their monthly pay was $6 per month), after having committed to six more weeks of service. Such was the difficulty of short enlistments, of which American generals complained throughout the war.[58] Still, Washington was left with only 3,300 Continentals, augmented by about 3,500 militiamen at or near Trenton under Cadwalader, Mifflin, and Ewing. These brave men would have to suffice for his next bold move.

Washington decided to remain at Trenton as Cornwallis's powerful column of troops neared Princeton. Hinting to Hancock, he wrote cryptically that "we are now making our Arrangements and concerting a Plan of Operations, which I shall attempt to execute as soon as possible & which I hope will be attended with some success."[59] The Virginian would take up a defensive position on the south bank of Assunpink Creek, on rising ground well-suited for Knox's 40 pieces of field artillery overlooking the town. The main road leading south from Trenton crossed the creek on a stone bridge, which channeled any attacker's formations into a narrow avenue of approach covered by American artillery and musket fire. Washington deployed his brigades along nearly three miles of the winding creek taking particular care to defend two vulnerable crossings: a lower ford near the Delaware, and another upstream from the bridge at Philip's Mill, which was "easily passable."

While the high ground south of the creek was indeed advantageous, Washington's plan to take up a defensive post was extraordinarily risky. Standing ground at Trenton when outnumbered meant giving up the initiative and opportunity to maneuver. If the British managed to cross the creek upstream, Washington's right flank would be turned, potentially collapsing the entire American line. Such a maneuver could allow Cornwallis to pin the American troops against the Delaware without enough time or boats to recross the river into Pennsylvania. The rebel army would be destroyed, and likely their entire cause of independence would collapse. Philadelphia too would certainly be lost. And if the Continentals were pushed off the high ground, where would they retreat and find provisions? Washington risked losing his force by gambling he could defeat Cornwallis. Most modern historians of the campaign and biographers of Washington (and soldiers at the time) see the general's stand along Assunpink Creek as a precarious point in the Revolution's history, a "make-or-break moment in the War for Independence." Still, he seems to have felt that a withdrawal would mean "destroying every dawn of hope which had begun to revive in the breasts of the Jersey Militia."[60]

After a 50-mile forced march southwest on the Great Post Road, Cornwallis and his breathless troops arrived at Princeton late on New Year's Day to join Brig Gen Alexander Leslie's infantry already at the small college town. Early on the 2nd, the British began their hurried march to Trenton with 8,000 men, leaving a detachment of three regiments at Princeton under Lt Col Charles Mawhood, an experienced soldier since 1752 and commander of the 17th Foot. Along the way the redcoats were fired upon and harassed for several hours by the adroit delaying tactics of Col Edward Hand's nimble Pennsylvania rifleman and Col Charles Scott's Virginians, deployed at creeks and defiles on the road to the Delaware, such that Cornwallis's exhausted soldiers did not arrive at Trenton until 4pm, with limping stragglers strung out for miles behind.

Hard pressed into Trenton, the troops of Hand and Scott barely managed to race across the bridge over Assunpink Creek with no time to spare, as British forces approached the stream at about 5pm. At this point, with sunset nearing, Cornwallis decided to attack the rebels' hillside positions across the creek by first probing the lower ford, then rushing the stone bridge. In this second battle at Trenton, the British and Hessian infantry made three heroic attempts to force their way across the bridge but were met with such a deadly hail of cannister shot and volleys of rifle and musket fire that none succeeded. One amazed Continental artilleryman wrote that "we fired all together again, and such a destruction it made, you cannot conceive. The Bridge looked red as blood ..."[61] Washington reported that "in this situation we remained till dark, cannonading the Enemy & receiving the fire of their Field pieces which did us but little damage."[62] In addition to defeating the British assaults, Washington's army was strengthened earlier in the day by the arrival in camp of more militia companies, putting about 6,800 men in the ranks.

Lord Cornwallis decided after nightfall that he would again attack the rebels with all his troops in the morning. The redcoats had suffered heavy losses at the bridge, but their officers expected they would finish off Washington's army soon after daybreak with a massive assault. His Lordship's decision turned out to be an enormous mistake.

Along the clear creek, many of the waiting American troops grew anxious that cold night. A worried Rhode Island officer wrote that "the stand at Assunpink [was] the critical moment of the war," while a Virginian saw this small battle as "the most awful crisis."[63] They need not have worried as Washington had no intention of clinging to his defensive lines overlooking the Assunpink. In fact, at a council of war that night, he and his senior officers decided upon a bold plan to withdraw secretly from their hillside positions and move by back roads to attack Mawhood's small enemy garrison left at Princeton. A Patriot informant had explained to Col Cadwalader the day before that the town was virtually unguarded on its southeast side and could be approached unseen by a seldom-used lane. Cadwalader provided Washington with a useful hand-drawn road map of the area as well. Moreover, Joseph Reed had just made a reconnaissance with a troop of dragoons confirming that the back route to Princeton was open. Washington was not only looking for a way to escape Cornwallis's expected onslaught in the chilly morning, but to find a way to deliver another blow to an unsuspecting, isolated enemy detachment: it was a golden opportunity.

Washington later explained his rationale for leaving Trenton that cold night. Once the fierce cannonade along the creek ended, he and his officers "discovered that the Enemy were greatly superior in number and that their design was to surround us." Prudently he "ordered all our Baggage to be removed silently [south] to Burlington soon after dark." Then, at midnight, "after renewing our fires" to deceive British patrols, and "leaving Guards at the Bridge in Trenton and other passes [fords]" on the creek, his cold, footsore army "marched by a roundabout Road to Princeton, where I knew they could not have much force left and might have Stores." As Washington had warned Congress in several recent letters, food was extremely scarce "in this exhausted Country." With an eye toward public morale, he noted that "One thing I was certain of, that [the attack on Princeton] would avoid the appearance of a retreat, (which it was of course[,] or to run the hazard of the whole Army being cut off) whilst we might by a fortunate stroke [cause the] withdraw[l] of Genl Howe [Cornwallis] from Trenton and give some reputation to our Arms." It is well to recall that Washington's weary soldiers in this winter campaign had just won their greatest victory to date seven days earlier, crossed a frozen river with artillery twice in four winter days, and defeated three bloody British assaults on their line that afternoon. And now their bold commander decided to pull all of them out of their defenses and lead them on a long night's trek on empty stomachs to make another attack early the next day.[64]

The ruse worked. Greene reported simply that the army "stole a march that night," and headed for Princeton. "We left all our sentries standing and moved off" to the right "as silently as possible."[65] While some enemy sentinels later reported the American movement that night to their commanders, Cornwallis remained confident he would defeat the outnumbered rebels at dawn.

Washington's intelligence network, including important sources colonels Reed and Cadwalader had heard from, paid off as he learned that only a small detachment of British troops was posted at Princeton, and that a route to the northeast could bring the army undetected to the town's vulnerable, unguarded side. At a council of war convened that night, the generals discussed their perilous situation and concurred that a nighttime attempt to cross the Delaware was out of the question with the enemy so close, and that a retreat south toward Philadelphia would likely collapse New Jersey's independence movement. Moreover, staying in their current positions invited a powerful British assault or flanking maneuver at dawn. The officers instead unanimously agreed to move the army north after slipping away unseen. They would trudge the 13 miles to Princeton and perhaps on to Brunswick afterwards to capture valuable enemy supplies and a priceless rumored war chest of £70,000 sterling.

The decision to slip away from Assunpink Creek was indeed audacious but also the only real choice that Washington and his cadre could make. Still, it's remarkable to consider how daring this maneuver was in the face of a dangerous enemy, made by officers who, in many cases, were not military professionals. The plan also demonstrates Washington's growing confidence and competence, a result no doubt of his recent victory on December 26.

Late that evening a few hundred soldiers were left in the darkness along the creek to tend campfires, act as sentries, and otherwise make the redcoats think the entire American army still occupied their positions. But the army had quietly slipped away at midnight. As it grew colder and began to freeze the muddy roads, Washington's long column of men, horses, cannons, and wagons first marched east to Sandtown, then turned north on the Quaker Bridge Road toward Princeton. When the troops reached a fork in the road near the Quaker Meeting House about two miles south of Princeton just after 7:30am, Washington divided his army in two. Mifflin's brigade continued directly north toward the Trenton-Princeton Road to block enemy forces coming from or going to Trenton, and to destroy the road bridge over Stony Brook. Most of the army, 5,000 men commanded by Sullivan accompanied by Washington, turned off to the right (northeast) on Saw Mill Road to come upon the town from the southeast, which was only lightly defended. This column neared the town at about 8am in cold but clear weather.

The British commander at Princeton, colonel Mawhood, had just set off that morning to march two of his foot regiments and a detachment of dragoons to Trenton to reinforce Cornwallis. He left two remaining infantry regiments at Princeton. As the unsuspecting redcoats stepped along the main road, American officers spotted them from the Saw Mill Road while closing on the town. At about the same time British officers with Mawhood's formation observed an unexpected column headed for Princeton; they initially mistook them for Hessians, whose dark blue coats resembled Continental uniforms. Concerned about leaving an unknown column in their rear, Mawhood turned his troops around and quickly moved back toward the town.

In the main American column Gen Mercer's 350 Continentals followed Sullivan's troops, along with Cadwalader's 1,100 militia. When Mawhood pushed his 500 soldiers toward high ground to intercept Sullivan's column approaching Princeton, Washington ordered Mercer, supported by Cadwalader, to attack these fast-moving redcoats. The two forces faced off in open grassland, violently colliding in an orchard at the William Clarke farm. The British charged Mercer's men with fixed bayonets, shoving them back, and mercilessly stabbing wounded American soldiers to death as they lay on the frozen ground. Cadwalader's Associators tried to support Mercer, but they too were pushed back in disorder. Only the timely deployment of a battery of Pennsylvania Associators artillery served by tough young waterfront laborers under 62-year-old former sailmaker Capt Joseph Moulder stopped the British advance from the orchard with deadly close-range grape-shot blasts from their two 4-pounder French guns.

From Saw Mill Road, Washington observed the fighting at the orchard and personally led troops from the brigades of colonels Hand and Hitchcock forward to strike Mawhood's redcoats from the east. Gen Mifflin, along Stony Brook, also sent part of his troops from the west to hit Mawhood's west flank. The British soon were overwhelmed, covering the ground with their dead and wounded. Washington displayed great personal courage rallying his unsteady troops during this crucial phase of the battle, led a decisive charge, and soon forced the stunned British to run from the field at about 9am. One soldier in the fighting that day wrote "I shall never forget, when I saw [Washington] brave all the dangers of the field, and his important life hanging by a single hair with a thousand deaths flying around him." Unfortunately, Gen Mercer, whom Washington praised as "a brave and good officer," was mortally wounded in the fighting on the Clarke farm by several British bayonet thrusts when he adamantly refused to surrender.[66]

With Mawhood's redcoats now in flight, the American troops turned toward the town of Princeton. There was at the college some resistance from British troops, but the surging American troops forced the redcoats to flee or surrender. About 300 British were captured, and 276 were killed or wounded in this violent contest. Flush with victory, Washington gathered his jubilant troops in town, where they heartily ate their first full meal in two long days. A witness wrote of the American soldiers "though they were both tired and thirsty some of them were laughing outright, others smiling, and not a man among them but showed joy in his countenance."[67] Despite the victory, however, some of the militia soon began deserting, even in whole companies. Washington was anxious, as he knew Cornwallis would soon learn of the attack in his rear and understand the meaning of the Americans' unexpected absence from the Assunpink's south bank. Washington briefly considered an immediate advance upon Brunswick but, seeing that his troops were thoroughly worn out, abandoned this possibility. The army was instead reformed and marched out of the town by noon, headed north for a winter encampment in the Watchung Mountains at Morristown, New Jersey, which they reached on the evening of January 6. "I shall draw the force ... at Morristown – where I shall watch the motions of the Enemy, & avail myself of every Circumstance,' Washington advised General Heath three days after the recent battle. The operations in New Jersey later called "The Ten Crucial Days," including the victorious battles of Trenton, Assunpink Creek, and Princeton, were over.[68]

Washington's letters written soon after reaching the army's well-protected mountain enclave at Morristown demonstrate his new optimism. He wrote with satisfaction that the enemy "appear to be pannick struck" only weeks after the British had driven the American army from New Jersey, though his men had deserted every day, and his force dwindled to less than 3,000 soldiers. But more remarkably, an audacious Washington was even looking to strike the British again. To Gen Putnam in Philadelphia he wrote "I am in some hopes of driveing them out of the Jerseys."[69] In a long letter to Rhode Island governor Nicholas Cooke on January 20, he implored him to raise the state's Continental regiments and commit to a common defense. "You must be sensible," the general wrote, "the Season is fast approaching when a new Campaign will open, nay the former is not yet closed; neither do I intend it shall unless the Enemy quit the Jerseys."[70] He went on to point out that new regiments would "give me an Opportunity in the fore part of the Campaign, before the Enemy can collect their force, or receive any reinforcement from home; to give them a fatal stab: such a blow in the beginning of the Season might terminate the Campaign to great advantage." Clearly Washington was not thinking of an inactive period of winter quarters. "I hope to close the Campaign gloriously for America," he concluded his letter.[71]

Today we can see that compared to the other large-scale campaigns, sieges, and battles of the Revolutionary War, the three American victories at Trenton and Princeton were small in scale in terms of the number of troops engaged. However, taken as a whole, their impact on the course of the war was decisive, in part because they happened at a crucial time in the American rebellion and changed the trajectory of the war. These combined victories were unquestionably a significant turning point in the war.

Historians have long assessed the battles' importance to the cause of independence and public spirit. Some argue that the campaign encouraged dispirited Patriots at a low point in the conflict. A recent author, Mark Malloy, concludes that "without Trenton and Princeton, the war likely would have ended in 1777," and that "these small victories breathed air into the dying fire that was American Independence. Without them the fire would have died in just a matter of months."[72] Historian David Price notes that Washington's "lightning sequence of triumphs reversed the momentum of the conflict just when it seemed that the quest for independence from Great Britain was on the verge of total defeat." He also concludes that "the impact on American morale was far out of proportion to the size of the engagement or its strategic significance."[73] Likewise, Washington biographer Edward Lengel concludes that "the fruits of victory were intangible," and the "patriots felt more confident and loyalists more discouraged than they had been before."[74] And acclaimed historian David Hackett Fischer describes a "double transformation" after the three rebel victories. American leaders went from despair to hope and confidence, whereas the British leaders went from a belief that the war would soon be over once they crushed Washington's army to a belief that they could never win the war. "The double transformation was truly a turning point," Fischer writes, and "the battles of Trenton and Princeton were not small symbolic victories."[75] Perhaps the pithiest assessment of the strategic results of the campaign is that of historians James Kirby Martin and Mark E. Lender in their study of the war, *A Respectable Army*. "So close to having reached the enunciated goal, the British had failed. So close to collapse, the Americans had survived."[76]

The importance of these battles was certainly understood by contemporaries. Richard Howe's personal secretary wrote that the battles "tend to revise the drooping spirit of the rebels and increase their force." And William Howe soon reported to Lord Germain about "the great encouragement it has given to the rebels," and that the three rebel victories had "thrown us further back than was at first apprehended, from the great encouragement it has given to the rebels." He also admitted "I do not now see a prospect for terminating the war, but by a general action ..."[77] British general James Grant wrote of the effects of the campaign as well, writing that "we have been obliged to contract our cantonments to Brunswick and Amboy ... in short is the most unpleasing situation I was ever in."[78] Another British officer observed that the Americans "are now become a formidable enemy."[79] One critical redcoat officer found that "by our continual blunders, which the enemy never fail to take advantage of, we seem more to encourage than dishearten them."[80] And in London, Lord Germain later complained in a speech to Parliament that "all our hopes were blasted by that unhappy affair at Trenton."[81]

The triumphant campaign's victors also recognized these ten days as salient. A Massachusetts sergeant in the campaign knew straightaway that the battle of Trenton would raise the people's "drooping spirits ... and string anew every nerve for our Liberty and Independence."[82] Maj James Wilkinson noted that "the joy diffused throughout the union by the successful attack against Trenton reanimated the timid friends of the revolution, and invigorated the confidence of the resolute,"[83] while a Philadelphia militiaman felt that the battles "gave a turn to the scale of American affairs." A Patriot chaplain recalled "the tidings flow upon the wings of the wind – and at once revived the hopes of the fearful, which had almost fled! How sudden the transition from darkness to light; from grief to joy!" An officer traveling home to Connecticut a few weeks after the battles wrote "You cannot conceive the joy and raptures the people were universally in as we passed the road."[84]

Just after the first fight at Trenton, Gen Greene wrote his wife that "this is an important period to America, big with great events ... everything wears a much better prospect than they have for several weeks past." The indefatigable Col Cadwalader also recognized the battles' importance immediately, reporting that Washington struck "a blow which has greatly changed the face of our Affairs, and if [the militia] can be induced to continue a few Weeks longer there is the strongest possibility that the enemy will be compelled to quit New Jersey entirely." The venerable John Adams, then serving in Congress, saw that after the battles the inhabitants of New Jersey "begin to raise their spirits exceedingly and to be firmer than ever. They are actuated by resentment now, and resentment coinciding with principle is a very powerful motive." These three small but crucial engagements, enhanced by the daring nature of their execution, turned a season of despair into a hopeful future.[85]

Several historians have pointed to Washington's renewed confidence in himself, and the restoration of his military reputation, which had suffered over the past four months, as further marking the campaign as one of the war's turning points. "Trenton and Princeton effectively quashed, at least for the present, every question as to Washington's military skill," writes Lengel.[86] Another popular biographer of the general, Steven Brumwell, asserts that the winter campaign was the "highpoint of Washington's military career," and that he "had redeemed his reputation, silencing, for the moment at least, those critics who were starting to question his capacity to lead the military struggle against Britain."[87] Historian John Ferling also finds that "in the aftermath of Trenton, the officers' confidence in his judgment had grown and Washington's self-confidence had swelled."[88] Add to these modern conclusions several contemporary assessments: even the British conceded that the battles of Trenton and Princeton were masterstrokes by their enemy. Scottish redcoat Lt Col Allan MacLean wrote that Lord Cornwallis "allowed himself to be outgeneraled by Washington ... at [the second Battle of] Trenton, and missed a glorious opportunity when he let Washington slip away in the night." Likewise, a fellow Scottish officer observed that "poor devils as the rebels are, they have outgeneraled us more than once."[89] Washington would have glowed had he known of the enemy's praise.

An additional significant result of the campaign was that the victories breathed new life into the New Jersey militia, which had previously done little to support Washington's army as it retreated to Pennsylvania.

Now with prospects seeming brighter, they turned out in droves to attack and harass British detachments, depots, and supply lines across the state. As one recent study of the Howe brothers states, "New Jersey was now swarming with motivated militia and a rash of small-scale actions erupted." And Loyalists were no longer safe, "as Howe limited the garrisons in the state to a narrow corridor along the Raritan River valley between Perth Amboy and New Brunswick."[90] After the clash at Princeton, small bands of elusive militia took the field to harass British foraging parties across the northern part of the state. Once Gen Howe reduced the British presence in New Jersey, his troops had a much smaller area from which to draw provisions, so they had to march into the countryside to procure them. Historian Arthur Lefkowitz concludes that now "Cornwallis had to send out foraging parties longer distances in search of fodder during the winter of 1777 ... which became the prey of Americans who could refer to partisan warfare manuals to help them plan their attacks."[91]

This hazardous situation for the British may be the most prominent result of the campaign. Crown forces now had to stay close to New York, abandoned New Jersey Loyalists, and left American Patriots to attack their vulnerable detachments in what modern historians called "the forage wars." Moreover, "the New Jersey government resumed normal functions, with the legislature often meeting at Trenton or Princeton." And many citizens renounced the loyalty oaths they had reluctantly sworn under heavy British pressure only weeks beforehand. Other than their outposts at Perth Amboy and Brunswick the British had lost their hold on New Jersey, and capturing Philadelphia was out of the question for the time being.[92]

The results of this remarkable campaign support the claim of modern historians as to its importance. Defeated at New York and chased 100 miles across New Jersey into Pennsylvania, by early December Washington had lost about 90 percent of his army. This was perhaps the lowest point in the entire war for himself and the new country. "The British never again came so close to snuffing out the rebellion as they did in 1776," write historians Martin and Lender.[93] Seemingly all Howe had to do was wait for better weather and lead his powerful army against the rebels in a final crushing blow. But Washington made his own luck. With the counsel of his senior officers, he turned desperation into victory knowing that only a few weeks remained before most of his small army would melt away. He had gambled and won, but the campaign was not a reckless one. It was carefully planned, bravely executed, and hard fought. True, placing his army on the south bank of Assunpink Creek to wait for a British attack was incredibly risky, perhaps needlessly so. But Washington prudently decided after the fighting at Princeton was over that an attack that same day on Brunswick was too much of an order for his hungry, tired, and worn out army to follow. We can leave it to Thomas Paine to describe the American triumphs in New Jersey perfectly.

> The conquest of the Hessians at Trenton by the remains of a retreating army ... is an instance of heroic perseverance very seldom to be met with. And the victory over the British troops at Princeton, by a harassed and wearied party, who had been engaged the day before and marched all night without refreshment, is attended with such a scene of circumstances and superiority of Generalship, as will ever give it a place on the first line in the history of great actions.[94]

Of the five turning points of the war discussed in this book, none were characterized by such a sudden, unexpected reversal of military fortune as Trenton, Assunpink Creek, and Princeton. Washington showed a newfound confidence, deftly motivated or enticed hundreds of his infantrymen to remain in the ranks beyond their enlistments, and led by example by showing fortitude and determination. He also demonstrated his competence by seeking advice from his officers, identifying an objective that was achievable, and struck at an enemy weak spot by using the element of surprise. During this ten-day period, he pushed on – at times in snow, ice, and darkness – despite the plan getting off schedule. "Keep with your officers," he was heard to say as the soldiers marched by him in the snow.[95] Washington and his troops turned what was essentially a raid on December 26 into a renewed offensive just days later at Trenton. He wisely recognized he had to escape from Assunpink Creek on January 2, made a bold night march to Princeton overnight, and won another victory there on the 3rd. This was a different general and a different army – despite being far smaller – than took the field at Long Island, Kip's Bay, White Plains, and Forts Washington and Lee.

The enemy also recognized what had occurred Capt Johann Ewald, a junior officer of the Hessian Jaegers, recorded in his diary some thoughts of the turning tide in January 1777, after the American victories. "Thus had the times changed! The Americans had constantly run before us. Four weeks ago we expected to end the war with the capture of Philadelphia, and now we had to render Washington the honor of thinking about our defense."[96] Gen Washington, true to his nature, was less dramatic. On January 20, he reported with considerable understatement that "our Affairs here are in a very prosperous train."[97] Indeed they were. These three battles staved off the collapse of the army, the war, and the cause of liberty, and renewed the struggle for American independence.

Triumph in the Wilderness: The Saratoga Campaign, 1777

The decisive Saratoga campaign of 1777 in the vast wilderness of northern New York was a sprawling combination of military operations, trans-Atlantic geopolitics, a dysfunctional British leadership structure in London, Quebec, and New York City, a siege in western New York, and six significant battles: Hubbardton, Fort Anne, Oriskany, Bennington, Freeman's Farm, and Bemus Heights. Also notable was a disputatious American command organization that included several prickly and ambitious rivals. Those who marched, fought, suffered, and died in the campaign were American Indian, British, German, Canadian, and American colonists – both Patriot and Loyalist. This campaign in New York, Vermont, and Canada took place in the some of the most inhospitable terrain for military operations in North America, where logistics would mean victory or failure. It was also the most important turning point of the Revolutionary War.

The origins of the complex campaign can be said to have started in Canada, British-held for over a dozen years. During the early years of the Revolutionary War, Canada figured prominently in British and American strategies. Troops of King George III occupied posts in eastern Canada, including Halifax, Montreal, and Quebec, and far-flung western forts, after their victory over France in the Seven Years' War in 1763. Once the Revolutionary War broke out in 1775, colonial military and political leaders looked northward to Canada in

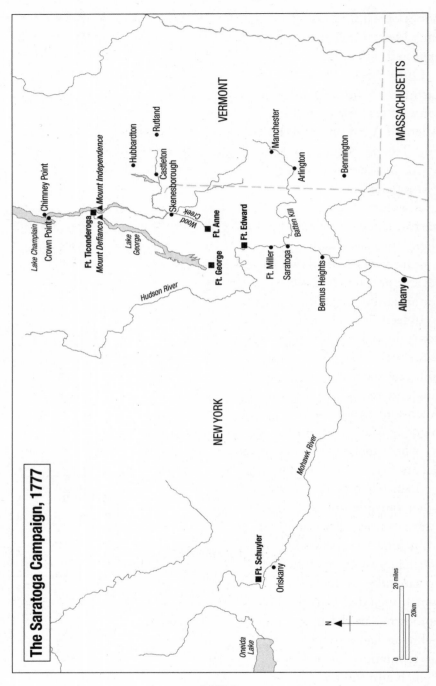

The Saratoga Campaign, 1777

MASSACHUSETTS

VERMONT

NEW YORK

Lake Champlain
Chimney Point
Crown Point
Ft. Ticonderoga
Mount Defiance
Mount Independence
Lake George
Hubbardton
Rutland
Castleton
Skenesborough
Wood Creek
Ft. Anne
Ft. George
Hudson River
Ft. Edward
Ft. Miller
Saratoga
Bemus Heights
Batten Kill
Manchester
Arlington
Bennington
Albany
Mohawk River
Ft. Schuyler
Oriskany
Oneida Lake

N

20 miles
20km

MAP 2

hopes of winning its allegiance to their nascent rebellion, striking an early blow at the British along the Saint Lawrence River and thwarting expected Indian raids.

Only weeks after the initial fighting of the war occurred at Lexington and Concord in Massachusetts in April 1775, a small force of scrappy New England militia jointly led by colonels Ethan Allen of Vermont and Benedict Arnold of Connecticut captured Fort Ticonderoga, New York, originally built by French forces in the 1750s in the vast northern wilderness. This now dilapidated bastion was perched above the southern end of Lake Champlain where the cold waters of Lake George flowed in from the south. The two large, narrow lakes, along with the Richelieu River to the north that drained them into the Saint Lawrence, made up a long-used water route linking lower Canada to New York City on the Hudson River with several portages. Possession of the stone fort was a key prerequisite for any military action against Canada.

Indeed Fort Ticonderoga, built during the French and Indian War, controlled the water route from Canada to New York. Its strategic value was an article of faith with British leaders, and its cannons and military materiel were a tempting target for the poorly supplied New England rebels. An attempt at its capture was not long in coming. Allen and Arnold stealthily stormed the fort with 200 militia on the night of May 10, and found only 50 careless British guards defending it, who quickly surrendered the far-off post without firing a shot. Allen's frontier Vermonters went on to capture another strategic post on Lake Champlain, Crown Point, ten miles to the north. Artillery and other valuable military stores from these forts were later moved to the American siege lines surrounding the British in Boston in early 1776.

In June 1775, the Continental Congress at Philadelphia appointed the haughty, aristocratic Maj Gen Phillip Schuyler of New York as commander of the new Continental Army's Northern Department, which included Canada. He was a wealthy, politically well-connected landowner in the upper Hudson River region. As his enemies knew, Schuyler had a touchy sense of personal honor and vigilantly guarded his reputation. He had served as a militia officer in New York during the French and Indian War and was well-respected by George Washington but was seen by others as being overly cautious when in command. Nevertheless, with Congress's blessing he began making ambitious plans to invade Canada. When Schuyler became ill, however, the small American force of less than 2,000 soldiers that marched toward Montreal and Quebec that summer and fall fell to the command of Maj Gen Richard Montgomery, a former British army officer who had relocated to New York in 1773.

Meanwhile, Benedict Arnold simultaneously led a force of 1,100 or so half-starved men on a grueling advance on foot and afloat through a barren wilderness from Maine to the Saint Lawrence River from September 13 to November 9. Arnold was a dynamic military leader, particularly in combat, was fearless to a fault, and typically led his troops from the front. He also had a disruptive habit of feuding with fellow officers and with Congress, with whom he had a bitter, perpetual grudge. But in the fall of 1775, his energy and drive ensured that his expedition arrived opposite Quebec. Weeks after his emaciated column combined forces with Montgomery's untested troops, they attacked the old French city on the snowy night of December 31. The quixotic assault failed, Montgomery was killed, and Arnold was seriously wounded. The surviving Americans eventually had to fall back, but many of their luckless comrades were captured. When thousands of British and German reinforcements fortuitously arrived at Quebec on May 6, 1776, once ice no longer choked the river, the Irish-born British commander of Canadian forces (and governor of Quebec) Gen Guy Carleton, attacked the rebels' lines and routed them on May 7. The defeated Americans were relentlessly pushed out of Canada, and eventually landed at Crown Point by July.

One of the British officers who landed at Quebec in May with the longed-for reinforcements from Great Britain was Lt Gen John Burgoyne. The 54-year-old officer had seen much dragoon service in the Seven Years' War, sat as a member of Parliament, and had married well, enabling him to pursue interests in the lively London theatre and smokey private clubs. English writer and politician Horace Walpole described him as a "vain, very ambitious man with a half understanding which was worse than none."[1] At heart, though, he was always an ambitious soldier. He first came to America at Boston in May 1775, and witnessed the battle of Bunker Hill in June, but took no active role in the bloody assaults that day. He sought military action in America and the glory that came with it and was not unwilling to actively promote his own ambitious career interests with the king and his ministers, who all lent a friendly ear.

Once on firm ground at army headquarters at Quebec, Burgoyne handed written instructions for Carleton from Lord George Germain, the British Secretary of State for the Colonies, regarding a planned campaign that summer from Canada south to Albany and eventually New York City. Germain was the government's chief minister and directed the British war effort from London, in close consultation with King George III. He ordered Carleton to capture the rebel-held forts at Crown Point and Ticonderoga, then proceed south. These operations were to secure the vital communications link from Canada to New York City and allow the Crown forces to divide and isolate New England from the rest of the colonies. To comply with his orders Carleton would have to construct a fleet to transport men and materiel swiftly up Lake Champlain from his jumping off position at St John's on the Richelieu River, 20 miles from Montreal.

Facing Carleton's powerful offensive in the deep New York forests was an American force of inadequate means. After the disastrous 1775–76 Canadian campaign ended in an inglorious flight of inadequate troops, the rebels began to regroup on the southern shores of Lake Champlain. Then a new Continental commander came to the frontier. Horatio Gates was a French and Indian War veteran, and an ambitious, argumentative personality who one historian calls "the war's most complex American general."[2] In late June Congress appointed him to the command of all Continental and militia field forces in Canada while Schuyler remained the overall northern department commander. Predictably this command structure created an awkward problem, because when Gates took over the "Canadian" army per his orders, it was now located at Crown Point, New York. Thus, a question arose as to who was now in command of the troops, Schuyler or Gates? After much squabbling, on July 8, 1776, Congress eventually confirmed Schuyler as head of the American forces since Gates was no longer "in Canada." The two contentious generals, now adversaries, would over the next two years have a tumultuous, competitive rivalry in the northern theater that did little to contribute to the Patriots' success. Their dispute was, in the words of one historian, "the most serious divisive force within both the army and Congress during the first three years of the war."[3]

After several months in Quebec preparing the expedition against American forces during the summer and early fall, including the disassembly of the powerful sloop *Inflexible* at the rapids of the Richelieu River and its reassembly on Lake Champlain, Carleton began his army's long-delayed advance on October 4. This was quite late in the fall to begin military operations in that part of the world where early winter weather could cripple the campaign. With over 20 ships and thousands of soldiers (commanded by Burgoyne) on board, Carleton's flotilla sailed south on the windswept lake toward Crown Point. A small American naval force at the south end of Lake Champlain led by and built at the direction of the ubiquitous Benedict Arnold, now a brigadier general, attacked the British ships on October 11 at Valcour Island, about 50 miles from Crown Point. Arnold's plucky force bravely battled the British ships for several hours in bloody naval combat but was soundly defeated by nightfall without appreciably delaying Carleton's advance.

The surviving soldiers and vessels of Arnold's defeated command raced to Crown Point the next day, pursued by Carleton's powerful fleet. Arnold quickly abandoned the weak American defenses there and fled south to Fort Ticonderoga and nearby Mount Independence on October 14, hours before the triumphant British occupied the point. At this time, Carleton had to decide whether to continue his army's advance to Fort Ticonderoga and perhaps Albany — as was expected by Germain — or return to Canada due to the lateness of the fall season, his lack of troops to take the fort by storm, and the lengthening of his long, overtaxed line of supply. He elected in the end to suspend his operations on the choppy lake for the year, much to the disappointment and disgust of Burgoyne and other officers, who urged Carleton to continue the campaign. Returning to Quebec now would make all the army's strenuous efforts meaningless, they protested, and certainly meant that the British would have to repeat their operations in 1777. Even American officers were surprised by the decision. "Why Retreat so percepetately after Vanquishing our fleet without attempting anything by Land?" wrote Pennsylvania Col Anthony Wayne from Ticonderoga.[4] Nevertheless, the stubborn Carleton could not be dissuaded, and the army sailed back north on November 4. Relieved American leaders welcomed the reprieve, but fully expected the British to make another attempt at reconquest from Canada in the spring.

Now with no prospect of taking the field in command of troops against Ticonderoga or Albany, a frustrated Gen Burgoyne received Carleton's permission to return to England for the winter months. The ocean voyage was, in historian Kevin Weddle's words, "ostensibly to carry Carleton's [campaign] report to Germain and deal with personal affairs – his wife had died while he was overseas."[5] But an ambitious Burgoyne knew that to secure the command of the inevitable 1777 campaign from Canada to New York, it would be wise to meet with Lord Germain in London and present his own operational plan, well thought out and based on his experience in the remote northern woodlands. From the Saint Lawrence River he sailed for England on November 9 and arrived there just one month later.

Burgoyne was not the only British leader who had been mulling over plans for the next year's campaign season on the Lake Champlain/ Hudson River corridor. Lord Germain and William Howe, commander of all British troops in the thirteen rebellious colonies, Nova Scotia, and Florida since October 1775, were also trying to figure out how best to operate in the northern theater. At the end of November 1776, as Howe's troops chased Washington's ragged army across northern New Jersey after the fall of Fort Lee, Howe wrote two letters to Germain with his concept for the 1777 campaign. His plan called for securing the Hudson River Valley by isolating the rebellious New England colonies, which British officials considered to be more radical provinces compared to the south. Dominating the Hudson corridor would also prevent the rebellious colonies from resupplying and reinforcing each other, and further secure British-held New York. To achieve this goal, Howe planned for 10,000 troops to move from New York City north to Albany in cooperation with an army of redcoats and Hessians moving south from Canada. Howe's plan required an additional 15,000 troops to be sent to America, which he had to know would be very difficult for London to provide.

Perhaps the officer thinking most about 1777 operations in America as he sailed east across the foggy Atlantic had to be Burgoyne. He arrived in London on December 9, and first met with the king, then Germain, to discuss the situation in America. His plan, titled "Thoughts for Conducting the War, from the Side of Canada," which he eventually presented to Germain and senior planners in London on February 28, was based largely on Carleton's memorandum for Germain, and discussions the two generals held in late 1776 for the coming campaign in New York. Burgoyne's bold operational plan called for an army of "eight thousand regulars rank and file" from Canada to advance south to reduce Fort Ticonderoga bolstered by "a Corps of Watermen; two thousand Canadians including Hatchet Men and other workmen; and a thousand or more Savages." Burgoyne, not Carleton, would command these forces sent southward. Just 3,000 troops would be left in Canada, under the governor's orders. One of Burgoyne's assumptions in his ambitious plan was that "General Howe's whole force should act upon Hudson's River, and to the Southward of it, and that the only object of the Canada Army be to effect a Junction with that force ..." He did not specify where Howe should act exactly, or where the intended junction should be. He also envisioned "an Expedition at the Outset of the Campaign by the Lake Ontario and Oswego [River] to the Mohawk River which, as a Diversion to facilitate every proposed Operation, would be highly desirable, provided the Army should be reinforced sufficiently to afford it." Lt Col Barrimore St Leger, an officer with extensive Canadian campaign service in the French and Indian War, was appointed to command the western diversion as he was the senior officer of that rank in Canada.[6]

Of great significance to the later stages of the campaign, and indicative of Burgoyne's strategy (approved by the king and Germain), was his statement in his plan about what he expected of Howe. "These ideas," he wrote, "are formed upon the supposition that it be the sole Purpose of the Canada Army to effect a Junction with Gen Howe, or after cooperating so far as to get Possession of Albany, and open the Communications to New York, to remain upon the Hudson's River, and thereby enable that General to act

water to Pennsylvania and to provide a sufficient force in New York to enable a junction with Burgoyne as his troops moved south. Clinton thought Howe's primary focus on the rebels' capital and thrashing Washington's army in battle was absurd. But the stubborn Howe refused to change his mind.

Howe wrote Burgoyne a week before his expedition set sail that "my intention is for Pennsylvania." By this time, Burgoyne was already south of Fort Ticonderoga, and seemingly unconcerned. In fact, on July 11, Burgoyne wrote a lengthy letter to Germain reporting recent successes including the capture of Crown Point, Fort Ticonderoga, Mount Independence, Skenesborough, and Fort Edward, as well as the battle of Hubbardton. The victorious frontier campaign was now further advanced than his expectations had been just 2 weeks ago. He complimented the "zeal and spirit of the troops" during the hardships of waging a wilderness war, and nowhere in his hundreds of words did he mention any expectations of Sir William Howe.[9]

On July 23, Howe's ships set sail out of New York Harbor, loaded with soldiers, supplies, horses, fodder, food, and arms. By this time, he heard that Burgoyne's army had taken Fort Ticonderoga, which made Sir William feel confident that the Canadian expedition was in fine shape, well ahead of expectations, and apparently in no immediate need of his military support in the Hudson River Valley. Howe's fleet departed the old city with 13,000 British and Hessian troops. This left Clinton with 7,000 troops to defend the several defensive positions at and around New York City, and to send a force northward if needed to ensure Burgoyne's success. In short, with Burgoyne's army now on the Hudson approaching Fort Edward, Howe was moving in the opposite direction with most of his troops, inaccessible at sea, and too far from New York to form a junction with Burgoyne. His departure also removed the large British army in New Jersey from its strategic position between the American forces and Clinton's defenses of New York, and now made it possible for Washington to send reinforcements north to Albany unimpeded.

In the end, poor communications over long distances, personal ambitions, and a bitter feud between Carleton and Germain made planning – and later executing – such a large-scale wilderness campaign extraordinarily difficult. London officials and the king did not fully understand the daunting challenges of conducting extensive military operations on multiple axes in America, especially the enormous logistical requirements involved and the rugged terrain to overcome. Additionally, having Germain in charge of directing the forces of Howe and Burgoyne from London rather than relying on Gen Howe was a mistake. In the numerous plans drawn up by the generals and Germain, and the flurry of letters from late 1776 to the spring of the next year, it should have been recognized that after the battles of Trenton and Princeton, Howe's emphasis was firmly on Philadelphia. He did not have command over troops in or from Canada; Carleton did. Howe was never ordered to make a junction with Burgoyne at Albany his objective. Even Burgoyne's plans did not call for a junction of the two forces but rather "cooperation" on the Hudson River with troops from the south. Burgoyne knew this before his army left Quebec, and as will be seen, he had other opportunities to revise his plan of operations later in the campaign when the seemingly high odds of success began to diminish as his troops marched farther south.

But this is getting ahead of the story of the military actions of June and July on Lake Champlain. Burgoyne's arrival at Quebec on May 6 carrying plans and letters from Germain to Carleton, who bitterly despised each other, pertaining to the summer campaign, did not please the latter. Canada's governor was angered to learn that he would not command the military operations in the field, but Burgoyne would. Additionally, he would be left with only 3,000 or so troops in Canada once Burgoyne went into New York. Germain's orders were so specific they even detailed which regiments would make up Burgoyne's offensive, and those to remain with Carleton. Sir Guy did not take out his fury against Burgoyne, but according to orders from London, his hands were tied as far as discretion in giving him assistance once the troops crossed into New York, out of the governor's jurisdiction.

Burgoyne's larger problem was that the detailed plans he made while in London over the winter failed to consider the limited resources and cooperative *habitants* among the small riverside farms and settlements along the Saint Lawrence – which he should have learned while on active service in Canada the year before. Burgoyne's military requirements for horses, wagons, carts, boats, food, fodder, Canadien militia,* Indian auxiliaries, and laborers were simply not available in Canada in the numbers he had planned for, nor would they ever be as his army made the long trek toward Albany in 1777. Carleton did what he could to make Burgoyne's army ready for the campaign, but in the end, Burgoyne had to make do with far less of everything than he'd planned over the London winter.

But he was likely pleased with his army. Burgoyne's redcoats included seven "foot" regiments. These troops and supporting artillery companies made up the army's right wing, led by Maj Gen William Phillips. Each of these regiments had a company of grenadiers, the tallest veteran soldiers in the unit that were used as shock troops. As most British commanders did, Burgoyne combined all these hard-hitting grenadier companies to make a single battalion. Likewise, each foot regiment included a light infantry company consisting of the most active, nimble soldiers who were more lightly armed, uniformed, and equipped than their comrades. These light companies were also grouped to make one battalion. Burgoyne also created a company of British rangers called the Company of Marksmen, who were outfitted for quick action in the dense American forests. The grenadiers, light infantrymen, the marksmen, and the 24th Regiment were joined to create the Advanced Corps, commanded by Brig Gen Simon Fraser, who had been on active British service for 30 years. Including four companies of the Royal Artillery Regiment to serve the 138 cannons and mortars on the campaign, Burgoyne's redcoats numbered about 3,750 men.[10]

The army from Canada also included German auxiliaries led by Maj Gen Friedrich Adolph Riedesel, which had arrived with his troops in Canada the previous year. Like the Hessian troops at Trenton, these units were hired in the thousands by the British government to deploy more redcoats to America, as seen in the previous chapter. This contingent consisted of four Brunswick (*Braunschweig*) infantry regiments, a battalion each of grenadiers and light companies, a Hessian infantry regiment and artillery company, and one regiment of Brunswick dragoons (unmounted). Although looked down upon by

*This is the 18th-century term used for French Canadians.

many of the British officers on the campaign, these 3,340 officers and men provided Burgoyne with much of the force's firepower and were actively engaged in heavy combat in the army's battles that summer and fall. These troops Burgoyne designated as his left wing.

Also making up Burgoyne's force initially were two corps of Loyalists, two Canadian militia companies, and a fluctuating number of Indians approaching 1,000 warriors from Algonquin and Iroquois native groups, some from hundreds of miles away. Finally, several hundred women and children accompanied the expedition, who were mostly families of soldiers, including Baroness Riedesel, the general's wife, and their three children.

By late May Burgoyne's force of about 9,500 troops was at Fort St John, downstream of Lake Champlain on the Richelieu River. On June 14, the general ordered his forces to move south from their camps to Lake Champlain, then into transports on the water. The army covered about 90 miles unopposed in hundreds of vessels and began to make camp on June 25 at the ruined fortifications at Crown Point, as well as Chimney Point, on the opposite (eastern) side of the lake. On July 1, joined by hundreds of Indians, Fraser marched out of camp with the Advanced Corps, headed south for Fort Ticonderoga just ten miles away, followed by Burgoyne's redcoats. On the east side of the lake, Riedesel's Germans also moved forward toward Mount Independence, opposite Fort Ticonderoga, through difficult swampy ground. The commanding general was expecting a stout defense from the Americans both in the forts and defending their outer field works. "The Army is in the fullest Powers of Health and Spirits," Burgoyne wrote to Howe on July 1. He reported having "a large Body of Savages" with his columns and expected more the next day. He curiously added that he would "implicitly follow the Ideas I communicated to Your Excellency in my Letters from Plymouth and Quebec," meaning the cooperation of their two commands. Howe was busy getting ready to sail his army south, which Burgoyne knew he had intended since early that year.[11]

On the south end of the lake awaiting the unchallenged British advance, the American forces at Ticonderoga and Mount Independence were commanded by Maj Gen Arthur St Clair, Schuyler's second in command. He was a Scottish-born soldier of the French and Indian

War who settled in Boston after that conflict ended. He had served with Washington's army at Trenton and Princeton, and in 1777 was assigned to the Northern Department. He had been appointed to command at Ticonderoga on June 12, and immediately recognized that the 3,500-man garrison was far too small to defend the forts and outer works. His garrison included Continental artilleryman, ranger companies, three New Hampshire Continental regiments, five from Massachusetts, and Col Seth Warner's Continentals from Vermont (an area then called the Hampshire Grants). New England militia forces also increased St Clair's nominal strength by around 500 men, though not all were well equipped. Schuyler also knew of the garrison's weakness and wrote Washington on June 28, "it is therefore highly necessary that a strong Reinforcement should without Delay be sent me," with artillery.[12]

On July 2, Fraser's light troops advanced unopposed through the dense woods and occupied Mount Hope, an elevated ridge just west of Ticonderoga's outer defenses. Without enough soldiers to defend it, St Clair had ordered it evacuated, and its log blockhouse burned. This was a "very advantageous" piece of terrain from which to observe and attack the fort's defenses. Its possession by Fraser's advanced troops also cut off the Americans from Lake George, a key potential withdrawal route.[13]

Burgoyne brought over 100 cannons up Lake Champlain to reduce Fort Ticonderoga, assuming its garrison would put up a resolute defense from its high walls, as the French had done in 1758. He need not have worried. The key to the American defensive positions at the head of the lake was, it turned out, an undefended mountain. Just south of Fort Ticonderoga was a steep wooded eminence known as Sugar Hill, also called Mount Defiance. St Clair and other American officers had recognized the significance of this high ground that dominated both Fort Ticonderoga to the north and Mount Independence to the east. They decided against placing defenses there. The hill was heavily forested, it was deemed by the garrison's officers to be inaccessible to the British, and they did not have enough troops to defend the position.

The British engineers and Burgoyne's second in command, artilleryman Maj Gen William Phillips, quickly recognized that possession of the unoccupied mountain was the key to dominating all the rebel fortifications at the lake and observing St Clair's movements.

On July 5, small British parties ascended Sugar Hill to prepare to bring field pieces to the summit and establish a suitable firing position for the guns. St Clair, engineer Thaddeus Kościuszko, and other American officers quickly saw the danger implied by enemy activity on the high hill. Additionally, the British approached Fort Ticonderoga with siege artillery. With these two dangers, St Clair moved immediately to begin an evacuation of both Ticonderoga and Mount Independence after dark. The Patriot officers collectively agreed that "a Retreat ought to be undertaken as soon as possible and that we shall be very fortunate to effect it." They hoped to quietly bring off as much as they could of supplies, arms, artillery, and ill soldiers to retreat south to Skenesborough, about 22 miles by water and farther by land, where the army had a supply depot and a shipyard. Their eventual objective was Fort Edward on the Hudson River, a 60-mile march south. The hasty and confused withdrawal began in the early morning hours of July 6 under cover of darkness.[14]

Led by St Clair, most of the garrisons' troops hurried south into Vermont by way of the tiny settlement of Hubbardton. There St Clair positioned a force made up of colonels Seth Warner's Vermonters and Nathan Hale's 2nd New Hampshire Regiment to await the arrival of the lagging rearguard commanded by Col Ebenezer Francis, while the rest of the army pressed on to Castleton. Col Pierce Long commanded the army's 200 supply-laden boats moving south on Wood Creek; this contingent reached Skenesborough at about 1pm.

The British learned of the Americans' retreat before dawn on the 6th. A log and chain boom made and emplaced by the garrison across the narrow waters of the lake was quickly broken by Burgoyne's ships, allowing the little navy to pursue Long's flotilla. To Long's surprise, since American commanders had expected the log boom to delay the enemy's ships for hours, British vessels and three regiments aboard soon appeared in South Bay near Skenesborough. Once foot troops landed, they overran the small village and harbor, which the Americans had abandoned after burning as much of the shipping, baggage, and supplies they could.

With the British on shore at Skenesborough in force, St Clair could no longer march his troops directly from Castleton to Fort Edward, as the redcoats now blocked his path to the Hudson. Instead, he was forced to lead his weary men on a wide detour through Vermont before safely reaching Fort Edward five days later.

Upon learning of the precipitous abandonment of the Ticonderoga defenses, the aggressive Gen Fraser quickly pursued the rebels with part of his Advanced Corps well before dawn, while Riedesel's Brunswick infantrymen occupied the now empty Mount Independence works. The following day, July 7, at 3am Fraser again took up the pursuit of St Clair's column over rough roads, and shortly after dawn he came upon the unsuspecting American rearguard on high ground at Hubbardton, about 1,100 men strong. He decided on an immediate assault on the Patriots.

The battle that ensued that morning was a hard-fought contest in which Fraser's impetuous attack was initially successful, but the stubborn New Englanders regrouped and struck back in the wooded hills by Sucker Brook. Fraser's 850 men were hard pressed and looked to be in real danger when a relief force of Riedesel's 150 Brunswick troops from Mount Independence came up on the American right flank. The Germans' charge against Warner's fortified position on high ground was bloody but soon forced the Patriot commander to order a hasty retreat east to Manchester. "They ran with the greatest precipitancy to save their lives," expecting no quarter from the surging Brunswickers. American losses were 371, most of them captured, but in this first battle of the campaign British and German losses were about 200 killed and wounded. These were soldiers who could not be readily replaced from Canada. Still, the rebels had been routed and Fort Ticonderoga was firmly in British hands.[15]

On July 8, Burgoyne made his headquarters at Skenesborough in the home of Philip Skene, a wealthy Loyalist landowner and British army veteran who served as a volunteer aide to the general. That same day, almost 200 soldiers of Col John Hill's 9th Regiment of Foot advanced twelve miles south to Fort Anne, along Wood Creek on the road to Fort Edward. Just north of the small blockhouse the redcoats fought a sharp engagement against 400 or so Albany militia men and 150 Massachusetts and New Hampshire Continentals who had escaped Skenesborough the day before. "The Enemy followed the [American]

Troops that came to Skenesborough as far as Fort Ann," Schuyler reported to Washington, "where [the British] were Yesterday repulsed, notwithstanding which, Colonel [Pierse] Long contrary to my express Orders evacuated that post."[16] Long's troops hurried on to Fort Edward, while the bloodied redcoats returned to Skenesborough, leaving their casualties behind.

Schuyler got word of the fall of Ticonderoga while in Albany. He arrived at the run-down Fort Edward a few days later. On July 12, St Clair's footsore Continentals marched in as well, having made a wearisome trek by way of Rutland. "I am here at the Head of a Handfull of [St Clair's] Men," wrote Schuyler, "not above 1500 without provision, little ammunition, not above five Rounds a Man, having neither Ball nor Lead to make any: the Country in the deepest Consternation." And Schuyler could see that Fort Edward "was once a regular Fortification, but there is nothing but the ruins of it left."[17] Although the American forces were bolstered by the arrival of Benedict Arnold, who had been ordered there by Congress to assist Schuyler in defending the region north of Albany, the Northern Department commander remained despondent. To Washington, he described the situation.

> Desertion prevails and Disease gains Ground nor is it to be wondered at, for we have neither Tents, Houses, Barns, Boards or any Shelter, except a little Brush – Every Rain that falls, and we have it in great Abundance almost every Day, wets the Men to the Skin – We are besides in great Want of every Kind of Necessaries, provisions excepted – Camp Kettles we have so few that we cannot afford above one to twenty Men. Altho' we have near fifteen Tons of powder, yet we have so little Lead, that I could not give each Man above fifteen Rounds, and altho' I have saved about thirty pieces of light Artillery yet I have not a single Carriage for them, so that my whole Train of Artillery consists of two Iron Field pieces.[18]

At least Schuyler did not have to worry about the British army chasing him. By July 10, most of Burgoyne's troops had regrouped at Skenesborough, where they spent weeks accumulating supplies, food, and carts to continue their burdensome campaign. At this point

Burgoyne had a crucial decision to make. He could continue to march toward Albany on the direct overland route by way of Fort Edward, or he could move his army back to Ticonderoga and then advance by water on Lake George to reach Fort Edward after trekking the ten-mile portage from the lake to the Hudson. The latter path was easier to move supplies, baggage, and artillery. Additionally, the portage road from Fort George, at the southern shore of the lake, to the Hudson was one of the best trails in the area, and would greatly benefit the use of wagons, carts, and wheeled artillery. The overland route from Skenesborough, however, was a poor road through numerous marshes and sluggish streams and could be readily blocked by the Americans with felled trees. Burgoyne elected to use both routes: the direct road for the troops and field artillery, and the water route for the army's heavy guns, baggage carts, and supply wagons back to Ticonderoga to cross Lake George and use the portage. He feared that if he moved the entire army back to Ticonderoga it would look like a reverse to area Loyalists, lower the morale of his troops, and encourage the enemy. As it turned out the water route would not have saved the army any time due to a critical lack of boats and the laborious portage near Fort Ticonderoga. The numerous obstacles the troops encountered on the trail from Skenesborough to Fort Edward lasted only several days, despite numerous historians' claims that the rebel obstructions on the road south fatally delayed Burgoyne's army.

Another thorny problem arose while Burgoyne's forces were still at Skenesborough: about 400 Native Americans and 170 Canadien volunteers arrived in the British camp. More Native Americans were expected soon, as Burgoyne had planned, but their deployment was often problematic for British leaders in the American war, as Burgoyne discovered. While he coveted the abilities of Indians in tracking, scouting, and wilderness warfare, these warriors were difficult to bring under British orders and so-called enlightened European standards of warfare. As much as he tried to rein in the Indians' common tactics of killing wounded soldiers and civilians, scalping, and expecting loot and hostages, Native American warfare frightened and outraged the region's Patriots. Burgoyne had given a lofty speech to the Indians that joined him in late June in which he told "Warriors – you are Free – Go forth in might of your valour and your cause – strike at the common enemies of Great Britain and America." But then he tried to bring their "most serious Attention to the Rules which I hereby proclaim for your invariable Observation during the campaign." These limitations included a ban on "Bloodshed when you are not opposed in Arms," killing "Men, Women, Children, and Prisoners," who "must be held sacred from the Knife or Hatchet."[19] He ended the address with a wish for their success, but many of his listeners were not about to follow these European rules of war.

Finally, after spending almost three weeks at Skenesborough, Burgoyne's troops advanced toward Fort Edward, beginning with the Advanced Corps on July 24. Patriot detachments had already completed their mission "to fell Trees across the Road between this and Fort Ann; to take up all the Bridges; drive off all the Cattle, and bring away the Carriages," Schuyler reported.[20] Passing the charred ruins of Fort Anne, the British neared Fort Edward on July 27 with about 6,600 troops. "The toil of the march was great," Burgoyne reported, "but supported with the utmost alacrity." In reaction, Schuyler and his soldiers retreated south to Saratoga, staying on the west bank of the Hudson.[21]

Reaching Fort Edward was an important waypoint for the British army's wilderness campaign. To date, Burgoyne had swiftly forced the American garrison out of Fort Ticonderoga, which had been considered their main defensive position before reaching Albany. The British had now driven the struggling Patriots from Fort Edward, the last significant defensible fort north of Albany. Moreover, there were at least two months of fair campaigning weather expected. A confident Burgoyne wrote to Clinton in New York predicting the army would be at Albany by August 23. Flushed with success, he made no mention in this message of expecting a junction with Howe's force on the Hudson.

In Philadelphia and elsewhere, American leaders were now gravely worried. "I am greatly concerned at the rapid progress of General Burgoyne's Army," Washington wrote tersely to Schuyler. By the end of July, the forts at Ticonderoga, Mount Independence, and Fort Edward had all been lost and American forces continued to retreat. The Continental Congress, frustrated by the increasingly dire news coming from the north, determined to make command changes in the Northern Department. Schuyler had certainly worked tirelessly to sustain Continental forces in New York, but limited resources and troops could not overcome Burgoyne's powerful army from Canada and his Indian allies. Schuyler was also not well-liked among New England delegates in Congress nor among those states' militiamen, who found the wealthy New Yorker haughty and condescending. Schuyler, a nervous and anxious man by temperament, did himself little good by the increasingly despondent tone of his reports to Congress, Gen Washington, and others. He even hinted at suicide in late July. The New York general wrote to John Jay, chief justice of New York's highest court, that should a battle occur "I Shall certainly be there, and In order to Inspirit my troops shall Expose myself more than It is prudent for a Commanding officer to do, [and] I may possibly get rid of the Cares of this life or fall Into [British] hands, in Either case I Intreat you to Rescue my memory from that load of Calumny that Ever follows the unfortunate." Washington became so apprehensive for the retreating northern army he sent Massachusetts-born Maj Gen Benjamin Lincoln to help Schuyler, notably because Lincoln was well-liked by militia officers of New England, "where the Spirit of Malevolence knows no Bounds, and I am considered as a Traitor," Schuyler complained to Washington. Granted, the military situation was not encouraging, but Schuyler's striking pessimism did not inspire confidence for future success.[22]

Congress relieved Schuyler of his command on August 1, and replaced him with Horatio Gates as the Northern Department commander. Two days earlier St Clair too was relieved of his duties for abandoning Fort Ticonderoga and its supporting defenses without putting up a fight. Although St Clair had nowhere near the number of troops needed to defend the fort, his failure to occupy Mount Defiance and his army's rapid retreat into Vermont could not be overlooked in the congressional process of affixing blame. Now it was up to Gates, Lincoln, and Arnold to somehow stop the British, Germans, and Indians from reaching Albany.

Although at the end of July American forces were in retreat down the Hudson and difficult command changes had to be made, hindsight shows that the earliest seeds of American victory in the

New York forests began to sprout in the first days of August, even if imperceptible to contemporaries. East of the Hudson River momentum began building in New England for increased defensive opposition to Burgoyne's oncoming force. On August 1, Brig Gen John Stark and his force of New Hampshire militia joined forces with Seth Warner's militia at Manchester, Vermont. These troops – and their commanders – were fiercely independent and held themselves apart from Schuyler's Continentals. Eight days later Stark moved his troops south to the town of Bennington, where supplies had been collected and guarded by the militia. This supply cache proved to be a tempting target for the British army as it continued its rugged march, with calamitous consequences.

The British army's Advanced Corps reached Continental Congressman William Duer's house eight miles south of Fort Edward by August 9, followed soon thereafter by the main column. Burgoyne made his headquarters at Duer's for several weeks, still on the east side of the river. At this point, Burgoyne's army was now about 60 miles south of Fort Ticonderoga, which stretched his supply line alarmingly thin. As historian Eric Schnitzer writes, "with St Clair's unexpected evacuation [of Ticonderoga], Burgoyne's timetable was advanced in such a way that the Army from Canada's supply lines were incapable of catching up."[23] And with militia forces gathering like a summer storm to the east, his overextended logistics were now even more vulnerable to attack and disruption. Moreover, the army's supplies were rapidly dwindling, and the need for more horses to pull wagons and carts was dire.

Burgoyne must have been pleased when reports reached the British headquarters that military stores, horses, "wheel carriages," and food supplies had been gathered at Bennington, about 35 miles to the southeast. Burgoyne ordered an expedition to capture the depot, led by the Brunswick dragoons' commander Lt Col Friedrich Baum, consisting of about 800 troops including German infantry and dragoons, Canadiens, American Indians, British Rangers, Loyalists, and two Hessian-served 3-pounder artillery pieces. The expedition left camp at Duer's on August 11, under the impression that only a weak collection of militia companies guarded the supplies at Bennington.[24]

Baum, who spoke no English and had little experience to recommend him, but was the only command option, reached the Walloomsac River about ten miles east of Bennington on the 14th, after an arduous march on a difficult frontier road. By the time Baum's troops arrived on the Walloomsac, Stark had mustered 1,500 New Hampshire militiamen at Bennington, and 500 more Vermonters commanded by Warner were at Manchester, about 25 miles to the north. These forces had been gathering since late July and were well-led and motivated. Baum soon learned that this strong force was ahead of him protecting the valuable supplies he was sent to capture. The German colonel prudently sent back a call for reinforcements to Burgoyne. Presumably he recalled his orders that it was his "discretion to attack [the Americans] or not, always bearing in mind that your corps is too valuable to let any considerable loss be hazarded on this occasion."[25]

On August 16, Stark attacked Baum's troops just inside the New York border with his larger force of 2,300 men, including hundreds of Warner's soldiers. The Germans were soundly defeated, Baum was mortally wounded, and but for the arrival of a heavy rainstorm and the mud-delayed relief column from Burgoyne under Lt Col Heinrich von Breymann with 640 men and two cannons, all would have been lost. Still, Stark's militiamen decisively won the day, inflicted 900 casualties including over 700 captured, and took all the Hessian field artillery – at the cost of only 70 casualties. "We used their own cannon against them, which prov'd of great service to us," Stark recalled with satisfaction. "Our Troops behaved in a very brave and heroic Manner," reported Lincoln to Schuyler, "they pushed the Enemy from one Work to another, thrown up on advantageous Ground and from different posts with Spirit and Fortitude until they gained a compleat Victory over them."[26]

Bennington was a severe setback for the British campaign. Baum's defeat reduced the British army on the Hudson by over 900 irreplaceable men, achieved none of its objectives, and disheartened regional Loyalists and Indian allies. Moreover, the failed raid now forced Burgoyne to await the arrival of the army's slow supply train from Fort George, buying Patriot forces much-needed time to concentrate more soldiers and supplies. Burgoyne seems to have recognized the significant unhappy shift in fortunes resulting from the hard-fought battle, and that the likelihood of success – so high just weeks ago at Fort Ticonderoga – now looked much less certain. His August 20 letter to Germain hints at his increased concern, for he closed it with the hope "that my Endeavors may be to some degree assisted by a Cooperation of the Army under Sir William Howe."[27] This clause was disingenuous, as Burgoyne knew quite well that Howe was focused on his campaign against Philadelphia by then. Or perhaps Burgoyne referred to a detachment under Clinton from New York City. It was the general's first reference to expecting Howe's support in a letter to Germain since leaving Canada, and he did not mention cooperation on the Hudson in his August 6 letter to Howe. Gone was the tone of his July 30 letter to Germain to report on "the successful progress which has been made by the Army" just 17 days before the battle of Bennington.[28]

On top of Baum's costly debacle, Burgoyne learned two weeks later of the fate of St Leger's diversionary expedition by way of Lake Ontario and the Mohawk River. This sundry force of 2,000 regulars, Loyalists, and Indian allies left the upper Saint Lawrence River on July 19, sailed into Lake Ontario, and on the 24th reached the mouth of the Oswego River. Their objective was Patriot-held Fort Schuyler (previously named Stanwix) on the Mohawk River in central New York, which they reached on August 2.

Fort Schuyler protected the six-mile portage known as the "Oneida Carrying Place," linking the Mohawk River with Wood Creek, then on to Oneida Lake and the Oswego River. Completed in 1762, the log fort was defended by 750 New York and Massachusetts Continentals in the summer of 1777, and had been commanded by Col Peter Gansevoort since May. Fortunately for the Patriots, the garrison had been resupplied just before St Leger's troops appeared.

As St Leger's force approached the earth and log fort, New York's Governor George Clinton called out the Tryon County militia downriver from Fort Schuyler to muster and march west to bolster the garrison. Quickly collecting 700 men in four regiments at Fort Dayton on the Mohawk, Brig Gen Nicholas Herkimer led them west on August 4, along with 60 allied Oneida Indians. Two days later, as the column trudged into a thickly wooded, confined area at Oriskany about six miles from Fort Schuyler, a mixed force of Indians and Loyalist light infantrymen from St Leger's besieging troops led by Sayenqueraghta (a Seneca war chief) ambushed the Tryon militia in the dark forest. The fighting was vicious, hand to hand, and without quarter. A Loyalist at the battle wrote that the Indians "made a shocking Slaughter among [the militia] with their Spears and Hatchets." Herkimer suffered a severe knee wound that would soon prove mortal, but he continued to command while propped upright against a tree. Casualties were appallingly heavy for the Tryon County men, with at least 250 of them killed and wounded.[29]

At the same time the battle raged at Oriskany, Lt Col Marinus Willett of the 3rd New York Regiment in Fort Schuyler led a sortie from the bastion to loot and destroy the Indians' empty camp behind the British siege lines. When the bloodied Seneca warriors at Oriskany learned of the Patriot soldiers' raid and their pillaging, they abandoned the battlefield after a torrential rainfall, which all but ended six brutal hours of fighting. Herkimer's survivors turned back to Fort Dayton, too bloodied and weary to go on, forced to leave hundreds of their neighbors dead in the woods.

With the Indians gone, Col Gansevoort's defenders resolute, and hearing that a brigade ordered by Schuyler was marching to reinforce the garrison, St Leger lifted the siege and began a retreat to Lake Ontario on August 22. Two days later reinforcements led by the indefatigable Benedict Arnold arrived from Albany, having been dispatched by Schuyler for the fort's relief. The British western diversion had been thwarted and turned back, although Herkimer's militia losses were substantial. Governor Clinton reported that the Tryon County men "suffered much and I fear that the Loss of their bravest Officers in the late Action will so dispirit them that unless they can be speedily succoured little more may be expected from them."[30]

The failure of St Leger's expedition to act as a diversion of American forces had little impact on operations along the Hudson. Burgoyne did not reinforce St Leger from his own troops, nor did Schuyler (or later Gates) send a substantial body of troops to Fort Schuyler. Even had St Leger's siege of the fort been successful, it is not clear that his command would have been able to reach Albany unimpeded. The real concern for both armies remained the situation between Albany and Fort Edward, which seemed to be getting closer to a violent resolution as summer came to a close.

In mid-August the American army, still led by Schuyler, moved down the Hudson from Stillwater to several islands about ten miles north of Albany at the mouth of the Mohawk River, which flowed in from the west. Schuyler then left the army two days before Gates arrived there at Van Schaik's Island to take command of the 4,000 or so troops in camp on August 19. Here Gates met with Gen Lincoln, whom he dispatched to Bennington to try to coordinate the operations of the various New England militia formations on foot in Vermont, including those of the talented but recalcitrant John Stark. "I am to return with the militia … to the northward, with a design to fall into the rear of Burgoyne," Lincoln wrote.[31]

The American army gathering near Albany had now grown substantially since early August. Two additional Continental regiments arrived in camp on the 22nd. Col Daniel Morgan and his veteran battalion of several hundred backcountry Pennsylvania and Virginia riflemen followed soon thereafter, sent by Washington to act as light infantry and scouts. Some militia from New York and Connecticut also arrived, but far less than called for by Gates (and Schuyler before him.) Many New England militia leaders were reluctant to join their commands with Gates for fear that Burgoyne would move his army eastward to the Connecticut River, especially after the Hubbardton raid. Still, Gates now had about 7,000 men in his camps, and expected more.

Over the next few weeks, Gates and Burgoyne steadily maneuvered their forces closer to each other on opposite banks of the Hudson. By September 9, the American army had returned to Stillwater. From there Gates learned that the British were moving south from Fort Edward, and that their artillery and wagons sent from Lake George had finally reached them. As reinforcements began to arrive at his camps Gates decided to take up a better defensive position farther north, knowing the enemy would eventually have to cross the Hudson. He tasked his young engineer, Col Kościuszko, to locate a strong position for the growing American army to block the British advance toward Albany.

The young Polish engineer chose Bemus Heights, a dominating ridge overlooking the main road along the flat bottomland by the Hudson River, at a place where 100-foot-high bluffs crowded close to the river and created a narrow area through which the enemy would have to pass. Artillery emplaced on the heights commanded this tight corridor and the low ground to the north.

On September 12, Gates posted his troops on Bemus Heights* in positions facing north on hilly, broken ground in thick woods, blocking the line of approach the British would have to assume. He deployed his army in two divisions. Arnold was on the army's left, commanding Poor's and Learned's Continental brigades. Gates personally commanded the Continental brigades under brigadier generals John Glover, John Nixon, and John Paterson on the army's right, nearest the river. Gates also positioned on the army's left Morgan's crack riflemen and a newly created light infantry battalion led by New Hampshire Maj Henry Dearborn, all of whom were under Arnold operationally. Including artillery, Stockbridge Indian scouts, and cavalry, Gates now commanded over 8,000 men, positioned behind strong earth and log defenses the soldiers constructed on strategic high ground.

Lt Col James Wilkinson, Gates's deputy adjutant general, described the American battle lines in detail.

> Gates' right occupied the brow of the hill near the river, with which it was connected by a deep entrenchment; his camp, in the form of a segment of a great circle, the convex toward the enemy ... about three-fourths of a mile to a knoll occupied by his left; his front was covered from the right to the left of the centre, by a sharp ravine running parallel with his line and closely wooded: from thence to the knoll at his extreme left, the ground was partially cleared, some of the trees being felled and others girdled, beyond which in front of his left flank, and extending to the enemy's right ... The extremities of this camp were defended by stoney batteries, and the interval was strengthened by breastwork without entrenchments, constructed of

---

*The spelling "Bemus" was originally used for this location in the 18th century and well into the 19th century, after the landowner Jotham Bemus.

the bodies of felled trees, logs, and rails with an additional battery at an opening left of the center. The right was almost impracticable; the left difficult of approach.[32]

This was an excellent position – much of it impregnable – from which the Patriot army could stand behind solid field works studded by field artillery, with interior lines and a secure right flank overlooking the river. Moreover, wooded terrain to their left and front made maneuver and reconnaissance difficult for the approaching enemy host. Defensive tactics suited Gates's strategy well – preventing the British army from reaching Albany.

Burgoyne's troops began crossing the Hudson on a floating bridge of batteaux just north of Saratoga on September 13; all but a few guards were on the river's west bank two days later. This was a tremendously risky move, as Burgoyne had now placed a major obstacle across his already tenuous supply line from Fort Ticonderoga, which could now be more effectively attacked and disrupted by swarming American militia units operating on the Hudson's east bank. Moreover, Burgoyne could not be sure he could recross the river if defeated or otherwise impelled to do so by American forces. He had effectively cut his extended line of communications to Canada and could only readily supply his army from the surrounding area – and it was now mid-September. Since Burgoyne's army had taken Skenesborough on July 6, they had only advanced 30 miles in 69 days. Time was limited; Burgoyne simply had to attack, defeat the rebels, and quickly reach Albany.

Once across the river, the British forces marched to Saratoga,* and then reached Sword's House four miles north of lofty Bemus Heights on September 17. Burgoyne's army numbered about 8,000 men, but only a handful of sullen Native Americans remained nearby, the rest having abandoned the British over the course of several weeks. At this point each army was sending out numerous scouting parties all over the heavily forested area, especially on their western flanks, where some maneuver could be possible, but movement was limited by poor roads, thick woods, and deep ravines.

*Now Schuylerville, New York.

After two more days at Sword's House, Burgoyne knew that dwindling supplies and the lateness of the season all but required him to attack the rebels' defensives and reach Albany, just 25 miles to the south. He ordered an advance to commence on September 19, with his entire army split into three columns. Fraser's Advanced Corps with artillery, Native Americans, and the Reserve Corps of Germans would move to the west by the British right flank to reconnoiter the American positions and to threaten the enemy's left and rear, forcing Gates to withdraw south. On Burgoyne's left, Gen Riedesel and the Brunswicker troops (along with some British forces) would march along the river road with much of the artillery and supply wagons, intending to divert Gates's attention from Fraser's flanking maneuver. A third column under Seven Years' War veteran Brig Gen James Hamilton consisting of the British foot regiments and four brass field pieces, accompanied by Burgoyne, would be at the army's center.

On the foggy morning of the 19th, the British and Germans packed up and advanced against the American defenses. The violent clash of the belligerents that warm day came to be known as the battle of Freeman's Farm, named for the deserted cabin and fields of Loyalist John Freeman in the center of the battleground. As Riedesel described it, "Freemann's Habitation … was the apple of discord during the whole of the day." Only a summary of this crucial engagement – and of the subsequent bloody clash on October 7 – can be given in these limited pages. Fortunately, the excellent recent scholarship of Eric Schnitzer, Theodore Corbett, John Luzader, and Kevin Weddle allows readers a detailed look at the complex fighting in the hills, ravines, and forests of Saratoga.[33]

On the British left Riedesel's 1,600 troops and artillery were slowed by damaged bridges and obstacles emplaced by Patriot forces along the river road. Meanwhile as Fraser's 3,000 men of the Advanced Corps troops moved west, they were followed by Hamilton's column of 1,700 troops, which turned south and then west to approach the Freeman farm. The Hessian Regiment Erbprinz remained at Sword's House as a rear guard.

American scouts alerted Gates to the enemy movements that morning. He elected to remain on the defensive behind his strong fortified lines in this his first battle as an army commander. The ever-aggressive Arnold, however, had other ideas. He urged a strong reconnaissance from the left flank to feel out the moving British columns in front of American lines and to disrupt their sweeping maneuver. Gates eventually consented by authorizing Morgan's riflemen and Dearborn's light infantry – 700 soldiers – to both observe and harass the British.

Morgan's foray turned into a far bigger fight than Gates had intended, and that afternoon saw heavy fighting with momentum shifting several times. Arnold had to deploy several Continental regiments and Connecticut militia into the growing struggle on the left directed by himself and Brig Gen Enoch Poor, while the hard-pressed British needed help from Fraser's corps and the Germans on the river road. When Arnold rode back to headquarters to urge Gates to send in additional troops, the army's cautious commander refused, concerned about Fraser's threatening force looming to his left.

From the British left Riedesel was finally able to bring 700 men and two 6-pounder guns to the east side of Freeman's fields to attack the rebels' right. The Brunswickers rallied the British troops still fighting on the "weed grown, stump studded farm." As evening fell, the American troops retreated through the darkening forest to their defenses, severely spent from the day's eight-hour struggle; the British made no attempt to pursue them, having suffered almost 600 killed, wounded, and missing, including 34 officers. This was almost ten percent of the army's strength, a staggering loss given the near impossibility of the redcoats getting reinforcements so far from Canada. Moreover, hundreds of wounded men overwhelmed the few British field hospitals at the main camp. By the tradition of this era, Burgoyne could claim a costly victory that day as his troops held the bloody field, but it did not feel like one. "It was soon found that no fruits, honours excepted, were attained by the preceding victory," Burgoyne admitted several weeks later.[34]

These heavy British losses also attest to the fierceness of the battle and the fighting quality of Gates's troops. "The courage and obstinacy with which the Americans fought were the astonishment of everyone, and we now became fully convinced they were not the contemptible enemy we had hitherto imagined them," a British observer conceded.[35]

The rebel troops had fought well for the most part, firing volley for volley against the redcoats for hours before yielding to the onrushing Brunswick infantry on their right flank at twilight. But they stopped the enemy's advance. And reckless Arnold had served well, inspiring the troops, frequently in the thick of the fighting.

Even before news of the battle and Burgoyne's now precarious situation spread, militia from New York, Massachusetts, New Hampshire, and Connecticut had mustered and marched to the American camps at Bemus Heights. Once Burgoyne crossed the Hudson, the British were suddenly far less of a threat to the New England states, so their soldiers poured into camps, raising Gates's strength to approximately 12,500 men. The American army "was practically overrun by thousands," historian Schnitzer writes, and food quickly became scarce.[36]

The outnumbered British remained in position where the fighting had ended, and dug in. "The Enemy have kept the Ground they Occupied the Morning of that Day [September 19]; And fortified their Camp," Gates reported to Washington.[37] In their lines the redcoats and Brunswickers regrouped, tended to their wounded, and prepared for more fighting. Burgoyne soon had it in mind to advance again and made plans to drive Gates's regiments off the high ground, when on September 21 he received a written message dated nine days earlier from General Clinton in New York, brought in by a stealthy courier, asking Burgoyne if a diversion from the south along the Hudson would be beneficial to the latter's operations. Burgoyne welcomed the timely offer and quickly replied by way of a daring messenger: "an attack or the menace of an attack" on American forts south of Albany "must be of great use, as it will draw away a part of this force and I will follow them close. Do it, my dear friend, directly."[38]

Burgoyne's imperative message starkly illustrates his increasingly perilous situation. Although he had advanced through a sparsely populated wilderness with his troops sustained by an overextended supply line with fickle (and fewer) Indian allies and disappointing Loyalists, he had arrived at a position close to Albany, his objective. But his need for Clinton's assistance made clear that his operations had stalled, particularly after the battle on the 19th, when the Americans not only put up a stout defense, but also responded aggressively.

To reach Albany he would now have to fight, and he now concluded he would surely need help.

The army of Canada's situation in mid-September again calls forth the dysfunctional command structure and planning failures among the top British generals and London officials. Clinton's offer of a diversion to support Burgoyne surely reminded the latter that his assumption of Gen Howe's army operating along the Hudson from the south was still in doubt. Germain, however, expected Howe to cooperate with Burgoyne as planned, even though he knew full well that Howe's focus was on Philadelphia. On August 16, Howe received a letter from Germain dated May 18 stating that whatever the general's operations against Philadelphia yielded he had to make sure he had time to coordinate with Burgoyne. Germain's letter, however, did allow for the Philadelphia expedition, and Howe chose to concentrate on that. In answering the letter on August 30 from Maryland, Howe advised the secretary that he would not be available to cooperate with Burgoyne at all. In fact, once Howe had decided on July 31 to change his route of approach to the rebel capital from the Delaware Bay to the Chesapeake Bay, he added another month to his campaign and "eliminated any possibility of aiding Burgoyne," writes historian Michael C. Harris.[39] Days before the fighting at Freeman's Farm, Howe soundly defeated Washington's army along Brandywine Creek, south of Philadelphia, and captured the city on September 26.

In New York, Clinton was as good as his word in helping his friend Burgoyne. On September 24, several thousand reinforcements arrived at New York from England. This allowed Clinton to take a force of 3,000 troops by ship and shore north on the Hudson on October 3. The British troops successfully attacked the Patriots' defenses at Forts Clinton and Montgomery about 55 miles from the city on October 6. The Americans also destroyed and abandoned nearby Fort Constitution by the 8th before the British arrived. Overall, the expedition to draw rebel troops away from Saratoga to face Clinton's expedition appeared to auger great success in Burgoyne's favor.

During these operations, Sir Henry received a verbal message from Burgoyne, still facing Gates near Saratoga, which greatly surprised him. With dwindling supplies, increasing casualties, and an American force growing daily, Burgoyne asked Clinton for orders on how to proceed. This was an entirely inappropriate request, in that Burgoyne's superior was Howe, not Clinton, who was under orders to support Burgoyne from New York City, not to command or advise him in a campaign that was largely Burgoyne's own design. It seems likely that at this point, Burgoyne realized he could not reach Albany, would get no more assistance from Clinton or Howe, and then began to look for scapegoats. In an October 8 message to the beleaguered Burgoyne, the punctilious Clinton wrote of his success against the rebels' forts, but also noted that with respect to the September 28 request, he could not "order or even advise [Burgoyne] for reasons obvious." Burgoyne never received this note.[40]

Back on October 3, the scarcity of supplies for Burgoyne's army had increased to the point that he cut the soldiers' rations by one-third. His commissaries advised him they had food to last only until October 20 or so. As emboldened American militia formations continued to "annoy, divide, and distract" the British rear and their stretched supply lines – even attacking at Ticonderoga, Mount Defiance, and the nearby Lake George boat landing – Burgoyne and his harried officers recognized that a major stroke against Gates's army had to be won for the endangered expedition to survive, or he had to order a retreat.[41]

After the costly engagement of September 19, the British and German soldiers had strengthened their field works by building a large log redoubt at Freeman's Farm for the Advanced Corps and artillery known as the British Light Infantry redoubt. To the north of it, they erected a poorly-built fortified camp occupied by the German troops of Lt Col Heinrich von Breymann. The British general officers now began to formulate their next move, with Burgoyne favoring an attack and Riedesel suggesting a retreat to Saratoga. On October 5, having consulted his senior officers, Burgoyne settled on making a reconnaissance in force against the American left from Freeman's Farm with 1,500 troops to "see whether [Gates] could be attacked or not," and to obtain much-needed forage for the starving animals.[42]

While the British leaders waited and planned, late September saw jealousy and quarrelling among the American officers on Bemus Heights, notably between the headstrong, glory-seeking Arnold and the insecure, defensive-oriented Gates and their respective supporters, a needless distraction for the Patriots' high command. Arnold felt slighted by Gates's failure to praise his troops' service at Freeman's Farm – or even mention his name – in a report to Congress, and had to be persuaded by supporters not to leave the army immediately. When Lincoln arrived in camp after the battle, he became by seniority the army's second in command in place of Arnold, as he outranked him, but the angry Connecticuter retained command of the left division. Fortunately, by early October the feuding generals were at least able to communicate without overt hostility and focus on confronting the enemy's intentions in their front.

On October 7, the last significant engagement of the campaign took place in a bloody, close quarters clash known as the battle of Bemus Heights, fought largely on and around Freeman's Farm. That morning Burgoyne – accompanied by Fraser and Phillips – led a corps of about 1,500 men southwest into the woods to scout the American left flank and gauge the likelihood of an effective attack. If successful, Burgoyne would promptly bring up the rest of the army to attack Gates's awaiting troops in their lines the following day. This plan was a bold throw of the dice, perhaps a desperate one, as the British high command knew of the superior numbers in Gates's ranks and his strong positions in front of them. The critical lack of supplies and the need to reach Albany, nonetheless, made this daring foray seem worth making.

Gates and his lieutenants were well aware of Burgoyne's critical predicament. They also knew that supplies for the British from Ticonderoga were now all but cut off. In a letter to Washington of October 5, Gates advised his superior that "from the best Intelligence he has not more than Three weeks provision in Store; it will take him at least Eight Days, to get back to Ticonderoga; so that, in a fortnight at farthest, he must decide, whether he will Rashly risque, at infinite Disadvantage, to Force [i.e., attack] my Camp, or Retreat to his Den."[43] Burgoyne's "rashly risque" reconnaissance was thus no surprise to his Patriot adversary.

Alert to Fraser's sweeping maneuver from his numerous forward scouts, Gates from his headquarters gave permission for Arnold, champing at the bit to get into the coming fight, to reconnoiter with

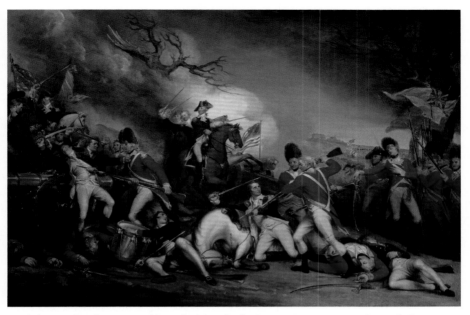

'The Battle of Princeton,' by John Trumbull. On 1st August 1977, General George Washington surprised and defeated British forces at Princeton, New Jersey. (Getty Images)

Engraved portrait of George Washington from the original picture painted by William Dunlap. (Getty Images)

Washington and his army crossing the Delaware River on December 25, 1776, prior to the Battle of Trenton. (Getty Images)

'26th December 1776: The Battle of Trenton' by John Trumbull. (Getty Images)

Site of Washington's troops' Christmas night crossing of the Delaware from Pennsylvania to New Jersey (distant shore). (Author's collection)

Maj Gen Horatio Gates, the victorious
American general at Saratoga.
(Getty Images)

British Lt Gen John Burgoyne surrenders
his army to Maj Gen Horatio Gates at
Saratoga in 1777. (Getty Images)

British Lt Gen John Burgoyne.
(Getty Images)

American Maj Gen Benedict Arnold
wounded at the second Battle of
Saratoga, 1777. (Getty Images)

The American position on Bemus Heights, overlooking the British line of advance towards Albany. (Author's collection)

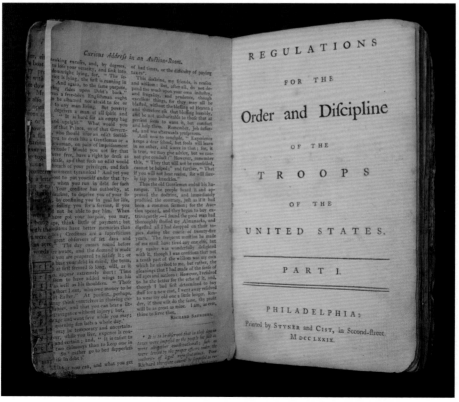

Regulations for the Order and Discipline of the Troops of the United States, also known as von Steuben's Blue Book. (The Society of the Cincinnati).

American troops march to Valley Forge, Pennsylvania, in 1777. (Getty Images)

Washington inspecting his soldiers' huts at the 1777–1778
Valley Forge encampment. (Getty Images)

Baron von Steuben, instrumental in improving the American Army during the winter at Valley Forge, 1778. (Author's collection)

Recreated winter huts at Valley Forge National Historical Park. (Getty Images)

Maj Gen Nathanael Greene, American commander at the Battle of Guilford Courthourse, 1781. (Getty Images)

Engraving of the Battle of the Cowpens, South Carolina, 1781 by Thure de Thulstrup. (Getty Images)

Lt Col Banastre Tarleton, an aggressive British cavalry leader in the Southern theater. (Getty Images)

Lt Gen Charles, Lord Cornwallis, commander of the British army at the bloody Battle of Guilford Courthouse, 1781. (Getty Images)

Greene's troops crossing the Dan River in Virginia to escape Cornwallis's pursuit. (Getty Images)

Maj Gen, Gilbert du Motier, the Marquis de Lafayette, a valuable French ally and Washington's key lieutenant in the 1781 Yorktown campaign. (Getty Images)

Above Washington's headquarters during the siege of Yorktown, 1781. (Getty Images)

Right French Admiral François Joseph Paul, Comte de Grasse. (Getty Images)

'Surrender of Lord Cornwallis,' by John Trumbull, depicting the British surrender at Yorktown to American and French forces. (Getty Images)

Morgan's crack shot riflemen, Dearborn's nimble light troops and a sturdy New Hampshire regiment. Arnold returned to camp after the initial fighting began, informed Gates of the developing situation, and convinced the American commander to allow him to attack with overwhelming might. Gates approved, and to the great encouragement of the troops, Arnold brought up additional regiments with him by late afternoon.

The fighting was heavy that cool, fall afternoon, the musket volleys "violent and incessant." Gradually the hard-pressed British troops had to fall back under intense fire, in which Fraser was mortally wounded. Soon the overwhelmed redcoats broke for the rear leaving eight artillery pieces behind, closely chased by bayonet-wielding American troops under Arnold's aggressive leadership.[44]

Arnold pushed the surging Patriot regiments onward against the main British and German fortifications, while Morgan and the light troops steadily worked their way around the British right rear. Burgoyne's troops put up a stout fight at close range from their defenses but as the day grew late the Americans captured Breymann's camp, shoved the German troops back with deadly volleys, and now threatened to envelop the entire right flank of the British lines. Arnold, however, was shot in the leg during the assault and had to be carried from the field in agony. By dusk the defeated army from Canada had been pushed back into a harried retreat. American losses for the day were about 150 killed and wounded, but the British and Germans suffered over 400 casualties shot down and strewn across the fields and woodlands, in addition to 200 men captured.

Gen Gates described the intense action to John Hancock, President of the Continental Congress, several days later. "From 3 o'clock in the Afternoon until almost Night the Conflict was very warm & bloody, when the [enemy] by a precipitate retreat determined the Fate of the Day leaving in our Hand eight pieces of Brass cannon, the Tents and Baggage of the Flying Army, a large quantity of … ammunition, a considerable number … wounded and Prisoner[s]…" This time he wisely made sure to applaud specifically "the gallant Major Genl Arnold whose Leg was fractured by a Musket Ball as he was forcing the enemy's Breast Work." He added that "too much Praise cannot be given to the Corps commanded by Colonel Morgan consisting of his [rifle] Regiment, and the light infantry."[45] It was a hard-fought and remarkable victory for the Patriot troops. Among the fallen leaves they triumphed over the enemy's professional, experienced troops who lost heavily in these terrible hours of close-in combat and were now retreating northward in haste. Burgoyne's veterans had been repulsed and thrown back – and so close to Albany.

With his western flank now dangerously exposed, Burgoyne ordered his demoralized troops back to the army's main camp near the Hudson River north of a deep draw called the Great Ravine. The heavy fighting that day cost him hundreds of casualties in a tremendous loss that gained his army nothing. The British commander must have known that the game was up. At this point the most he could hope for was a breakout to Lake George; any possibility of reaching Albany was gone. Most of the weary troops must have known it too. The day after the fierce battle was glum in British and German camps. Fraser died of his wound from a rifle bullet fired by one of Morgan's marksmen and was buried within the British "Great Redoubt," while the hungry army began its solemn withdrawal that night at 8pm, north toward Phillip Schuyler's riverside plantation and elegant house at Saratoga. Most of the 300 badly wounded British and German soldiers were left behind.

Late the next evening, the retreating redcoats and Germans halted at Saratoga. Without hope of succor or resupply, by the 13th they were surrounded by Gates's army and other militia forces. The inactivity of the British high command at Saratoga allowed time for Gen Stark to position a militia force of 2,000 men to their north, effectively closing off Burgoyne's only avenue of retreat. At this point, all of the British leaders in the camps at Saratoga recognized that the American army was too strong to be defeated, and the British army was too weak to get away to the north. The British commander regretfully sent an initial message to Gates about discussing surrender terms, thus beginning negotiations for capitulation. The first meeting between American and British officers to discuss surrender occurred on October 14, and the British called a truce the following day.

Initially, Gates astounded the British by agreeing to their easy terms quite quickly. Some anxious drama was added to the tense negotiations when the British learned of Clinton's relief force operating toward Albany on October 13. Burgoyne suspected that Gates was rushing the surrender negotiations so that this rescue attempt would not reach him or Albany in time. The expedition led by Maj Gen John Vaughan, however, did not reach Albany, and turned back to New York City on the 18th after burning Kingston, New York's capital, 60 miles south of Albany. Burgoyne received the advice of his officers that once capitulation negotiations had begun, he could not honorably break them off, and on October 17, the British commander agreed to a "convention" so that his beleaguered command would in effect surrender to Gates at Saratoga.[46]

At this point, within Gates's camps some of the bitter seeds of discord that grew into a command crisis within the Continental Army over the ensuing winter were deliberately sown. The victorious Gates decided to use his decisive triumph to snub his commander, George Washington, whose army had just been defeated at Germantown, Pennsylvania. Gates sent his senior aide, James Wilkinson, to officially report the news of the Saratoga victory to Washington, that "this fortunate Event [that] took place on the 17th Inst., & put us in possession of Six General officers, five thousand Combitants, five thousand stand of Arms, and twenty Seven Peices of well sorted brass Ordnance with fixed Ammunition Compleat."[47] But Wilkinson took his own sweet time to arrive at Washington's headquarters, while Gates snubbed Washington by reporting the news first to Congress, calling it "a signal & important event, [made] the more glorious, as it was effected with so little loss to the army of the United States."[48] The prickly, protocol-conscientious Washington – at the time still under the threat of Howe's large army at Philadelphia – instantly recognized Gates's studied act of disrespect. The fallout from this ugly episode will be taken up in the following chapter.

The immediate effect of the stunning American victory in the Saratoga campaign was the elimination of an entire enemy army of over 7,000 British, German, and Loyalist troops, not including casualties from St Leger's unsuccessful operations on the Mohawk River. Moreover, the dozens of pieces of artillery surrendered or captured in battle and at fortified posts during the campaign were invaluable to the Patriot cause, as cannons had to be imported to America with difficulty at this point in the war. Gates's army also gained an enormous quantity of muskets, ammunition, camp equipment, and other supplies quite difficult to procure in America.

The British loss of men and materiel could not be replaced in Canada and ended any future operations from there on the scale seen in 1776 and 1777. The strategy of 1777 was over. Although the terms of the "Convention" signed by the British and Americans on October 17 stipulated that the surrendered soldiers would soon be transported back to England, Congress quickly ignored this inconvenient stipulation and none of the prisoners sailed home until the war was over. Additionally, the British defeat led many Indian warriors to sour on campaigning with the redcoats, even before the surrender; by mid-October none remained in Burgoyne's camp. In effect the northern campaign had collapsed for Great Britain. Overall, the reconquest of America, writes historian Gordon Wood, seemed "beyond British strength."[49]

Official news of the disastrous surrender in the far-off New York forests reached London on December 2 in a dispatch from Sir Guy Carleton, although some ominous rumors of disaster had previously trickled into the sceptered isle. Strong vocal reaction was immediate from the opposition members in Parliament. "Ignorance had stamped every step taken during the course of the expedition," an angry parliamentarian complained in a typical remark.[50] Another MP wrote critically of the poorly executed campaign, and with some sense of military science: "no man with common sense would have placed two armies in such a position as from their distance made it absolutely impossible that the one should receive any assistance from the other." Fearful of "the gathering storm," the renowned old Whig William Pitt, now the Earl of Chatham, introduced in the House of Lords a provocative motion that stated, "if an end is not put to this war, there is an end to this country." And noted socialite, politician, and historian of Ancient Rome Edward Gibbon wrote that he refused to support "the prosecution of a war from whence no reasonable man entertains any hope of success." News of the disaster galvanized the political opposition to the king's ministers in London, shocked the public, and dearly undermined the country's sinking morale.[51]

The king and Lord North now had difficult choices to make regarding British leadership. Should they keep Lord Germain and the Howe brothers in their posts? All three received disparagement (especially Germain) for their failed efforts to crush the rebellion in 1777, and the loss of an entire army on the banks of the Hudson. In the end, Germain was not sacked, but North did allow a Parliamentary inquiry into the campaign from Canada. Sir William Howe, who had already tried to resign in October, was soon permitted to do so in February 1778, and Admiral Howe resigned months later; both brothers claimed that North had failed to support them in the American war. Carleton too requested that the ministry recall him; he was replaced in 1778 as both governor and military commander of Canada by the Swiss-born officer Sir Frederick Haldiman. The Saratoga disaster resulted in changes in British commanders in America along with a significant change in the king's strategy to crush the rebellion. Such were the sour fruits of defeat among its leaders. George III and Lord North recognized upon the news of the debacle on New York's distant frontier that the military situation required what has been called a "strategic reappraisal." Eminent British historian Piers Mackesy observes that "some new plan was needed," and the king now wanted "a radical review of strategy."[52] But this critical reassessment, Kevin Weddle observes, oddly did not include input from military officers in America, those "commanders on the ground with the most extensive knowledge of the overall situation."[53] Some lessons are never learned.

The king and London officials decided that the new focus in America would be on the southern colonies, where British officials believed there was far more Loyalist support than they had seen in New England and northern New York. In this belief they were encouraged by Loyalists from the South, eager for the crown to divert resources to reconquer Georgia, the Carolinas, and Virginia – which historian Mackesy terms "the soft underbelly of the rebellion."[54] A new emphasis would also be placed on naval operations – blockading ports and making coastal raids – to cripple America's warfighting capabilities, and to reclaim some of the more valuable colonies. There would be no more major offensives on land by the British army in the north. Although many Britons, including some in Parliament, called for an end to the war, George III and Lord Germain had no intention of giving up even after the impact of the Saratoga humiliation had settled in.

The most significant consequence of the Saratoga campaign was the entry of France, Great Britain's bitter enemy, into the war on the side of the United States. On March 13, France announced commercial and military treaties of alliance with the new United States, in effect a declaration of war with Britain, stipulating that "the two contracting Parties shall each on its own Part, and in the manner it may judge most proper, make all the efforts in its Power, against their common Enemy." The disparate American diplomatic delegation in Paris – Benjamin Franklin, Arthur Lee, and Silas Dean – had long urged the Comte de Vergennes, King Louis XVI's foreign minister, to recognize American independence, and continued with a renewed insistence once reliable news of Burgoyne's defeat reached Paris on December 4. The French had provided barely covert military aid to the Americans since early in 1776, including arms, gunpowder, naval stores, and other military necessities, but "Saratoga was the sign for which France had waited." Vergennes did not need to be pushed, as it turned out, nor did the French crown. King Louis exalted that "America is triumphant and England abashed," further concluding that Gates's victory "totally changed the face of things." "The American victory at Saratoga," observes historian Larrie Ferriero in his acclaimed study of the role France and Spain played in the Revolutionary War, "combined with somewhat optimistic reports that Washington had been only narrowly defeated at the battle of Germantown [on October 4, 1777, near Philadelphia], provided the outwardly reluctant Vergennes the pretext for the decision he had already made." Talks with eager American representatives began in early December, and the longed-for treaties were eventually signed in Paris on February 6, 1778.[55]

Louis XVI needed no excuses to go to war with Great Britain. After the overwhelming British victory in the Seven Years' War against France and Spain, both Bourbon monarchies sought revenge and the restoration of the colonies they had lost in 1763. In Paris, most believed that "England is the natural enemy of France," in the words of Joseph Matthias Gerard de Rayneval, under-secretary of state to Vergennes. Of the two enemies of Britain, France was the senior partner.[56] Spain was

France's ally in the war, but never recognized the United States officially. The Spanish were worried in early 1778 that if they formally recognized the American rebels, the British navy would attempt to capture the priceless annual silver convoy they expected from Mexico, and attack Spanish troop ships returning from Buenos Aires, Argentina. King Charles III of Spain did however agree not to make any separate peace with the British, on whom they declared war in June 1779, until the latter recognized American independence.

The French entry into the war had a hugely momentous effect on the military situation in America and Great Britain in several ways. Now that Britain and France were openly at war, the financial and military support from King Louis to the Americans was no longer covert. Thus, in addition to the loans, arms, and supplies furnished by the French, they could deploy troops to America along with naval forces, which would also threaten Britain's ability to resupply its forces in America. French regiments did in fact serve in several campaigns from 1778 to 1781, including the siege of Savannah, the battle of Rhode Island, and the war's culminating operations of the victorious Yorktown campaign. French ships also won the salient "Battle of the Capes" in September 1781, to make the crowning victory at Yorktown all but inevitable.

For King George III and Lords North and Germain, the American alliance with France created a sudden need to rethink their strategy, which fundamentally affected the military situation in their rebellious colonies. First, the British were now forced to redeploy thousands of soldiers and dozens of warships away from the American theater to other areas of operations. "After 1778, the British army and navy were engaged not only in the war for America, but in the protection of the British possessions in the West Indies, the Mediterranean, Africa, and India," writes award-wining historian Andrew O'Shaughnessy.[57] The British also "had to garrison 27 different posts in America, not including Canada." Additionally, the dreaded fear of a devastating cross-channel invasion of the home island by France – later joined with Spain – meant that fewer troops could be sent to or kept in America for the duration of the conflict. "In 1779, the danger of invasion was greater than at any time since the Spanish Armada in 1588." And once they joined the war, the Spanish quickly began an exhausting siege and blockade of the British-held base at Gibraltar at the western entrance to the Mediterranean Sea from June 1779 to February 1783. It was the largest battle of the war in terms of the numbers of British, Hanoverian, Spanish, and French troops involved. The British garrison there included over 5,000 troops, which could not be depleted for campaigns in America. Similarly, the already-stretched Royal Navy now had to safeguard Britain's vital commercial shipping trade from enemy warships and privateers, while at the same time protecting Great Britain from a likely seaborn attack. As Kevin Weddle concludes, "Great Britain now faced a global war without allies and without enough resources to conduct the operations it needed to undertake to achieve its end – preventing American independence."[58]

Most significantly for Americans, the Franco-American alliance made the West Indies and India the focus of British strategic thinking for the rest of the conflict. "The object of the war being now changed," the British Admiralty Board in London wrote to Admiral Richard Howe, "and the contest in America being a secondary consideration, our principal objects must be distressing France and defending ... his majesty's possessions." To France and Britain alike, the wealthy tropical islands of the Caribbean Sea were too valuable to leave unguarded, the source of immensely valuable sugar, rum, coffee, chocolate, indigo, and cotton. And the chance of planters losing thousands of their slaves was unacceptably risky. The islands became the main theater of the American conflict, drawing army and naval assets there and away from the former British mainland colonies. This redirection of British strategy had immediate results. In 1778, thousands of British troops now had to garrison and defend vital posts at Canada, Florida, Rhode Island, and New York City, while others sailed off for offensive operations in the West Indies.[59] Gen Clinton, who replaced William Howe at Philadelphia, received word at New York from Lord Germain that he would receive no reinforcements that year, and that he must ship 5,000 troops south to the West Indies to invade St Lucia, and redeploy 3,000 more soldiers to protect Florida and Canada. These troops' redeployments were the direct result of the refocusing of the war effort to the islands of the West Indies – because of the American success at Saratoga.

Clinton thus had to abandon Philadelphia and its numerous Loyalists and march his army back to New York in the early summer of 1778. Germain's instructions to the frustrated Clinton directed him to assume a defensive posture in American ports and garrisons. Lord Jeffrey Amherst, who in early 1778 had become commander-in chief of the Forces, wrote that "our principal object must be distressing France and defending and securing our own possessions against their horrible attempts."[60] This was a reactionary strategy. The lack of sufficient troops would prevent the British from meaningful offensive operations in New England and the mid-Atlantic region for the duration of the war. Perhaps a perceptive King George III summarized the critical change in circumstances in the American war best in a letter to Lord North of March 13, 1778. The French alliance with the United States

> must entirely overturn every plan proposed for strengthening the army under the command of Lieut. Gen. Clinton with an intent of carrying on an active war in North America; what occurs now is to fix what numbers are necessary to defend New York, Rhode Island, Nova Scotia and the Floridas; it is a joke to think of keeping Pennsylvania, for we must from the army now in America form a corps sufficient to attack the French islands, and two or three thousand men ought to be employed with the fleet to destroy the ports and wharfs of the rebels.[61]

Certainly, the most important result of the alliance with France in 1778 – made possible by the improbable Saratoga victory – was that now the American cause had a military asset it could not create for itself: a powerful navy. The vital importance of the French navy for the eventual victory for the United States can hardly be overstated. "It was the presence of French warships, not additional arms or men, that would change the fundamental nature of the war," historian Larrie Ferreiro concludes.[62] The Continental Navy, authorized by the new Congress in 1775, was far too small throughout the war to counter George III's huge Royal Navy of almost 300 warships. These sailing ships gave the British the dominating capability of securely transferring troops, cannonading seaports and shorelines, and limiting American commerce on the high seas – none of which could be countered by the under-sized Continental Navy. With France now fully in the war, bolstered by the Spanish navy the next year, the United States's new ally was an effective counter threat to the British fleets in the Caribbean Sea and on the Atlantic Ocean, as well as a serious threat to Great Britain itself. As will be seen in a later chapter, after many frustrating twists and turns in the joint military operations of French and American forces for three years, the alliance paid off brilliantly in the most spectacular way imaginable for the cause of independence at Yorktown, Virginia, in the summer and fall of 1781.

With few exceptions, historians rightly judge the Saratoga campaign to be the most decisive military event of the American Revolution. The morale-boosting victory was proof "that the American country with its armed population might be beyond the power of Britain to reconquer with any force which she could raise and sustain in America," writes Mackesy, and it was "the clearest turning point of the war."[63] The consequent French alliance, Ferriero concludes, "breathed new life into the cause of independence ... America was now assured of a military campaign on more equal terms."[64] Further examples abound.

The importance of the victory was not lost on contemporaries either. Having heard unofficial news of the impending Saratoga victory on October 18, Washington exulted that it was "the happy moment which Heaven has pointed out for the firm establishment of American Liberty." He later magnanimously called it "the great and important event to the Northward" which "must be attended with the most fortunate consequences," and a "singular Instance of Providence."[65] These "consequences" included not only the loss of a large British field force, but an end to major military operations in the northern provinces, an alteration in British strategy in America, and French recognition of the United States along with a military alliance. The latter proved decisive, the *sine qua non* of American victory in the Revolutionary War.

3

The Army's Reformation: The Winter at Valley Forge, 1777–78

"It is not easy to give you a just and accurate idea of the sufferings of the Army at large," wrote George Washington to the state government of New Hampshire, just nine days after moving his suffering troops to their bleak winter camps at Valley Forge, Pennsylvania, about 25 miles west of Philadelphia. "Were they to be minutely detailed, your feelings would be wounded, and the relation would probably be not received without a degree of doubt & discredit."[1] Thus did the army's commanding general allude to and foretell in one letter the Continental Army's trying experience from December 19, 1777, to June 19, 1778. The story of this desolate winter encampment has been colored by myths and legends ever since American troops left Valley Forge to pursue the British who abandoned Philadelphia, headed for New York. Revising this overly nostalgic narrative has been the work of recent historians Mark Lender, Ricardo Herrera, Wayne Bodle, and John Buchanan, who each offer a modern look at the American army's trying experience along the Schuylkill River's southern bank. These historians have adeptly detailed the American army's trials and tragedies, which thus need only be generally recounted in this chapter. Rather, how the American army's Valley Forge experience decisively contributed to its ultimate victory and helped establish the independence of the thirteen new states is the focus of this study.

As seen in the previous chapter, the military events in Pennsylvania in the summer and fall of 1777 were intertwined with the decisive Saratoga campaign that led to Burgoyne's surrender to Gates. That spring Washington had moved out of the army's winter camps at Morristown, New Jersey, on May 28 to get closer to New York and observe British movements from Bound Brook. His command numbered just over 8,000 men in the ranks, many of whom were serving three-year enlistments.

Based on plans he had begun to form the previous November, General Howe planned to lead a large part of his force at New York to capture Philadelphia, the putative American capital, and the largest city in the colonies. Howe's campaign precluded a strong effort to coordinate operations with Burgoyne's army from Canada attempting to reach Albany. Despite the expectations of Germain and Burgoyne for the British commander in chief to coordinate with the Canadian army's operations along the Hudson River in some meaningful way, Howe set sail with about 20,000 troops on July 23 on his expedition to the south. He left about 7,000 troops at New York under Clinton to protect the port city from an opportunistic attack by Washington. In early July, Howe heard of Burgoyne's unexpectedly rapid progress and his capture of Fort Ticonderoga, which convinced him that the northern army no longer needed support from New York City. Initially Howe planned to sail south and then move up the Delaware River to close in on Philadelphia, but he subsequently changed his approach to the Chesapeake Bay. This decision added weeks to the long voyage and gained him nothing. Not until August 25 did British and Hessian troops begin disembarking from their cramped transport ships at Head of Elk, Maryland, at the north end of the bay.

Until Howe's actual destination was known, Washington had to be careful how he reacted to his enemy's movements. When Howe's soldiers boarded their ships in early July, Washington could not have known if they intended to sail up the Hudson or to Boston, or possibly to southern waters. Once Washington concluded that Howe was bent for Philadelphia, he quickly shifted troops from northern New Jersey to the capital city's environs. By early September the American army came to occupy a defensive position on the left (east) bank of the Brandywine

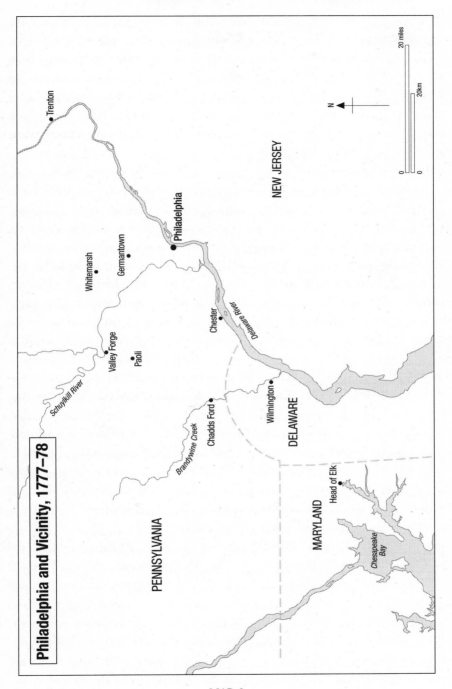

Philadelphia and Vicinity, 1777–78

Trenton

Philadelphia

Germantown

Whitemarsh

Chester

Valley Forge

Paoli

Schuylkill River

NEW JERSEY

Delaware River

Wilmington

DELAWARE

Brandywine Creek

Chadds Ford

MARYLAND

Head of Elk

PENNSYLVANIA

Chesapeake Bay

N

20 miles

20km

0

0

MAP 3

River about 20 miles west of Philadelphia, having cautiously fallen back from northern Delaware as the enemy slowly advanced.

A major battle was not long in coming. On September 11, Howe sent most of his troops on a wide flanking march under Lord Cornwallis and struck Washington's troops on their right flank and rear. After fierce fighting for several hours during which the hard-pressed American troops fought well, Washington ordered a retreat north over the Schuylkill River to Germantown that evening. His tired army had suffered 1,300 casualties, more than double those of the British, but the officers and soldiers were generally in good spirits. Howe, as was his habit, did not pursue them immediately after the battle. Congress had already recognized they were in danger, and hurried west to York, Pennsylvania, by September 18.

Washington's dilemma in September was that he faced two competing imperatives. If he took up a position to defend Philadelphia – Howe's primary objective – his army could not protect its supply collections to the west on the Schuylkill River at and near Reading. Conversely, if the Continentals defended their supply depots, Washington risked losing the capital city. In a series of marches, maneuvers, skirmishes, and small engagements – including the "massacre" of an unsuspecting American detachment under Brig Gen Anthony Wayne at Paoli Tavern on September 20 – Howe managed to occupy Philadelphia unopposed on the 26th. Washington had been outgeneraled but given the size and condition of his army at that time, it is doubtful he could have prevented Howe's success anyway. The British army would now have adequate winter quarters, although scarcely luxurious, and as many as 2,000 soldiers at times made up the lengthy sick rolls.

Washington and his lieutenants, however, were not thinking of ending the campaign for the year so early. In fact they saw an opportunity to strike a blow at about 8,000 enemy troops positioned around Germantown, north of Philadelphia. On October 4, the American army attacked the redcoats and Hessians on a foggy morning, advancing in four separate columns. Washington's bold thrust was initially successful, but early fog caused some confusion, too much attention was devoted to neutralizing a British-fortified stone house on the main line of advance, and Washington's battle plan was overly complex. The Patriot army was forced to retreat – in good order – 25 miles northwest to Pennypacker's Mills, having come so close to victory. By the end of November, the British army and navy were able to clear the Delaware River south of Philadelphia and secure their riverine supply lines by eliminating the stubborn rebel forts Mifflin and Mercer.

In early November Washington marched his army forward to Whitemarsh Creek, a dozen miles northwest of Philadelphia, where his troops occupied strong defensive positions on high ground supported by well-sited artillery. By this point, however, the increasing logistical difficulties of the Continental Army's supply system had practically immobilized the troops. Now, Howe decided to advance against the rebels before winter set in but then hesitated to order a frontal assault once he saw the daunting rebel lines. The Americans had also been reinforced by thousands of footsore troops arriving from Saratoga after Gates's decisive victory. Howe couldn't tempt the cautious Washington to attack him, and after unsuccessfully trying to flank the Americans, he withdrew his army in frustration to their strong Philadelphia lines. Now with cold and wet weather setting in, the British and their Hessian allies settled into their winter quarters and camps.

Once Howe withdrew his troops from Washington's nearly impregnable position, the American commander had an important decision to take: "whether the army should wage a winter campaign or take up winter quarters," in historian Ricardo Herrera's words, "which was as much a political decision as it was a military matter." Washington's army had to "deny the British Army the ability to sustain itself from the region" by keeping a threatening force on foot nearby, but far enough away from the enemy to avoid a sudden strike Howe might lead from the city's garrison. The Continentals also had to protect their invaluable supply depots off to the west and safeguard the vulnerable populace living in the area around Philadelphia from British depredations. They had to be "far enough from the Enemy not to be reached in a day's march, and properly interposed between the Enemy and the most valuable part of the Country on this side of the Schulkil," wrote Washington's young aide John Laurens of South Carolina.[2]

Many Congressmen pressed Washington to continue active military operations. Likewise, some of Washington's generals called for the army to attack Philadelphia, a risky option especially given the American soldiers' lack of clothing, shoes, and provisions for active winter operations. But others urged caution. An attack "would be Hazardous and must End in Ruin to the Army & to the American Cause," Gen Sullivan warned. Lafayette too argued against a "project" with so many "difficulties, inconveniencies, and bad chances," while artillery chief Henry Knox suggested moving the army instead to a place of "tranquility." After scouting the British defenses around Philadelphia in late November, Washington decided against an assault, due in part to his army's "distressing" condition.[3] Gen Greene was of a similar opinion. "The probability of a disappointment is infinitely greater than that of success," he wrote to Washington, and "we must not be governed in our measures by our wishes."[4] Washington decided to move the troops to a suitable place for a winter encampment. Historian Herrera succinctly summarizes the army's eventual course of action. Washington wisely listened to voices that "counseled caution, restraint, and patience; voices that foresaw waste, ruin and disaster; and voices that varied in temperament, learning and vision – but all of which were united in their opposition to another effort against Howe's army. The Continentals needed to enter winter quarters."[5]

Washington gave orders for the troops to march out of the defensive lines at Whitemarsh on December 11, cross the Schuylkill River, and head west to Gulph Mills, where in a heavy snowstorm they arrived two days later and remained for six days without tents. He announced that "the army [was to] to take such a position, as will enable it most effectually to prevent distress & to give the most extensive security; and in that position we must make ourselves the best shelter in our power." The commanding general was still unsure where their encampment would be. His aide Col Laurens wrote on the 15th that "the precise position is not yet fixed upon, in which our huts are to be constructed; it will probably be determined today; it must be in such a situation as to admit of a bridge of communication over the Schuylkill for the protection of the country we have just left." From the Gulph, Washington announced prior to moving once again that he "persuades himself, that the officers and soldiers, with one heart, and one mind, will resolve to surmount every difficulty, with a fortitude and patience, becoming their profession, and the sacred cause in which they are engaged: He himself will share in the hardship, and partake of every inconvenience." These were high expectations for every soldier.[6]

The hungry army of as many as 19,000 men marched on December 19 from Gulph Mills to a wooded area around two high hills, Mount Joy and Mount Misery, which was known as Valley Forge.[7] This position was just south of the Schuylkill River, about 20 miles from Philadelphia, and had several advantages for a cantonment. The area was "densely wooded" rolling terrain that made it a strong defensive position. Soldiers, scouts, and spies could keep an eye on the British in Philadelphia, and the open terrain between the camps and the city meant that an enemy advance against Valley Forge could be promptly detected. Additionally, if the British launched operations against them, the Continentals could cross the river to their rear at Fatland Ford, where a bridge was later built.

Washington's fatigued troops that struggled into Valley Forge were already in bad shape. The weary soldiers' trail to the new cantonment, according to Private Joseph Plumb Martin, could be "tracked by their blood upon the frozen ground." And "during this march we had nothing to eat nor to drink," a Massachusetts officer recalled.[8] An American commissary agent warned of an "approaching calamity that threatens our Army for want of Provisions." Likewise, Brig Gen James Varnum of Rhode Island wrote at the time that "three days successively, we have been without bread. Two days we have been intirely without meat … The men must be supplied or they cannot be commanded." This was quite an ominous observation that would indeed be realized in the coming months.[9]

Adding to the supply difficulties were the 400 or so women and their children who accompanied the soldiers and also had to be fed. They were wives, washerwomen, seamstresses, cooks, and nurses. All but a few are nameless to history. Many managed to survive the long marches, scant food, disease, and weather of life in camp and on campaign with the army. The Continentals did not clothe them and barely fed them. Washington tried to rid the army of all women not useful to the troops and regarded them as a nuisance. They were often seen as an impediment to the army's movements and were typically ordered to march at the dusty or muddy rear of the columns with the wagons. The British and Hessians too had camp followers, a common sight in armies of the 18th century.

The first order of the day was for the soldiers to build shelters. At Washington's direction the troops built 14- by 16-foot log shelters for themselves, each with a "fire-place made of wood and secured with clay on the inside," laid out in orderly streets. On the 18th, Washington ordered his brigade officers

> to superintend the business of hutting [and] to oversee the building of huts for his own regiment; which officer is to take his orders from the field officer of the brigade he belongs to, who is to mark out the precise spot, that every *hut*, for officers and soldiers, is to be placed on, that uniformity and order may be observed.[10]

He directed that the troops were "to be divided into squads of twelve, and see that each squad have their proportion of tools, and set about a hut for themselves." Washington offered an incentive "as an encouragement to industry and art ... to reward the party in each regiment, which finishes their hut in the quickest, and most workmanlike manner, with *twelve* dollars."[11] Over 2,000 huts were eventually constructed that winter. The soldiers "appeared to me like a family of beavers," wrote Thomas Paine, "every one busy,"[12] although tools and nails were in short supply. Many huts were poorly insulated and ventilated, with harmful health effects on the troops. Hundreds of drafty shelters were dug a few feet into the ground which increased dampness inside them, and some had no doors or floors. Lafayette described them as "little shanties that are scarcely gayer than dungeon cells."[13] Not until February 8 did Washington report that most of the army was housed in log huts.

Images and legends of the Valley Forge winter often depict the weather as being severe, but in fact it was not unusually cold that year and there were no major blizzards to endure. The army's Morristown winter encampment of 1779–80 in New Jersey was much worse in terms of snow and bitter temperatures; Washington called it "intensely cold and freezing." During the Valley Forge months, however, winter temperatures were below freezing about 30 days, which was not notably harsh. In fact, the troops' hardships were not primarily the result of the weather, though the rain, snow, and cold certainly contributed to their misery. Rather, as historians conclude, "it was the result of exposure, given the impact by the poor shelter, inadequate clothing, and malnutrition from which the men suffered."[14]

While the soldiers began to build their rustic huts as soon as they arrived in the frosty hollows and hills of Valley Forge, the army had other critical needs that plagued them throughout their time on the banks of the frigid Schuylkill. In short, they lacked almost everything. Indeed, much of the story of Valley Forge in 1777–78 is really about the failure of logistics, its effect on the soldiers, and how Washington worked with Congress directly to try to alleviate the army's precarious position.

One of the most persistent problems the ragged army and civilian leaders faced was clothing the troops properly for military service and warding off the winter elements. One veteran of Valley Forge wrote a vivid description of the typical suffering Continental: "There comes a soldier, his bare feet are seen through his worn-out shoes, his legs nearly naked from the tattered remains of his only pair of stockings; his breeches not sufficient to cover his nakedness; his shirt hanging in strings."[15] Washington struggled with the troops' persistent lack of adequate clothing supplies all winter and spring. Even at the beginning of the encampment he wrote about his dilemma to Patrick Henry, Virginia's first governor. "It will be a happy circumstance, and of great saving, if we should be able in future to cloath our Army comfortably. Their sufferings hitherto have been great, and from our deficiencies in this instance, we have lost many Men & have generally been deprived of a large proportion of our Force."[16] The lack of proper uniforms – regimental coats, hats, breeches, shirts, waistcoats, stockings, and shoes – led to deaths, desertions, and thousands of men unready for service. Washington later wrote to Governor Henry at the end of the year that "the Articles of Shoes – Stockings & Blankets demand the most particular attention, as the expenditure of 'em from the Operations & common accidents of War we find to be greater, than of any Other Articles." He also reported with some alarm that just days beforehand, "not less than 2898 Men [were] unfit for duty by reason of their being bare foot & otherwise naked" in their squalid camps.[17] Gen Greene agreed, reporting in January that military "operations are greatly facilitated by having the soldiers well cloathed, and their health preserved."[18]

Greene warned Rhode Island's governor Nicholas Cooke in January of the soldiers' plight. "It is very necessary that large supplies of cloathing be procured and sent forward for the use of the officers as well as the soldiers," he advised, as "they suffer very much for want of cloathes.' Tis peculiarly hard that added to all the necessary hardships of a soldiers life we should suffer so much in this respect."[19] Likewise, Gen Wayne reported in February to Pennsylvania's president Thomas Wharton Jr, that "some Hundreds of our poor worthy fellows have not a single ragg of a shirt … I have not been able to draw a single shirt from the store, for the want of which our men are falling sick in numbers every day – contracting vermin and dying in Hospitals, in a condition shocking to Humanity, & horrid in Idea – for God sake procure a Quantity for me [even] if you strip the Dutchmen [German speaking settlers] for them."[20] At one point, tents were used to make shirts for lack of an alternative cloth. Washington eventually ordered army detachments to seize clothing from area residents, an expedient that caused "the greatest alarm and uneasiness even among our best and warmest friends."[21] By the first week of February, an alarming 3,989 men were unfit for duty because they lacked shoes or clothing. Long after the crisis at Valley Forge, Baron von Steuben would recall that "the men were literally naked in the fullest extent of the word."[22]

Reputedly, the observation that "an army marches on its stomach" was coined by Napoleon or Frederick the Great. Undoubtedly, all the troops at Valley Forge would have agreed to the primary importance to a soldier of adequate food rations delivered regularly in maintaining the army's morale and overall health. The persistent lack of food plagued Washington's troops from their initial arrival at Valley Forge and did not begin to improve until well into the spring of 1778. As congressmen and army officers eventually recognized, the Continental procurement system and a lack of adequate transportation were the primary causes of the food supply problem.

A complete account of the many hardships and suffering of the troops for the entire Valley Forge winter is beyond the scope of this brief chapter. It is worth noting, however, that the bleakest part of the winter encampment experience was in February 1778, which saw one of the gravest crises for the cause of independence during the entire war. A marked downturn in the weather exacerbated the supply shortages. Even in late January Greene reported that "our troops are naked, we have been upon the eve of starving, and the Army of mutinying."[23] Hungry soldiers shivering in damp huts were heard to mumble "no bread, no soldier" and "no meat no soldier." On some occasions they boiled leather scraps for soup or ate the bark off trees, a sure sign of desperation. The soldiers also ate squirrels, rabbits, and raccoons. Not infrequently the troops had no meat or flour for days at a time. "The resources of this Country in point of fresh Provision are nearly exhausted," Washington reported on February 6, "and the Army under my command is in consequence litterally reduced to a starving Condition."[24]

Provisions began to improve in March, and in April more shad fish was available from the nearby Schuylkill River for several weeks. But until the weather improved, food supplies in camp were so low as to alarm the army's leaders. In early February Washington wrote to the army's inept commissary general that "the occasional deficiencies in the Article of provisions, which we have often severely felt, seem now on the point of resolving themselves into this fatal crisis – total want and a dissolution of the Army," which would of course result in "the most ruinous consequences." The army's commander warned that due to food shortages "the spirit of desertion among the sold[i]ery never before rose to such a threatening height, as at the present time. The murmurs on account of Provisions are become universal, and what may ensue, if a better prospect does not speedily open, I dread to conjecture."[25] Maj Gen William Alexander, known as Lord Sterling due to his unrecognized claim to a disputed Scottish earldom, advised Washington that "the Complaints of the want of provisions and forrage are become universal and Violent, every officer speaks of it with dread of the probable Consequences." In mid-February, Gen Varnum alerted Greene that "the Situation of the Camp is such, that in all human probability the Army must soon dissolve – ——Many of the Troops are destitute of Meat, & are several Days in Arrear," adding that many horses were dying for want of fodder.[26]

The lack of food concerned the army's leadership, as morale plummeted in the Valley Forge camps. Commissary officer Ephraim Blaine wrote in mid-February that the soldiers' daily rations had reduced by half, and "god only Knows when we shall have it in our power to Afford them a plentiful supply."[27] Earlier that month Washington wrote to Jeremiah Wadsworth, former Deputy Commissary General of Purchases, that "the present unsettled State of the Commissary's department in this quarter, makes me fearful, that unless some Measures are fallen upon to reconcile the jarring Interests of these who act, or pretend to act, under the Appointments of Colo. [Joseph] Trumbull, that the Army will in a little while want Supplies of every kind." Washington also warned of "the alarming situation of the Army on account of provision."[28]

Surely no one was more concerned with the army's dire situation in February 1778 than its commander in chief. Washington wrote to Govenor George Clinton of New York on the 16th about "the present dreadful situation of the army," reporting that "for some days past, there has been little less, than a famine in camp. A part of the army has been a week, without any kind of flesh & the rest three or four days." Always alert to the danger of mutiny among the cold, hungry, unpaid troops, he admitted that "strong symptoms … of discontent have appeared in particular instances; and nothing but the most active effort[s] every where, can long avert so shocking a catastrophe." He also worried that the dwindling stockpiles of supplies ("magazines") provided by New Jersey, Pennsylvania, Delaware, and Maryland "will not be sufficient to support the army more than a month longer, if so long."[29] By the end of the month almost 5,000 men were sick, and about 3,700 troops had no shoes or clothing and were consequently hors de combat.

One of Washington's most vivid letters during the February provisions crisis was to Patrick Henry. Wasting no words, Washington described "the melancholy prospect before us, with respect to supplies of provisions." He added that "the situation of the Commissary's department and of the army, in consequence, is more deplorable, than you can easily imagine. We have frequently suffered temporary want and great inconveniences, and for several days past we have experienced little less than a famine in camp." The general worried he "had much cause to dread a general mutiny and dispersion" of the troops. Food was so scarce that

> our future prospects are, if possible still worse: The magazines laid up, as far as my information reaches, are insignificant, totally incompetent to our necessities; and from every appearance, there has been heretofore so astonishing a deficiency in providing, that unless the most vigorous and effectual measures are at once, every where adopted, the language is not too strong to declare that we shall not be able to make another campaign.[30]

Thus, no food, no army.

When supplies did not arrive in sufficient quantities for the hungry soldiers in camp despite the pleas of Washington and Congress for help, the army had to rely on the odious expedient of impressment, which meant seizing private property for the army's use, "a lawful yet deeply resented practice." Impressment was "subject to considerable abuse, was often overly broad in scope, and became a license to steal in the hands of some disreputable agents." But often this was the commissaries' or quartermasters' only choice.[31] Many army leaders knew the risks associated with taking the property of citizens. "We take all the Horses and Cattle, Hogs and Sheep fit for use," General Greene wrote, "but the Country has been so gleaned that there is little left in it ... How far necessity may sanctify the seizing and stating the value of private property for public purposes, I shall not pretend to say," thought Greene, "but the fewer the instances the better, as it militates with the first principles of civil government, by destroying that security and confidence in the public faith plighted to every individual, to protect him in the enjoyment of personal liberty, and the free disposal of his property."[32]

Not only were the men in the ranks hungry but so were the horses, crucial for the army's transportation of supplies, deploying artillery, and cavalry operations. One of Washington's aides, Tench Tilghman, wrote of "the alarming Situation we are in, in regard to provision and Forage." He implored Clement Biddle, commissary general in charge of forage, to seize every "Carriage that can be found and send them forward to

Camp loaded with Forage. If some is not got in soon, it will come too late as I fear we shall not have a Horse left alive to eat it. You know our distress and I am sure you will endeavour to alleviate it." Numerous plaintive letters among army leaders warned Washington that "the Horses are dying for want of Forage," and that "our horses are dying by dozens every day for the want of forage." One observer in camp noted that without horses "almost every species of camp transportation is now performed by men, who without a murmur, patiently yoke themselves to little carriages of their own making, or load their wood and provisions on their backs."[33]

The lack of food and fodder that winter was also caused by the enemy. The British captured supplies around Philadelphia by raiding mills, farms, and homes with large detachments. Moreover, they frequently bought supplies from eager Americans near the city, who were quite willing to sell their produce to the occupiers – for which they received precious hard currency rather than Continental receipts of dubious value. American forces often patrolled the roads leading into Philadelphia to interdict this trade that impeded the flow of valuable supplies to Valley Forge and treated severely those they caught red-handed. One unlucky Pennsylvania civilian was "tried for attempting to carry flour into Philadelphia, [and] found guilty of the charge." He was sentenced to receive 250 lashes on his bare back. Another man was "tried for attempting to drive Cattle in to the Enemy," convicted, "and sentenced to pay the sum of one hundred pounds and to be confined in the Provost Guard 'till that sum is paid to the Adjutant General, out of which twenty dollars shall be paid to each of the Light-horsemen who apprehended the prisoner as an encouragement for their Activity & good conduct[,] the rest to be applied to the use of the sick in Camp." But Washington admitted in early February that "in spite of every thing hitherto done," this commerce was "still continuing, and threatening the most pernicious consequences."[34]

In mid-February, Washington learned through his extensive intelligence network that the British "intend making another grand Forage into this Country," a major sweep outside of Philadelphia to procure supplies for their troops, and to deny them to the rebels. To get a jump on the redcoats, the Continental Army commander ordered over 1,500 of his men to make their own "Grand Forage" to collect food, fodder, and militarily useful supplies. This major procurement expedition would be led by his reliable lieutenant, Gen Greene. In his February 12 orders, Washington authorized Greene "forthwith to take[,] Carry off & secure all such Horses as are suitable for Cavalry or for Draft and all Cattle & Sheep fit for Slaughter together with every kind of Forage that may be found in possession of any of the Inhabitants," and to cover "within Fifteen or Twenty miles west of the River Delaware between the Schuylkil and the Brandywine." Always wary of antagonizing the local citizenry, he ordered Greene to make sure that proper "Certificates [were] to be given to each person for the number[,] value & quantity of the horses Cattle Sheep & Provender so taken."[35] He did not have to add "if possible," as the two generals knew that such niceties could not interfere with the mission's goal.

Gen Wayne acted as Greene's deputy commander for the operation, "helping to score important successes, such as several hundred head of cattle, dozens of horses, loads of forage, wagons, harnesses, and other supplies," in New Jersey. Capt Henry "Light-Horse Harry" Lee also conducted foraging operations along the northern Chesapeake Bay in Delaware. "Forage the country naked," Greene told his officers, "We must take all their Cattle, Sheep and Horses fit for the use of the army."[36] The foraging endeavor was not easy. Greene reported on the scores of disaffected farmers encountered, many of whom hid their livestock, wagons, and food. But out of necessity, he had to be ruthless. "The Inhabitants cry out and beset me from all quarters," he wrote Washington, "but like the Pharoah I harden my heart." He continued "I determine to forage the country very bare. Nothing shall be left unattempted."[37] After Greene's troops were back at Valley Forge, Greene summarized his expedition for Henry Knox: "I executed my orders with great fidelity," but added "we are still in danger of starving."[38]

Modern scholarship has documented that in 1778 supplies were sufficient and sometimes plentiful in the area around Valley Forge and beyond. The fall of 1777 had seen a productive local harvest as well. The agriculturally rich region had long been considered as "the best poor man's country." For most of the winter, the problem was not a persistent lack of nearby food and fodder or heavy snows blocking roads.

Rather, it was the lack of transportation to bring supplies to the army's camps. "We are starving in a land of plenty," observed Washington's aide John Laurens, "perishing by Cold and surrounded by Cloathing Sufficient for two Armies but uncollected." Trussel concludes that "the root cause of the army's difficulties in the winter of 1777–78 ... was the basic inability of the transportation system to meet the requirements of the situation."[39] Roads were often poor and muddy, inadequate to provision thousands of troops and the army's horses. Congress also paid unrealistically low rates to hire wagons and teamsters than did the local economy, making it difficult to let contracts. Wagons and horses were simply not available for the army's use to transport supplies to Valley Forge, in a rural location with a road network ill-suited for supplying thousands of soldiers for six months.

Inadequate food, a lack of clothing, and poor housing inevitably led to the widespread decline of the soldiers' health. Even in June 1778, long after winter was over, about 2,300 troops were on the brigades' sick lists at Valley Forge. Men suffered from influenza, typhus, pneumonia, and dysentery, brought on by unsanitary camps, bad water, and the lack of blankets. Frostbite too was a concern, as was smallpox outbreaks. Lafayette observed that "the unfortunate soldiers were in want of everything; they had neither coats, hats, shirts nor shoes; their feet and legs froze till they became black, and it was often necessary to amputate them."[40] An estimated 2,000 to 2,500 soldiers died during the winter, most of them from March to May.

During the winter and spring months, Washington had other difficulties to face besides the army's critical lack of clothing, supplies, forage, and medicine. As if those enormous challenges were not enough for him, he also confronted administrative crises within the army, including widespread discontent among his disgruntled junior officers, congressional interference with the army's leadership, and what appeared to be a determined effort by a clique of generals and congressmen to supplant him as commander in chief with a now prominent rival.

Once the straggling army reached its camps along the right bank of the Schuylkill, officer resignations erupted as a significant problem during the early months at Valley Forge. Congress and the states had been planning a reorganization of the Continental Army for months, an effort met with much opposition by many of the army's officers, some of whom would be reduced in rank or no longer retain their commands. The widespread discontent among the officers caused low morale, and their numerous resignations caused much disorder in the army's organization, training, and readiness. It also irked the commander in chief to no end. Historians James Kirby Martin and Mark Edward Lender have concluded that

> Washington's officers were growing as restless and angry as the soldiery. To the officers, any needless tampering with rank became an attack on personal honor. Washington's lieutenants wanted the respect they thought due them as propertied citizens, who now held high military rank. Congress, however, treated them as if they were professional soldiers – and a possible threat to society.[41]

The frustrated commander called for unity in the struggle, not division: "we should all be considered as one people, embarked in one cause, in one interest; acting on the same principle into the same end." But he recognized a growing divide between the army's leaders and a largely unsympathetic Congress, which he considered worrisome.

Washington's subordinates were growing increasingly upset for good reason. They had spent a lot of money "maintaining themselves in the field" as gentlemen and feared being financially ruined at the end of the war by a stingy Congress. Many demanded half pay pensions for life, to begin at the end of the war, as just recognition for their sacrifices and lost income (a common practice in the British army). These officers were "wasting their fortunes, impairing their constitutions, [and] depriving themselves of every domestic pleasure," wrote Gen Greene. He also worried that "this discontent has arisen to such a height and is so general as to forebode the most alarming consequences." Greene held that "if [officers] lose the confidence in the justice of Congress it is easy to foresee the fatal effects that will result."[42] Washington was not unsympathetic to their demands. For a long time, Congress opposed any plan for half pay or pensions, fearing that the creation of an officer class or faction wielding political power was dangerous to American liberties. Others were wary of a professional standing army posing a military threat to the new republican government, an ideology that went back well over a hundred years in English political philosophy. Only in the late spring of 1778 did "Congress come to reality" and approve pensions but restricted them to only seven years – and nothing allowed for widows of those men who died in the service. Still, this disgruntlement was a needless distraction for the general, and alienated the officers and Congress from one another at a critical moment in the struggle for independence. And this friction would resurface dangerously in 1783.[43]

The discontented Continental officers were not the only ones unhappy with the state delegates meeting in York. Many enlisted soldiers at Valley Forge blamed Congress for their cruel hardships that winter. For instance, a New Jersey diarist in the army in January, 1778, wrote that "the cry against Congress still continued as high as ever: men of no less rank than Colonels spoke of them with the greatest contempt and detestation."[44] Though many factors led to the American troops' misery that winter, a poorly conceived, ill-timed attempt by Congress to reform the army's chaotic logistical organization during active military campaigning in 1777 significantly contributed to the army's woes by the end of that year. A leading scholar of supplying Washington's troops, Erna Risch, notes that "the timing [of the reorganization] inevitably led to shortages of rations at Valley Forge," which contributed to the suffering in the encampments. "The shortage of food at Valley Forge," she concludes, "has to be understood in terms of subsistence supply developments in the six months preceding the encampment of the troops there."[45] Likewise, historian E. Wayne Carp concludes that "Congressional reform of the Commissariat resulted in the host of resignations at all levels of the department, leaving it demoralized and unprepared for the army's winter encampment at Valley Forge."[46]

Adding to these woes, Joseph Trumbull, Commissary General of Stores and Provisions responsible for buying and distributing food and clothing, resigned in disgust with Congress in July 1777. Congress did not allow him to appoint his own assistants, but they held him responsible for them while in office. And Trumbull was not granted the typical commission for himself on purchases – a common allowance within 18th-century armies to attract successful merchants and businessmen to accept burdensome logistical posts. Given these restrictions, he quit. He was replaced by Baltimore merchant and former militia officer William Buchanan on August 5, 1777, but he was "as incapable as a child," a congressman wrote, and eventually resigned on March 20, 1778, during a congressional inquiry "into the causes of the deficiencies in the department of the purchasing commissaries."[47]

The quartermaster department was equally ineffective. The army's quartermaster department supervised an astounding number of staffers, agents, and deputies across a broad spectrum of responsibilities, spread far and wide. Historian Risch reports that the department "employed storekeepers, clerks, barracksmasters, express riders, laborers, and artificers, as well as superintendents of government property, roads, stables, wood yards, and horse yards." It also included a forage department with "clerks, foragemasters, measurers, collectors, weighers, stackers, superintendents, and laborers," and a wagon department, which hired "wagonmasters, wagoners, packhorse masters, and pack horsemen." And in its boat department, there were "superintendents, masters of vessels, mates, and boatmen."[48] This was a huge organization operating across a large territory with little money, and a largely unsupervised staff that was not always dependable or honest.

Other problems with the army's logistical administration had major effects. Maj Gen Thomas Mifflin resigned as quartermaster general on October 8, 1777, and retired to Reading – without sending word to Washington. His departure came at a critical time for the army, and he was not immediately replaced by Congress. This inexcusable failure of the delegates to appoint a competent replacement for Mifflin at such a crucial moment greatly added to the soldiers' distress at Valley Forge.

Soon after arriving at Valley Forge – if not before – Washington came to believe that the public and Congress did not understand the extent of suffering among the troops in the camps. "It is not easy to give … a just and accurate idea of the sufferings of the Troops at large," he wrote, "were they to be minutely detailed, the Relation so unexpected – so contrary to the common opinion of people distant from the Army, would scarcely be thought credible."[49] Washington requested that a delegation from the Continental Congress or the Board of War visit the camp to confer with him and his senior officers, and to witness the bleak conditions the soldiers were enduring. On January 10, Congress decided to send a committee from York to Washington's headquarters to assess the army's situation and try to improve the flawed logistical system as much as possible. Some of the committee members were skeptical of Washington's complaints about the scarcity of provisions before they arrived at Valley Forge and were initially unsympathetic to his pleas.

During the weeks it took Congress to consider sending several of its members to Valley Forge, Washington wrote to Henry Laurens, President of the Continental Congress, that "respecting the state of the Commissary's Department," he did "not know from what cause this alarming deficiency, or rather total failure of Supplies arises: But unless more vigorous exertions and better regulations take place in that line and immediately, This Army must dissolve." This would be "a melancholy and alarming Catastrophe."[50] The poor condition of the troops also affected the army's readiness for battle. "Had a body of the Enemy crossed Schuylkill [River] this morning, as I had reason to expect from the intelligence I received at Four oClock last night, the Divisions which I ordered to be in readiness to march & meet them could not have moved. It is unnecessary for me to add more upon the subject."[51] This was an alarming situation that could have been fatal to the cause of independence, and a more active British general than William Howe would likely have taken advantage of it.

Washington wrote again to Laurens the next day even more emphatically, stating "I am now convinced beyond a doubt, that unless some great and capital change suddenly takes place in that line this Army must inevitably be reduced to one or other of these three things. Starve – dissolve – or disperse, in order to obtain subsistence in the best manner they can. Rest assured, Sir, this is not an exaggerated picture, and that I have abundant reason to support what I say."[52]

This shocking letter certainly put Congress on notice of the disturbing supply hurdles, and the Continental Army's collapse would likely have ended the war.

The "Committee at Camp" that Congress created to visit Valley Forge and investigate the problems supplying and equipping the army originally consisted of three members of Congress' Board of War – Horatio Gates, Thomas Mifflin, and Timothy Pickering – along with four congressmen: Francis Dana, Joseph Reed, Nathaniel Folsom, and John Harvie. But soon Congress decided not to send the Board members, as all three were considered to be critical of Washington; that could have created an awkward atmosphere at the army's headquarters. Instead, two additional congressmen were appointed, both Washington supporters. The committee resided at Moore Hall, a few miles from Washington's headquarters, after arriving on January 24, "to reform the army." Although some congressmen thought that the army's situation had been exaggerated prior to the committee's appearance at the encampment, very quickly they discerned the horrible conditions endured by the suffering troops. From the camps, Congressman Dana reported that "every regiment has been destitute of fish or flesh four days," adding that "we do not see from whence the supplies of meat are to come. The want of it will infallibly bring on a mutiny." Conditions at camp and their effects on morale were clear to the committee almost immediately.[53]

Gen Greene reported in late February that "we are still in danger of starving; the Commissary department is in a most wretched condition; the Quarter Masters, in a worse. Hundreds and hundreds of our Horses have actually starved to death. The Committee of Congress have seen all these things with their own eyes."[54] A month later in a letter to Rhode Island's Supreme Court chief justice, Greene reported on the congressional visitors.

> There is a Committee of Congress here at Camp to establish the army anew. They were astonished at our situation and declare they had no conception of our condition, although they were within 60 miles of us. They seem to be very sensible of the great inattention paid to the Army and of the mismanagement of the three great departments. They are striving to correct and amend them as fast as possible. But it will be a work of time to bring about a general reformation.[55]

Accounts such as these make the claims by a few modern historians of Washington exaggerating the army's plight to get Congress and the states to act more quickly to remedy the army's dire situation seem unfair and indecorous.

In the end, the delegation recognized that the army's procurement process was hopelessly flawed and complicated, with poor accountability and fraudulence of its purchasers, wagon masters, forage buyers, and other personnel. The committee angrily described these unaccountable deputies and assistants as "little piddling pilfering Plunderers." In short, they blamed Congress for allowing such a chaotic system to continue, and more forcefully, for not promptly filling the position of quartermaster general after Thomas Mifflin resigned in October.[56]

Working closely with Washington and his staff, the camp committee advised Congress that the power of the quartermaster general should be substantially increased and centralized to promote efficiency. They also concluded that the quartermaster general had to be an officer of authority and influence. The new appointee would also require two capable assistants. The delegates recommended Philadelphia businessman and militia colonel John Cox to serve as the main purchaser and examiner of received supplies, and New Jersey attorney Charles Petit to be the bookkeeper in charge of accounts – a civilian appointment that also came with a Continental Army colonel's commission. No longer would Congress oversee the regulations in supply operations that were decentralized and inefficient. Most notably the Committee at Camp called for the appointment of Nathanael Greene as quartermaster general (after initially recommending Philip Schuyler), despite his strong reluctance to accept a role he knew would be frustrating, tiresome, and thankless. Moreover, Greene hesitated to give up his field command in the army for a thankless staff position. "Nobody ever heard of a quarter Master in history," the Rhode Island general lamented, but at Washington's persistent urging he took the assignment. Congress made the appointment on March 2. As an incentive, "Greene and his two assistants ... were granted a 1 percent commission on all funds expended in their department."[57] Similarly, Congress improved the Commissary Department by appointing Connecticut merchant Jeremiah Wadsworth as its chief in April, with a similar structure of power, authority, and commission on expenditures as had Greene. By centralizing the system of supply in the hands of a few appointees Congress gave these men considerable power and latitude in their roles. "Men of character and ability were installed at the head of the quartermaster and commissary departments and given free rein to direct them as they saw fit," historian Carp observes.[58] It must be noted, however, that these attempts at solving the supply crisis offered some relief in 1778 but did not create long-term effective processes to benefit the army.

As the committee endeavored to fix the army's logistical difficulties, a major disturbance for Washington and many of his senior subordinates emerged early in 1778 concerning the oversight of the army, command appointments, and even Washington's tenure as commander in chief. Not surprisingly these difficulties emanated from the Continental Congress. Their roots went back many months but arose as a crisis during the cold months of the Valley Forge cantonment.

In June 1776, Congress had created the Board of War to oversee the new nation's military efforts, the Continental Army and its officers, and the raising and supplying of troops. Originally it was staffed by five congressmen, not military officers. This civilian board soon became inundated with military responsibilities to address for which its members had little or no experience, and almost no time. By December 26, 1776 − as Washington's army defeated the Hessians at Trenton − Congress called for a revised board on which military officers, not congressmen, would serve. The new board went into effect on July 18, 1777, but no members were elected until November, just weeks before Washington's troops came to Valley Forge. One of the members was General Mifflin, who had fought at Trenton and Princeton, but had just resigned as quartermaster general in October. He had become increasingly disenchanted with Washington's tenure as commander of the Continental Army after the defeats at Brandywine and Germantown and resented the growing influence Nathanael Greene had with the commander in chief. The delegates at York also appointed Horatio Gates as the board's president, which created an awkward command situation for the army's leadership. Fresh from the laurels he had justifiably earned at Saratoga just weeks beforehand, Gates's role as president of a congressional board in effect made him Washington's superior as a civilian, but Gates also remained in uniform and kept his rank. He was also known to be critical of Washington's leadership and effectiveness. The Board of War "moved to take control of the American war effort." Washington's victories at Trenton and Princeton now seemed a long time ago to his detractors. "This army will be totally lost unless you come down and collect the virtuous band," Mifflin wrote to Gates in November. Some congressmen concluded that Washington should be replaced as the army's commander in chief as well. Declaration of Independence signer and Continental Army surgeon Dr Benjamin Rush, for example, called Washington's army "an unformed mob" and saw Washington as "outgeneraled and twice beaten." Even Washington supporter Henry Laurens admitted that some of the criticism in Congress of the Virginia general had merit.[59]

This unstable situation in Congress and the Board of War was exposed when Washington became aware of the criticism of his leadership in November 1777. He received an alleged extract from a recent private letter written to Gen Gates by Thomas Conway, an Irish-born officer with decades of prior service in the French army who volunteered for duty in America. Supposedly Conway had written "Heaven has determined to save your Country; or a weak General and bad Councellors would have ruined it." This was an obvious reference to Washington and his top lieutenants – Greene in particular. The commander in chief quickly confronted Gates and Conway in writing, breaking open in public what later became known as "the Conway Cabal." Conway did not deny he wrote the letter (though not that particular line) while Gates, playing the victim, was more upset that his private correspondence was made public.[60]

Some historians have questioned whether a cabal or conspiracy to remove Washington even existed, including Knollenberg, who doubted "there was ever any serious movement in the Continental Congress to deprive Washington of his command." Even Washington himself held that "no whisper of the kind was ever heard in Congress."[61] Most recently, however, Mark Lender has concluded persuasively that not only did three senior generals – Mifflin, Gates, and Conway – act to supplant Washington, opposition also came from about a dozen Congressmen. But "the chief threat to Washington's command lay in the Board of War," where Mifflin and Gates "sought control of setting military policy and strategic goals." The board was "at the crux" of the efforts to replace Washington, and "the cabal was less an organized plot than it was a gradual attempt at an administrative-political takeover of the war effort."[62]

Washington certainly saw the situation as an effort by some army officers to replace him with the heralded Gates, who he called an "inveterate enemy."[63] Writing in late May 1778 to Landon Carter, a wealthy tidewater Virginia planter, the general reported "that there was a scheme of this sort on foot last fall [that] admits of no doubt but it originated" not in Congress but "in another quarter – with three men who wanted to aggrandize themselves," i.e., Gates, Mifflin, and Conway. He also saw Conway as a threat to the honor and morale of his officers when, late in 1777, Congress appointed Conway inspector general of the army with the rank of major general, leaping over the seniority of several of the army's brigadiers. He would be answerable to Congress, a direct affront to Washington, and the appointment was strenuously objected to by offended officers who were not promoted to the position. Washington made his opposition to Conway known to Congress and treated him with stiff formality at headquarters. Greene too thought "him a very dangerous man in this army,"[64] and deplored the covert machinations against Washington. "A horrid faction had been forming to ruin his excellency and others," he wrote, "Ambition, how boundless! Ingratitude, how prevalent! ... General Mifflin is said to be at the head of it. And it is strongly suggested that General Gates favours it."[65] Greene was right.

Eventually the boastful Conway overplayed his hand by offering to resign, especially given Washington's icy reception of him. Tired of the controversy, Congress accepted it on April 22, ridding the army at Valley Forge of an unwelcome distraction. Gates's congressional supporters had been "firmly rejected." Washington triumphantly concluded that Gates, Mifflin, and Conroy, "finding no support" for their plot, "on the contrary," were seen as scheming, and realizing "that their conduct, and views when seen into, was like[ly] to undergo severe reprehension they slunk back – disavowed the measure, & professed themselves my warmest admirers." Gates, tarnished by the scheming, was soon dismissed by Congress from the Board of War, and in November 1778, left to take command of the Continental Army's Eastern Department in New England. And yet although Washington retained command of the army, he could hardly have enjoyed the victory, and must have been angered by the effort to replace him.[66]

Another foreign officer appeared at Valley Forge that winter who, unlike Conway, had a profoundly positive effect on the American army and in fact the war. On a cold day in early December of 1777, a ship docked in the harbor of Portsmouth, New Hampshire, after a long trans-Atlantic voyage. A group of red-coated officers disembarked soon afterwards, but they were not of the British army. Rather, the party consisted of Baron Friedrich Wilhelm August Heinrich Ferdinand von Steuben, a Prussian-born officer of significant military experience, and his entourage of several junior French officers, whose language the baron also spoke. All had made the oceanic journey from France to serve the American cause of independence. Steuben was a 40-year-old officer from Magdeburg, in Brandenburg-Prussia. He was born into a noble family, though not a wealthy one, so it was entirely proper for him to use "von" in his name, despite the contrary claims of numerous historians over the years.

Steuben had served in the Prussian forces of Frederick the Great beginning at age 16. As a junior infantry officer during the Seven Years' War (1756–63), he was wounded at the battle of Prague in 1757, and then again at the battle of Kunersdorf in 1759, in what is now Poland. Toward the end of the war, he was promoted to captain, and served as a junior aide on Frederick's staff. But not long thereafter, he ran afoul of an influential Prussian general, and was dismissed from the army in 1763. The following year, however, he began his service in the army of Josef Friederick Wilhelm, the prince of Hollenzollern-Hechingen, a small Roman Catholic principality in southwest Germany, during which time he was awarded the Order of Fidelity, with the title of *Freiherr*, which is commonly given as "baron" in English.

By 1777, Steuben was in Paris, seeking military opportunity in America, as did so many other ambitious European officers. After some stops and starts, with the financial support of high French officials, American diplomats Benjamin Franklin and Silas Dean arranged for his voyage to America, with a heavily embellished letter of recommendation in his pocket that falsely claimed he had been a lieutenant general in Prussian service. Nevertheless, Steuben was a seasoned veteran and, perhaps most important to the Continental Army, he had years of experience drilling, disciplining, and caring for soldiers as a company commander and staff officer to the greatest European general of the age. He was also in desperate need of a military position, and came to America not because of any idealistic, enlightened ideas about liberty, rights, and republican government, but for money, glory, and preferment. In this he was not atypical.

Steuben arrived in early February at York, Pennsylvania, seeking from Congress no rank or salary; he would cheerfully begin his service as a volunteer with the Continental Army. Pleased by the magnanimous offer, Congress sent him and his aides off to Valley Forge, where Washington received him on February 23. The Virginian soon came to respect the baron's vast military experience, especially in training troops, along with his impressive history of service with the Prussian army. The American commander quickly recognized that these skills made Steuben perfectly suited for the position of inspector general, including drilling the army, supervising the soldiers' discipline in camp and while on the march, and assisting the commissaries feed and clothe the troops. Washington was in a bit of a quandary, however, as the position of inspector general was still held by the finagling Gen Conway, Washington's political enemy. Conway, however, was off on a ludicrously impractical, Board-initiated expedition led by Lafayette to again invade Canada from Albany, a winter enterprise Lafayette canceled in March when he recognized how few troops were available for northern operations and the obvious supply challenges he would face. Washington thus assigned Steuben as acting inspector general over the 7,500 soldiers fit for duty at Valley Forge, although the baron was not yet given a formal Continental rank.

Steuben worked tirelessly to visit the American brigades in their miserable camps, inspecting their health, food, huts, and clothing. He was an indefatigable, larger-than-life personality, much admired by the persevering men and their officers, who were in awe of him. An impressed young American soldier soon wrote "never before or since have I had such an impression of the ancient fabled God of War, as when I looked on the baron." Steuben also saw that regulations for camp hygiene, marching order, guard duty, etc., were few, and each regiment seemed to have its own drill, depending on the colonel's preference. Clearly, he and his aides had much work ahead of them, but the question remained: how would one officer train and drill the entire army spread out at Valley Forge?[67]

Steuben's answer was innovative and effective. The Prussian created a model company of Washington's 50-man "General's Guard" at headquarters and an additional 100 picked veterans from other units. Starting on March 19, with this oversized company he worked out the details of the simplified drill, firing procedures, and precise movements he created during long hours spent in his quarters planning the next day's instructions. His new system was based on simplicity and uniformity, so that it was easy to learn, and so units would be better able to effectively maneuver when engaged with larger formations on the march and in battle.[68]

On March 25, Steuben began the instruction of the entire army by using the soldiers of the model company to return to their units and train others. He insisted that officers should drill their men, not the sergeants. He also made vigorous bayonet drill an important part of turning the regiments into regulars. Steuben taught battlefield maneuvers such as going from marching in column to the formation of a battleline, advancing and firing by the platoon method, proper fire discipline, wheeling to the left and right, refusing a flank, and attacking a position obliquely. All these skills were needed to make the army quick to deploy, more lethal, and more effective to control in battle.[69] "I was kept constantly, when off other duty, engaged in learning the Baron de Steuben's Prussian exercise," wrote one of the tired Continentals, "it was a continual drill."[70] The American officers greatly respected Steuben's attention to detail and thoroughness, and appreciated his innovated reforms of army discipline. Col Henry Livingston Jr of New York reported on the day drilling began that Steuben "is now teaching the most simple parts of the exercise such as position and marching of a soldier in a manner quite different from that they have been heretofore used to, in my opinion more agreeable to the dictates of reason and common sense than any mode I have before seen." Even Horatio Gates, who observed the soldiers training during part of the winter, concluded that "few armies want discipline more than ours ... Our time is short, and we have much, too much to do; therefore, we should only attempt to do that which is most for our present benefit."[71]

Steuben's new drill and formations were not only simpler, they also took into account the peculiar nature of the American soldier. Unlike long-term professional troops who served in the harshly disciplined forces of France, Prussia, and Great Britain, Washington's men were amateurs who had volunteered (or been drafted) for short enlistments, in some cases having elected their junior officers, and who would never have endured the brutal corporal punishments of a European army. Steuben treated the troops with a mixture of intimidation, patience, and performative anger, which endeared him to the ragged rebels in the ranks. "He seems to understand what our soldiers are capable of," wrote Col Laurens, one of Washington's aides-de-camp. Even the baron would later write that "my enterprise succeeded better than I had dared to expect." And as he spoke no English, he tasked an American officer to translate for him while drilling the soldiery, often swearing in more than one language, to the adoring amusement of the troops.[72]

At the same time, Steuben began writing a drill manual titled *Regulations for the Order and Discipline of the Troops of the United States* (1779), which was eventually translated into English and printed on blue paper covered boards and was thereby known as "the Blue Book." Impressed, Washington wrote to the baron "I very much approve the conciseness of the work – founded on your general principle of rejecting everything superfluous."[73] In March 1779, Congress officially adopted these *Regulations*, which "also included official regulations for military conduct, from administration and courts-martial to sanitation and hygiene, and a guide to the duties and responsibilities of each rank in the army."[74] For all of his efforts he was appointed a major general by Congress in May 1778 while still in camp at Valley Forge, and officially became the army's inspector general. It was surely telling when a foot soldier wrote that month that "the troops are instructed in a new and so happy a method of marching that they soon will be able to advance with the most regularity, even without [drum] music and over the roughest grounds."[75] Thus, it seems the troops approved of him as well. And so did many senior officers, who gave him their thanks at the end of the conflict. At the war's conclusion Gates wrote to him that "the Astonishment with which I beheld the Order, Regularity and Attention, which you have taught the American Army; and the obedience, exactness, and true spirit of Military Discipline, which you have infused into them, does you the highest honor."[76] Similarly, on December 23, 1783, Washington wrote Steuben from Annapolis in "the last Letter I shall ever write while I continue in the service of my Country," that he wished "to make use of this last moment of my public life, to signifie in the strongest terms my entire approbation of your conduct, and to express my sense of the obligations the public is under to you, for your faithful & meritorious Services."[77] High praise indeed.

As winter turned into spring in 1778, Washington began to think about the coming season for an active campaign against the enemy still firmly ensconced at Philadelphia. An assault on the city's defenses was out of the question. The troops at Valley Forge – numbering about 13,000 by May 2 – were still hungry and poorly clothed, and many were too sick to take the field. The frustrated Continental commander also had to continue his efforts to get states to raise, equip, and march their militia regiments to his support. With an excellent intelligence network in the Philadelphia environs, Washington received many reports of the impending change in British commanders – Clinton for Howe – and rumors of a planned evacuation of the riverside town. Washington needed to learn what the redcoats where doing, as he was becoming increasingly intent upon striking a blow against the British as they departed Philadelphia. "There is reason to believe that the enemy mean to evacuate Philadelphia," he wrote to the governor of Maryland, and "it is necessary therefore to draw together as great a force as can be provided for, with the utmost expedition."[78] Anxious to strike at the enemy, in mid-May Washington entrusted a detachment of 2,200 men to the young Marquis de Lafayette, who would be leading his first independent operation. The Frenchman's object was to gather intelligence of British intentions and interfere with their movements by controlling three major roads into the occupied city. But he was warned not to risk too much. The expedition left camp on May 18, and moved about ten miles east to a position on Barren Hill, an exposed and isolated location about 11 miles northwest of Philadelphia. Lafayette imprudently ignored Washington's admonition not to remain at a stationary position where the British could bring to bear their superior numbers against him. Washington's inklings were correct. On May 20, Howe's 9,000 to 10,000-man force attempted to surround Lafayette's exposed force on Barren Hill with a three-pronged attack. Advised of the rebels' static position by a Continental deserter, the redcoats came close to crushing the Frenchman, but he was able to extricate his troops from this dangerous situation by rushing to safety across the Schuylkill River at Matson Ford. The frustrated British marched back to Philadelphia. Washington generously praised the detachment's escape as "the brilliant retreat by which [Lafayette] eluded a combined maneuver of the whole British force."[79]

Washington's favorable assessment was putting quite a spin on what had really occurred. His decision to appoint the inexperienced Lafayette with one fifth of his effective force on a reconnaissance mission across a major river was risky. The marquis showed poor judgment staying put on the high ground, did not properly secure his army's perimeter, and almost lost his command. But the steady troops, having been drilled and trained by Steuben for months, showed poise and proficiency in moving off the hill and over the river in their rear under pressure from thousands of determined enemy redcoats. They had marched quickly and expertly from line into column and kept their cool. "American soldiers, properly trained, could maneuver with disciplined precision and order as well as most European armies," Steuben's recent biographer concludes, and "this was proven by their escape at Barron Hill."[80] Lafayette's stalwart detachment certainly did not panic. They forded a high river in proximity to the enemy and retreated, staying in their ranks. Much of their success could be a result of poor British generalship that day, especially by the veteran Maj Gen James Grant, an inflexible, defensive officer known for failing to deliver a battle's telling blow. Time would soon tell if Washington's new army had been drilled and trained enough to secure American independence.

To conclude this chapter on the crucial importance of the American army's six-month stay at Valley Forge, and all its misery, sacrifice, desperation, and eventual transformation, a cursory look at events through June is necessary. As detailed in the previous chapter, French recognition of American independence and the treaty of military alliance they signed with the new nation drastically changed British military and geopolitical priorities. "The war must be prosecuted on a different plan," wrote Lord Germain, so now the king's military emphasis turned to defending the British Isles and protecting its most valuable assets – the rich sugar islands in the warm Caribbean Sea. Thousands of troops and naval assets now had to be sent off to the West Indies for active operations, transferred from the rebellious North American colonies. Clinton replaced Howe as the new British commander in America after Howe was granted permission to resign. The new British commander in America promptly ordered the evacuation of Philadelphia, per royal instructions, and began to march his army, long wagon train, and a great number of Loyalists across New Jersey toward New York, beginning on June 15, 1778. Washington quickly recognized that this was a golden opportunity to strike at Clinton's vulnerable rear guard as the slow British column made its way to the defenses around New York. And a bold attack would quiet the muted grumblings of some men in Congress about the army's continued inactivity now that fair weather had arrived.[81]

Washington's Continentals stepped off smartly in pursuit of Clinton's army crossing New Jersey while the state's swarming militia companies harassed the British and impeded their march with tedious obstacles and sudden attacks. Washington wished that "every possible expedient should be used to disturb and retard their progress, by hanging on their flanks and rear, breaking down the Bridges over the Creeks in their route, blocking up the roads by falling trees and by every other method, that can be devised."[82] Clinton moved his men through Monmouth County headed for Sandy Hook on the Atlantic coast for transport to New York City and other destinations, all the while guarding his supply train in scorching summer temperatures that soon became extreme.

Washington sought to attack the retreating enemy column on the move, but at a council of war most of his generals urged caution. Some of his lieutenants urged him to beware of a sudden enemy attack if Washington's army were to get caught by strong British battalions in open country, without high wooded ground in which to act defensively.

After some additional deliberation, he decided to advance "a select and strong detachment" of 4,000 picked soldiers led by the petulant Charles Lee, the army's second in command, who had recently returned to American service after being exchanged from his lengthy captivity. Lee was ordered to move quickly and take advantage of opportunities to strike the British wagon train and any isolated detachments they encountered. "[We] mean to harrass them as much as possible," Washington said, and he would follow warily with the remainder of the army in close support. On June 28, the two forces clashed in a sprawling, confusing battle in sweltering heat among the hills and ravines near Monmouth Courthouse, about 30 miles from Sandy Hook. The trained American Continentals stood firmly in what was for them largely a defensive battle during which they held off Clinton's aggressive attacks with his rear-guard troops. "All our Troops behaved with the greatest Bravery," Greene proudly reported, having been in the thick of the fighting. By early evening Clinton broke off the British attacks and cautiously retired to the courthouse area. Then, after dark he ordered his troops to continue their march to Sandy Hook, leaving Washington's army in possession of the bloody battleground. "We forced the enemy to retire, and encamped on the Field of battle," Washington bragged to Gates.[83]

While the battle might be called a draw or inconclusive, the American commander was quick to praise his soldiers for what he publicly declared as their victory over "the Flower of the British Troops."[84] The strong effort by Washington and his lieutenants to "shape" the indecisive outcome of the battle into a victory was crucial in enhancing Washington's military reputation, bolstering public morale, and keeping his army – still the symbol of the cause of independence – intact. Notwithstanding Clinton's bitter comment that Washington's claim that Monmouth was an American victory was ridiculous, Washington's spin on events was for the most part successful, especially among Patriots. This was also the last battle in the northern states in which he would command troops.

Valley Forge is perhaps the most mythologized episode of the Revolutionary War. It has often been depicted as an epic endurance story of the Continental Army's painful rebirth in the snow and freezing climate of Pennsylvania. It was, it is said, a metamorphosis of an untrained band of ragged citizen soldiers into a well-drilled professional army that was then able to take on the superior British enemy, as "proven" at Monmouth. The architect of this unlikely transformation is always given as Baron von Steuben. The magic he worked as drillmaster turned rank amateurs into trained soldiers who fought the June 28 battle by going toe to toe with British regulars that day, making Valley Forge the "birthplace of the American army." And many accounts of the inhospitable winter encampment conclude that the painful shortages of clothing, supplies, and provisions hardened the soldiers into a superior fighting force that emerged from the ordeal united to win the war.

It is not the purpose of this chapter to debunk the myths of Valley Forge. Rather, the following pages will instead show why the winter encampment there makes the dreary six-month experience along the Schuylkill River a decisive turning point of the war.

Perhaps the most apparent consequence of the Continental Army's time spent at Valley Forge was an improvement in the soldiers' discipline, drill, and morale. This was a "noteworthy achievement" that demonstrated the "maturation" of the troops into a force resembling a professional army. This gradual transition toward an improved and cohesive body of troops was even more impressive given the abysmal conditions the soldiers survived during the encampment. And it cannot be denied that much of the credit for this transformation goes to the persistent efforts of Steuben's expertise and methods.[85]

It is important to have a clear understanding of the extent of the army's transformation in the six months of the grim encampment. Washington's troops who arrived at Valley Forge were not a loosely formed horde of musket-dragging civilians with no sense of what it meant to be a soldier. Many of them had been on active service in the army for over a year. Some had just arrived from northern New York, where they had been battle-tested during the victorious Saratoga campaign, while others had fought bravely and competently at Brandywine and Germantown. There were in camp veterans of the fighting at Trenton and Princeton too. These men knew how to stand up to redcoats on the battlefield and fire deadly close-range volleys into the enemy's ranks. They had endured many trying hardships, suffered from the lack of just about everything, and received little pay while in the ranks. And their endurance had been proven to be astonishing, as demonstrated during Arnold's 1775 march to Quebec, the 1776 retreat across New Jersey, and the defeats near Philadelphia in the autumn of 1777. Those who would be subject to Steuben's system of military discipline in the hopeful spring of 1778 were not all inexperienced but had seen some fighting, a lot of marching, and far too much misery.

Steuben turned Washington's core army into regulars. They did not become, to be sure, the well-trained, long-serving rankers and sergeants of the British or Hessian regiments, nor would they ever do so – although the frequent modern assertion that the British army was, at this time, the best in the world is highly questionable. The Continentals were not on lengthy enlistments and did not intend to make the military their vocation. But they did become well-disciplined in the 18th-century meaning of *disciplined*: not in the sense of punished (though some soldiers might disagree) but trained, drilled, and competent in the skills and routines of full-time soldiers. The baron simplified the army's basic drill in musketry and maneuvering, the later having been seen as problematic at Brandywine. "Ignorant officers, as well as men, had been schooled in their duties, and a level of standards of performance had been established," concludes historian Philip Greenwalt. The men now knew how to change position on the battleground under fire, and to move from one position to another, all the while keeping together as a company or regiment, "competently and responsibly led" by junior officers who knew what they were about. As one study of the encampment concludes, "the winter of 1777–78 saw the development of the Continental forces into what was for the first time a genuine army." And it must be added that at no time during the war to that date had there been another opportunity to properly drill and train the army.[86]

It has been understandably common for historians to evaluate the efficacy of the Continentals' development at Valley Forge under Steuben by looking at their conduct at the battle of Monmouth Courthouse. "If anything proved the worth of the training program at Valley Forge, it was the performance of the continentals at Monmouth," Steuben's recent biographer concludes.[87] During the exhausting battle, in which the advancing Americans led by Lee were forced to retreat to well-situated defensive positions from which they inflicted significant losses on the attacks of the British rear guard, Washington's troops and their leaders no doubt acquitted themselves well. "There was no chaos" when the Continentals initially had to fall back, write the authors of the definitive study of the battle, and "the Americans displayed considerable competence ... thus it is not too much to credit Steuben's training regimen with enabling officers to maintain control of their commands in difficult circumstances." The hard-pressed troops did maintain their order, kept together with their officers, and showed great discipline on an unbearably hot day: "they were better prepared than ever before."[88] And this was in the face of determined attacks by the best of the enemy's troops. It should be kept in mind, though, that the American army fought largely a defensive battle in which the Continentals fell back and occupied high ground studded with artillery to ward off British attacks. It was not an engagement where Washington's troops made coordinated offensive maneuvers or assaults, so the "testing" of Steuben's training was not seen much on the field. But the well-drilled Patriots did demonstrate the value of their winter exercises. Notably, the thousands of troops led by Lee at Monmouth were picked men, meaning that the healthiest, sturdiest, and most reliable soldiers were chosen from several regiments, and placed in new formations for the battle under officers with whom many were unfamiliar. And yet when attacked that day, these troops behaved well under fire because all knew the drill – how to maneuver, to show fire discipline, to stay with their officers and in the ranks. This was because of the tireless efforts of Steuben. Prior to resigning his military commission in late December of 1783, Washington wrote his final letter while on military service to offer effusive praise to the man he had the most to thank. It was not to Knox, Greene, Lafayette, Sullivan, Schuyler, or Wayne. It was to Baron von Steuben.[89]

Did all that happened at Valley Forge change Washington too? As we have seen, he decided to strike the rear of the British Army marching from Philadelphia to New York once the enemy left Philadelphia. This was a risky plan, as his army would be operating against a dangerous foe in open terrain, not secure behind rivers, ridges, or strong defensive fieldworks. Such a scenario he had long sought to avoid. Would he have chased and attacked Clinton's column without the confidence he now had after consolidating his position as commander in chief? Did he now have greater confidence in his well-trained army? Could this also be considered an important result of the Valley Forge winter?

The success that American arms achieved that hot and bloody late June day was not lost on those who fought in the swirling battle of Monmouth Courthouse. Washington commended "the gallant officers and men who distinguished themselves upon the occasion and such others as by their good order & coolness.[90] And his young aide Alexander Hamilton reported that "the behavior of the officers and men in general was such as could not easily be surpassed. Our troops ... behaved with more spirit and moved with greater order than the British troops," surely attributable to their incessant spring drilling.[91] Perhaps the greatest praise the Continental Army received after the battle was from a British general at the engagement who wrote that the redcoats had received "a handsome flogging. We had not received such a one [before] in America." That was high praise indeed. It was a much improved, confident army that marched out of the camps at Valley Forge and went toe to toe with Clinton's veteran battalions in the fields near Monmouth Courthouse. Moreover, several American officers who fought that day praised the deadly effectiveness of Knox's expertly deployed Continental Artillery.[92]

Washington's professional reputation was also secured and enhanced by the army's winter experience in 1777–78, a contributing factor to Valley Forge's role as a decisive event in America's revolution. The so-called "Conway Cabal" was perceived by Washington and his supporters as a threat to his authority and reputation. It is certain that several officers and congressmen were highly critical of Washington, and some hoped to replace him with Gen Gates. But the artful Gates and Mifflin were discredited, Conway was gone, and Washington's authority was thereby strengthened, as loyal supporters rallied to defend and exalt the commander in chief. He had rid himself of his three army adversaries. Washington came out of the tempest "in a stronger position to manage military matters," write historians Martin and Lender. "Moreover, Congress would listen to him more carefully." Congress and Washington communicated more effectively going forward. Congress caved in on the issue of pensions, "a sign of its reinvigorated respect for

Washington's opinions. In the long run, that may have made a critical difference in maintaining a proper balance in civil-military relations."[93]

A second event that consolidated Washington's control of the army was his successful effort to have a congressional committee visit camp from York. The general lobbied Congress to confer with him in person at the army's camps to resolve the supply and organizational difficulties that had plagued the army during the 1777 campaign. And, to preemptively seize the initiative and control the agenda, by the time the delegates arrived at headquarters Washington (with Hamilton's assistance) was ready to present them with a 16,000-word summary he had prepared of the myriad deficiencies in the commissary and quartermaster departments. The committee emerged from the Valley Forge visit with a better understanding of the logistical difficulties Washington faced and was more sympathetic to the army's requirements. The "Committee at Camp" quickly became the voice of Congress, and made decisions on its behalf, mostly in accord with the commander in chief's wishes. Once the committee had spent a few days observing the squalid camps at Valley Forge there was no question among the delegates about the army's doleful plight.[94]

Washington worked closely with the committee to make reforms in the supply departments and the army's structure. Crucially, he was able to convince Congress to immediately put the supply departments under his control – not Congress's or the Board of War's. This productive collaboration established the precedent of cooperation of the army's leader with the civilian authority of Congress, which increased his support in that body. It also contributed to the demise of the anti-Washington faction and the rival Board of War, which soon became focused on trivial concerns. Going forward, Washington would command the quartermaster and commissary departments and appoint their leaders – not Congress. The commander in chief faced no additional threats to his authority or tenure throughout the war. The importance of Washington's secure role as head of the army may be assessed by considering who else was suitable for top command, especially after Gates's reputation had tarnished that winter. No one else fit the bill.

And perhaps above all, Washington had kept the army together. In the face of hunger, cold, and disease most of the weary soldiers stayed in camp. They had "suffered temporary want and great inconveniences," Washington reported, and he "had much cause to dread a general mutiny and dispersion." But the troops saw their general share many of their hardships, and knew he never left Valley Forge for the entire six-month duration of the cantonment. While some men deserted and over 2,000 died, others came into the cantonment that spring, so that when the army broke camp in mid-June, about 16,000 men in the ranks marched off. As noted above, a battle was looming as the Continentals moved to catch up with the British rear guard in New Jersey. Washington would now encounter future events with an improved fighting force, dedicated officers, capable quartermaster and commissary generals, and the support of Congress. The years ahead through 1783 would not be easy, but the Valley Forge experience turned the trajectory of the war toward eventual victory. It was most likely, as American poet Thomas Buchanan Read wrote 85 years later, "a midnight storm of woes/To clear the sky for Freedom's morn/the hour when Liberty is born."[95]

4

Long, Bloody and Severe: The Battle of Guilford Courthouse, 1781

Before beginning an overview of military events in the southern theater of the war in 1780 and 1781, a few key concepts should be explored to help make sense of this momentous struggle so crucial to American independence. Some misconceptions about the most significant campaign in the South during the Revolutionary struggle must also be addressed. First, the widespread notion too often used in print and on the web that there was a single overarching "southern campaign" during the Revolutionary War that encompassed all the military events in the South from 1775 to 1783 is an inaccurate oversimplification, and a distorted interpretation. Historians of the war do not typically cover, for example, the battles from Quebec in 1775 to Sullivan's Iroquois expedition in 1779 in one chapter called "the Northern Campaign," so why should such a sweeping interpretation be fitting for the American South? Simply put, the complexity of warfare south of the Potomac River, including not just the major battles but also the brutal Loyalist versus Patriot civil war, the years-long conflict with the Cherokees, the divide between the backcountry and coastal areas, slavery, the unique geography in which war was waged, and many other factors, make a "one-chapter view" of the southern theater incomplete and inaccurate.

Second, not every battle fought in the Continental Army's Southern Department, comprised of Virginia, North Carolina, South Carolina, and Georgia, can be said to have its own separate campaign associated with it. Most of the southern battles and smaller engagements were elements of larger campaigns, such as what may be called the Charleston Campaign of 1780, or the Yorktown Campaign of 1781. Just as there was no single all-encompassing "southern campaign," it is misleading to claim that there was, for instance, a "Camden Campaign" or a "Cowpens Campaign," in which each battle has its own discrete set of circumstances uniquely distinct from events immediately before and after it. Instead, it is more historically accurate to look at the long war in the South in terms of time frames, such as the early years of British operations in the Carolinas, or the military campaign beginning in late 1778 and the associated fighting at Savannah, Augusta, and Charleston the next year. Thus, for this study of one of the most decisive turning points of the entire Revolutionary War, the more accurate concept of "the Carolinas Campaign of 1780–81" as an interpretive framework will be used, which sets parameters on both time and place.

This southern focus of course begs the question, what was the critical turning point in the 1780–81 Carolinas Campaign, and one of the most important of the war? This question is often debated by scholars, authors, soldiers, history buffs, and museum professionals at conferences, during military staff rides, in print, on bus tours, through lectures, and of course online. While this chapter will argue that the answer to this question is the battle of Guilford Courthouse fought on March 15, 1781, in North Carolina's Piedmont, other battles and campaigns are often put forth as decisive turning points, two engagements in particular, and these will be discussed at the conclusion of the chapter. In looking at the crucial year of 1781, and particularly at the clash at Guilford Courthouse, a brief overview of prior events will put this salient battle in its immediate contemporary context.

In late 1779, British army commander in chief Henry Clinton launched a massive seaborne expedition from the British base at New York to capture Charleston, South Carolina, to support beleaguered southern Loyalists in the Carolinas and Georgia, and to help restore royal authority across the South. British authorities in America and London believed that in the South, concealed Loyalists were in great number and only needed a committed show of force by British troops to rise up in arms and put down the rebellion. Moreover, the fine harbor at Charleston would provide a well-supplied, convenient base to operate against the French in the West Indies.

About 9,000 of Clinton's soldiers crammed on board transport ships at New York's wharves in late December 1779, and after a miserable voyage of several storm-tossed weeks landed south of Charleston on February 12, 1780. Clinton's army slowly closed in on the fortified city and began their siege on April 1. Six weeks later, the city's chief defender, Continental Maj Gen Benjamin Lincoln, surrendered the garrison of 5,600 troops on May 12. The captured militia were paroled to their homes, but the Continentals were imprisoned in deplorable conditions. The major British victory was "an unfortunate event," Washington wrote with understatement, and a significant blow to American hopes for a southern victory.[1]

With the southern army wiped out at Charleston, a new force had to be created. But against Washington's advice, on June 13 Congress appointed Horatio Gates, the victorious American commander at Saratoga in 1777, to command what was left of Continental forces in the South, along with Maryland and Delaware troops Washington had previously ordered sent to the Carolinas. These latter 1,400 soldiers were commanded by a German-born French officer, Maj Gen Baron de Kalb, who urgently called for Virginia and North Carolina to mobilize their militia forces to bolster Gates's newly forming army.

A month before Charleston surrendered, the North Carolina assembly had appointed former governor Richard Caswell as the state's militia commander in the field. By early August Maj Gen Caswell positioned his troops across the border into South Carolina ahead of de Kalb's Continentals moving south.[2] Gates reached de Kalb's camp at Cox's Mill on the lower Deep River in North Carolina on July 26. Almost immediately Gates elected to advance into South Carolina and take the direct road to Camden, where the British had maintained a strong outpost. This sudden decision – taken by Gates with little knowledge of supply conditions in the theater – was opposed by the American officers in camp due to a lack of provisions along this route, which led through an inhospitable country teeming with armed Loyalists. Instead, Gates's officers recommended marching to Camden via Salisbury and Charlotte to the west, where they would find more friendly support,

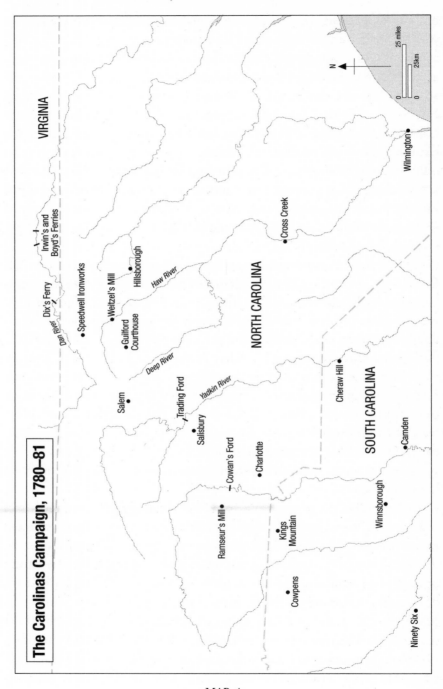

The Carolinas Campaign, 1780–81

VIRGINIA

Irwin's and
Boyd's Ferries

Dix's Ferry

Dan River

Speedwell Ironworks

Weitzel's Mill

Hillsborough

Haw River

Guilford
Courthouse

Deep River

Salem

Trading Ford

Yadkin River

Salisbury

Cowan's Ford

Charlotte

Ramseur's Mill

Kings
Mountain

Cowpens

Ninety Six

Cross Creek

Wilmington

NORTH CAROLINA

Cheraw Hill

SOUTH CAROLINA

Camden

Winnsborough

N

25 miles
25km

MAP 4

but the stubborn Gates would not change his plan. On August 7, his small force combined with Caswell's 2,000 militiamen as they marched south toward Camden. Virginia militia troops led by Edward Stevens joined them several days later to bolster Gates's ranks.

Gates was not the only general on the move in South Carolina in August. The British forces in the province were now commanded by Lord Cornwallis, since Clinton had left Charleston in June to sail back to New York. It was good riddance for each general, as these two redcoat officers politely despised each other by early May. Aware of Gates's approaching force in the South Carolina backcountry, Cornwallis and his escort left Charleston and arrived at Camden on August 13, where there were about 2,300 troops at the fortified post. Always aggressive, Cornwallis planned to strike the approaching Americans unawares north of the rustic village. Gates too tried to move quickly on the British at Camden, but rather than attack their well-defended camps head on, he sought to occupy a strong position behind a sluggish creek several miles north of the town, close enough to oblige the British to attack his larger, threatening army.

Coincidently, at 10pm on a sultry August 15, both generals ordered their weary troops to advance toward the enemy in a night march through tall pine forests on sandy roads. In the darkness, the leading elements of each column crashed into each other about seven miles north of the town at about 2am. After a short and confusing firefight on the road, both startled vanguards withdrew a short distance and prepared for a major contest early the next morning. They did not have long to wait.

At first light, the British troops deployed on both sides of the road, shaking out their best troops on the right. Several regiments also lined up on the left of the road, with a Highlander regiment to their rear. Tarleton's British Legion dragoons waited on the road in the rear, keen to exploit any break in the rebels' line with a mounted dragoon charge. The redcoats numbered about 2,200 veteran soldiers. For reasons he never explained, Gates arranged his troops in a defective manner that led to a shocking disaster. He placed his veteran Continental regiments on the right side of his line, with one regiment of Maryland troops on the road as a reserve. In the center waited Caswell's North Carolina militia, and on the left stood the inexperienced Virginians. Thus, with this arrangement there were few experienced troops on the American left or center. All told, Gates's army numbered over 3,500 men.

At dawn Cornwallis quickly assaulted the American line by first advancing his regiments on his right flank, where his hardened infantry smashed into Gates's untried militia after firing a deadly musket volley. The redcoats then charged with leveled bayonets directly at the Virginia militia units. With few bayonets among the militiamen and little experience with the steel blade, the panicked Virginians and most of the North Carolinians in the center instantly fled for the rear, many without firing a single shot. The veteran Maryland Col Otho Holland Williams, Gates's adjutant general, described the sudden rout: "they threw down their loaded arms and fled, in the utmost consternation. The unworthy example of the Virginians was almost instantly followed by the North Carolinians."[3] After the militia bolted, generals Caswell and Gates frantically tried to rally them, but could not get the frightened troops to rally on the road to Charlotte. The surging British regiments next attacked the stalwart Maryland and Delaware men to their left. Eventually, the Continentals were overwhelmed and ran from the field into the nearby woods and swamps. Gen de Kalb fought on foot that morning and was struck down with multiple bullet and bayonet wounds, which soon proved mortal. One of Gates's aides wrote "we owe all our misfortune to the Militia, [h]ad they not run like dastardly cowards, our Army was sufficient to cope with theirs, drawn up as we were upon a rising and advantageous ground."[4] The battle was an ignominious debacle for Gates and the American fortunes in the South.

Coming just three months after the devasting loss of troops and artillery at Charleston, the stunning rebel defeat near Camden seemed to eliminate any hope of preventing the victorious British from overrunning South Carolina and crushing the Patriots across the state. In his flight from the battlefield Gates stopped briefly at Charlotte, then raced on to Hillsborough, in central North Carolina, where he attempted to collect what worn down soldiers and limited supplies he could for future operations. Most of the dispersed militia would not rally after the battle, and there were hopelessly few men left standing in the ranks, little money, and barely enough sustenance for man or beast. The situation for those desperately fighting for independence in the Carolinas now looked grim indeed.

Cornwallis's resounding victory over Gates secured South Carolina for the British and left North Carolina vulnerable to an enemy invasion. The battle near Camden also allowed armed southern Loyalists to embody and regain political and military power. Now victorious, Cornwallis planned to advance directly north about 80 miles to Charlotte, to support cowering Loyalists in North Carolina, scatter any remaining American forces in the field there, and reestablish the king's authority across the province. He had contemplated such an advance earlier in July, and Clinton was favorable toward conquering North Carolina, but only *if* South Carolina had already been secured. "It at present appears to me that I should endeavor to get, as soon as possible, to Hillsborough," Cornwallis wrote to Clinton a week after the victory at Camden.[5] Although he was skeptical of the armed support the British would see when they entered the state, Cornwallis expected to "assemble and try to arrange the friends who are inclined to arm in our favour, and endeavor to form a very large magazine for the winter of flour & meal from the country, and of rum, salt, &c." Yet with less than 3,000 troops available to move into North Carolina, Cornwallis surely must have known that a conquest of the huge state with thousands of its angry inhabitants actively supporting independence was highly unlikely. His real goal was defeating the rebel army and interdicting supplies transported farther south. In fact, the British march in 1781 through North Carolina from January until early May was more like a raid than a permanent conquest, and an attempt to shore up the Loyalists along the Cape Fear and Haw Rivers. The king's friends "continue ... to give me the strongest assurances of support when His Majesty's Troops shall have penetrated into the interior parts of the Province." Likewise, he hoped that "upon the appearance of a British army in North Carolina, a great body of the inhabitants were ready to join and cooperate with it." This questionable optimism marked the beginning of the invasion of North Carolina starting in early fall of 1780.[6]

By September 26, the advance column of 1,200 British troops reached Charlotte, the courthouse hamlet Cornwallis hoped to make "a fixed post" with several earthen redouts to defend it. Here the redcoats encountered determined resistance from mounted Patriot troops under the young English-born Col William R. Davie, a 1776 Princeton graduate. The invaders eventually pushed Davie's men out of the small village, but they found the area to be a pesky nest of "rebels." The British remained there for several weeks. During this trying time Cornwallis issued a public proclamation announcing his intention to "restore as much peace and quiet to the country as may be possible, during the operations of war," and calling on the locals to "faithfully deliver up their arms, and give a military parole to remain thenceforth peaceable at home, doing no offence against his Majesty's government."[7]

At the same time Cornwallis's troops pushed into North Carolina, a supporting militia column off to the west advanced along the foothills of the Blue Ridge Mountains. This column of 1,100 armed Loyalists was commanded by the Scotsman Maj Patrick Ferguson, a regular British army officer whom Clinton had earlier appointed inspector of the Loyalist militia. This role made Ferguson responsible for raising, drilling, and commanding Loyalist military units in the South for service with the regulars. Despite the young Scotsman's success in raising troops, Cornwallis was never an enthusiastic supporter of Ferguson's efforts as he regarded the major as one of Clinton's favorites, not his. He also placed little confidence in the efficacy of Loyalist troops on campaign in general. Nevertheless, Ferguson took the field with confidence and set out with his mounted companies for North Carolina's hostile, far backcountry settlements.

Late in September, Ferguson's column reached Gilbert Town (near modern Rutherfordton), to the west of Charlotte and Cornwallis's main army. Perhaps the major was too confident or bold, for at this point he made a fatal miscalculation. He sent a provocative proclamation to the distant backcountry settlers and those living across the rugged Appalachian Mountains in Virginia, the western Carolinas, and present East Tennessee. He announced, "if you do not desist your opposition to the British Arms I shall march this army over the mountains, hang your leaders, and lay waste your country with fire and sword." Such a needless inflammatory declaration provoked and incensed the well-armed Overmountain men to rendezvous in the mountains, hollows, and valleys, then ride southeast toward Fergusson's command. Hardy Virginia frontiersmen also struck out from around Abingdon and joined hundreds of mounted North Carolinian riflemen along their way. These combined forces were met by rugged South Carolinians at Cowpens, a large open pastureland west of Charlotte where about 1,400 armed men assembled. They moved quickly east toward Kings Mountain, where Ferguson's Loyalists took up a defensive position on a high wooded ridge about 30 miles from Charlotte. Aware of the frontier forces gathering to oppose him, the young major anxiously called on Cornwallis for support.[8]

For Ferguson and his Loyalists, no rescue was coming. On October 7, 1780, the gritty American frontier militia commanded that day by the prominent, well-educated Virginia pioneer Col William Campbell surrounded and defeated the Loyalists on Kings Mountain in a fierce battle in the autumn forest in which Ferguson was killed. "The victory was complete to a wish," Campbell boasted a few weeks later.[9] The defeated Loyalists lost 119 men killed (some after they surrendered) and about 700 reluctantly surrendered, fearful of the Patriot woodsmen's brutality. Campbell's victorious Overmountain fighters did not linger long on the wooded heights after the shooting stopped, as their officers knew that once Cornwallis learned of Ferguson's annihilation, he would come after them to rescue the unlucky captives. The backcountry frontiersmen dispersed, and the North Carolina and Virginia troops quickly rode north with their prisoners toward Gilbert Town. Along the march several prominent Loyalist leaders were tried quickly and hanged there before wiser Patriot commanders stopped the extralegal executions.[10]

The total American triumph on Kings Mountain eliminated over 1,000 organized Loyalist militiamen and dampened the enthusiasm among other "Tories" to enlist or even openly gather in groups. Southern Patriots won a morale-building victory after the disasters at Charleston and Camden. Ferguson's defeat also led Cornwallis to postpone his further advance into North Carolina by over two months. Instead, the British general retired 65 miles south to Winnsboro, South Carolina, by the end of October. It was a "healthy spot, well situated to protect the greatest part of the northern frontier" of that province in

Cornwallis's estimation. The worn out British troops, many of whom were ill with fever, regrouped there, and expected to be reinforced by troops from Virginia's Chesapeake Bay by January. This unexpected respite allowed Gates and other officers time to collect supplies and more men at Hillsborough, Salisbury, and Charlotte, though very few North Carolinians showed up at camp – especially those who had fled the shocking musket fire and bayonets at Camden.[11]

Significant Continental Army leadership changes in the South came that autumn. In October, at Washington's insistence, Congress appointed Nathanael Greene to supersede Gates as commander of the Southern Department. Washington ordered the Rhode Islander to "proceed without delay to the Southern army, now in North Carolina, and take the command accordingly." Baron von Steuben was tapped to accompany Greene to his new, distant assignment. Then, Daniel Morgan of Saratoga fame was promoted to brigadier general to command the southern army's light troops in the Carolinas, where he had recently come out of retirement from Virginia to assist Gates's struggling army. After a long journey from West Point, New York, Greene and his staff rode into the small village of Charlotte, North Carolina, on December 2 and relieved Gates, who departed for his Shenandoah Valley farm the next day.[12]

Although he had been warned during his tiresome southward journey that soldiers, supplies, and arms were hard to come by in the department, Greene was still startled upon his arrival at Charlotte by the shockingly poor condition of the soldiers. His first of several letters to Congress, governors, and North Carolina officials that week are often quoted, and for good reason, as they vividly describe the dispirited army's plight. "The Difficulty of carrying on the war in this Department is much greater than my imagination had extended to," he wrote to North Carolina's governor Abner Nash, and his troops were just "the Shadow of an Army in the midst of Distress."[13] And to Governor Thomas Jefferson in Virginia, upon whom he planned to rely for much of the army's needs, he made a detailed report.

I find the troops … in a most wretched condition, destitute of every thing necessary either for the comfort or convenience of soldiers.

It is impossible that men can render any service ... whilst they are starving with cold and hunger. Your [Virginia] troops may be literally said to be naked and I shall be obliged to send a considerable number of them away into some secure place and warm quarters until they can be furnished with clothing. It will answer no good purpose to send men here in such a condition, for they are nothing but added weight upon the army, and altogether incapable of aiding in its operations ... The life of a soldier in its best state is subject to innumerable hardships, but when they are aggravated by a want of provisions [and] clothing, his condition becomes intolerable, nor can men long contend with such complicated difficulties and distress – deaths, desertion and the hospital must soon swallow up an army under such circumstances.[14]

Unfortunately for the neglected American soldiers serving down south, these conditions in the Southern Department improved only marginally over the next few years.

At Charlotte, Greene commanded about 1,000 poorly clothed and armed Delaware and Maryland Continentals, in addition to an always fluctuating number of short-term militia companies of mixed reliability. These men needed to be fed, supplied, and rested, so the new commander had to adopt a new course of action for the immediate relief of his broken-down soldiers. With Cornwallis about 60 miles to the south, Greene adopted a risky plan of dividing his troops into two elements. He would personally march the main force to a "camp of repose" along Hicks Creek, a small tributary of the Pee Dee River in the Cheraw region, just across the border in South Carolina. This spot would put him far to the east of Cornwallis, so that he could threaten British outposts in South Carolina and appear to be on the offensive. A smaller but more mobile light force detachment under General Morgan called the "Flying Army" was ordered to move west of the Catawba/Wateree River southwest of Charlotte to help secure the Carolina backcountry for Patriot militia and civilians, and to threaten the fortified British outpost at Ninety Six. This deployment separated Greene's already weak army by 120 miles with the stronger redcoats and Loyalists between the American detachments and made both rebel wings vulnerable to British attack. But Greene adopted the risky plan to better feed and supply his troops, although provisions and clothing were still scarce. Shockingly, some of the ragged troops on the Pee Dee had no clothes at all, "except a little piece of blanket in the Indian form round their waists."[15] It is a wonder they stayed in the ranks.

North Carolina at this time was almost helpless concerning resources and logistics. An exasperated Governor Abner Nash wrote a vivid letter to Congress back in October to report that "all the funds of this State have been exhausted in the course of the late [1780] campaign [and] the horses, wagons, tents, arms, camp equipage of every kind, the pay and bounty of the militia, and the provision of beef, pork, flour, spirits, sugar, coffee, wine, medicines, etc., etc., all fell upon us, besides the payment of very large sums on Congress[ional] draughts, & all was lost in a single hour" at Camden. Thus, only dire necessity made Greene wager that he could unite his separated army quickly enough if need be.[16]

The British now grew active in January. Lord Cornwallis, as described earlier, was an experienced soldier and an aggressive campaigner. Learning of Morgan's backcountry foray to his left as he moved northward toward Charlotte – resuming his active operations to enter North Carolina – he detached a 1,200-strong, fast-moving column of foot regiments, artillery, and British Legion dragoons led by the aggressive Col Banastre Tarleton to overtake and destroy Morgan off to the west. The young, hard-hitting commander of the short green-coated British Legion had already made a notorious reputation for fast movements and violent attacks, and was especially feared by American militiamen. His swift assault on a Virginia Continental detachment commanded by Col Abraham Buford at the Waxhaws settlements near Charlotte back in May 1780 helped establish his "no quarter" notoriety but also showed that his pugnacity could be marked by impetuosity – as Morgan's small command would soon see.

Alert to Tarleton's rapid approach, Morgan moved his men – over 1,000 strong, and increasing daily – north to avoid the oncoming enemy. Morgan, however, did not want to have his men on the march or crossing the nearby Broad River when Tarleton inevitably caught up to his column. Accordingly, about six miles south of the river, the new brigadier halted his troops on January 16 at the Cowpens, the open area of grasslands that was a Patriot rally point before the battle of Kings Mountain. This ground offered an excellent defensive position with secure flanks so that the hard-pressed militia and Continentals could make a determined stand. Morgan placed his battle-tested Maryland and Delaware Continentals in his rear line on an open knoll. He also deployed hundreds of militiamen from Virginia, North and South Carolina, and Georgia to his front. Typically, militia troops were unwilling to fight in lines trading volleys with red-coated veterans charging at them with fixed bayonets, as seen at Camden. Still, southern militia had won impressive recent victories in South Carolina at Musgrove's Mill (August 19, 1780) and Kings Mountain, so Morgan may have had more confidence in their reliability. He placed the militia, led by the dour Col Andrew Pickens of backcountry South Carolina, in line several hundred yards in front of the Continentals, asking them to fire two or three volleys when Tarleton's troops attacked, then to fall back behind the main force. He also advanced about 100 or so skirmishers bearing their long, deadly accurate flintlock rifles out in front to help slow the expected initial British attack.

At dawn's first light on the frosty morning of January 17, Tarleton spied the American lines in the growing light. He impetuously ordered an attack – even though not all his troops had come up. Morgan's innovative deployment worked well, as the militia for the most part fired a few volleys and fell back in order. Tarleton's infantry and cavalry drove forward, but after some early confusion the Continentals held fast, and a bold, well-timed cavalry charge from the American left flank by Col William Washington's dragoons blunted Tarleton's assault. Remarkably, a simultaneous bayonet charge by the Maryland Continentals on the American right routed the stunned enemy in what was in effect an unplanned double envelopment. Hundreds of fearful redcoats and Loyalists surrendered, and the rebel victors also captured two 3-pounder field artillery pieces. Only Tarleton and several dozen mounted dragoons managed to escape east back to Cornwallis's camp south of Charlotte at Turkey Creek. The loss of so many British soldiers at Cowpens – over a quarter of the army – was a major blow to the British army in the Carolinas, and in Morgan's words, "a compleat Victory."[17]

American losses were about 150 killed and wounded, compared to about 900 of the British including the captured troops. The many British dead lay stiff on the cold battleground, unburied.

Morgan and his jubilant soldiers had little time to celebrate though, knowing that Cornwallis would soon be after them once news of the rebels' remarkable victory reached his headquarters. Morgan hurried his men east on the 18th toward the Catawba River, which they managed to cross at Sherrald's (also called Sherrill's) Ford by January 23, after evading Cornwallis – who wasted two valuable days of the pursuit marching in the wrong direction. Morgan's position now placed a major water obstacle between his light troops and the oncoming British. Still, he was apprehensive about the fast-approaching enemy and suggested to Greene that he move the main army closer to the Catawba.

Morgan's plan was wise as the British followed his troops into North Carolina after the battle of Cowpens. Cornwallis was reinforced on January 18 by 1,200 troops led by Maj Gen Alexander Leslie, just arrived from the Chesapeake Bay. Now his force of 2,500 men was made up of redcoats of the Royal Welch Fusiliers, the 33rd and 71st regiments, along with a picked amalgamation of the Guards, the Hessian Regiment von Bose, a Hessian light infantry company (Jaegers), Tarleton's British Legion, and the Royal North Carolina Regiment, a Loyalist formation. After failing to catch up with Morgan's column – and liberate the Cowpens prisoners, now headed for Virginia – the British advanced to Ramsour's Mill, 35 miles northwest of Charlotte on the west side of the swift Catawba River. Cornwallis wrote that "my situation is most critical," but he was "determined to go on." Unable to keep up with Morgan, the British general decided to "lighten" his own column for faster pursuit marches. He ordered much of the army's excess baggage, wagons, tents, and supplies destroyed, including that of the officers. He "determined to burn all my wagons except those loaded with rum, salt, spare ammunition and hospital stores." One of Cornwallis's two brigadier generals, Charles O'Hara of the Guards, wrote of Cornwallis's daring decision: although the British were in "a barren, inhospitable, unhealthy part of North America," still "it was resolved to follow Greene's army to the end of the world."[18]

Local Patriot militia units tried to defend the Catawba crossings but "the fords were so numerous, and our force so small," Greene lamented. Finally, after scouting for a suitable place to cross the chilly river, the British foot soldiers forced their way across the Catawba under deadly rifle fire at Cowan's Ford on February 1, and pushed back the hundreds of North Carolina defenders led by Brig Gen William Lee Davidson, who suffered a mortal wound in the fighting. Tarleton and his dragoons splashed across at an upstream ford, chased the fleeing militia, and violently dispersed about 400 of them that afternoon at Torrance's Tavern on the Great Salisbury Road. Cornwallis reported that "this stroke, with our passage of the ford, so effectively dispirited the militia, that we met with no further opposition on our march to the Yadkin [River]."[19]

Two days prior to the fight at Cowan's Ford, Greene arrived at the banks of the Catawba to confer with Morgan. The southern army commander had ordered the rest of the army at the Cheraw camps to march west under South Carolina's Brig Gen Isaac Huger to join Morgan's troops at the rustic town of Salisbury, a few miles from Trading Ford on the Yadkin River. A hopeful Greene implored Huger to "hasten your march towards Salisbury as fast as possible … we should take every possible precaution to guard against a misfortune. But I am not without hopes of ruining Lord Cornwallis if he persists in his mad scheme of pushing through the country."[20] When the British crossed the Catawba, however, it was obvious to Greene and his lieutenants that they could not stand and fight due to Cornwallis's superior force and the flight of the militia. Instead, Greene ordered Morgan to move farther northeast to Guilford Courthouse, a hamlet on the Great Salisbury Road about 55 miles away, where Huger's troops and wagons were also diverted on February 1.

Morgan moved his troops from Salisbury across the Yadkin at Trading Ford, closely pursued by the British. Using all the boats and rafts he could find, Morgan managed to get his command across the flooded river with no time to spare, as the enemy's leading units appeared on the western riverbank just as the Patriot troops got over to the east side. And the rebels had all their boats safely with them, which frustrated Cornwallis's hopes of catching the fleeing enemy in retreat.

Although none of the troops could have known it, this narrow escape would be repeated on a larger scale just two weeks later.

Greene's troops began to arrive at Guilford Courthouse on February 7, including Huger's weary soldiers coming from the banks of the Pee Dee on the following day. Of great significance, the bold and capable Lt Col Henry "Light-Horse Harry" Lee and his legion (a mixed force of Continental dragoons and infantry) arrived two days later, having served with rebel partisans in eastern South Carolina earlier in 1781. Bivouacked in the cold around the little wood-framed courthouse, the army counted about 2,000 soldiers in the ranks, including 1,426 Continentals, "many of whom are badly armed and distressed for the want of clothing." The small force was organized in two brigades, with Williams commanding the two Maryland regiments and Huger leading the Virginians, per Greene's orders of January 27.[21] Greene's urgent pleas for Carolina militia to turn out went largely unheeded. He also implored Steuben, then serving in Virginia, to procure and forward arms, supplies, and new recruits to the army.

While the American army gathered around Guilford Courthouse, the British forces were on the move. Cornwallis led his army upriver from Salisbury and crossed the Yadkin at Shallow Ford on February 7. From there the plundering British column quickly moved to the prosperous Moravian towns of Bethania, Bethabara, and Salem, settled by German Protestant pietists in the 1750s. By the 10th, the British were at the latter village, just 25 miles or so west of Greene's army and on the same side of the Yadkin. Given how quickly the British army could cover distances at this point in the campaign, their position at Salem created a longed-for opportunity for Cornwallis to close with the rebels and defeat them in battle. A major defeat for American arms would crush Patriot enthusiasm and support in North Carolina, the British general assumed, and perhaps bring the southern province to heel.

At the courthouse, intelligence received by Greene about the British arrival at Salem alerted the Rhode Island general to the danger his army was in. This was one of the most crucial moments of the Carolinas campaign for Greene, who now had little choice but to hurry his forces away from the British and place his harried soldiers behind yet another water course for safety. This meant moving northeast to cross the muddy Dan River across the state border and take up a defensive position in Virginia.

At a brief council of war at headquarters including Greene, Morgan, Williams, and Huger on February 9, "it was determined unanimously that we ought to avoid a general action at all events, and that the army ought to retreat immediately over the Roanoke [Dan] river." This hasty plan was the true beginning of what came to be called "the Race to the Dan," a charitable name for what was really a successful, albeit dramatic retreat. The critical decision now for Greene to take was where to cross the muddy river, and how to get there quickly. The American army was too weak to face the British in a general engagement, all the officers recognized. "It would be inevitable ruin to the army and no less ruinous to the American cause to hazard a general action," Greene prudently decided. During his first week in command at Charlotte he had already concluded that the best course of action for American arms was a cautious one, a lesson he had learned serving several years with Gen Washington. "While so much depends upon the opinion of the people both as to men and money, as little should be put to the hazard as possible," he had observed, and "until we have a more permanent force ... if we put things to the hazard in our infant state before we have gathered sufficient strength to act with spirit and activity and meet a second misfortune all may be lost."[22]

The anxious Patriot commanders quickly had to determine where to cross the Dan to avoid being attacked *en route* by the enemy at their heels before they could ferry across the river. Moreover, Greene's troops would be slowed by "heavy rains, deep creeks, bad roads, poor horses and broken harness, as well as delays for want of provisions," in the general's bleak assessment on February 9. The Americans had two viable options to get over the Dan. They could move north to Dix's Ferry (at present Danville, Virginia) almost 50 miles away at what was called the "upper crossing," where the river was narrower, and likely to be less flooded. But the quick-marching British at Salem were themselves just 65 miles from Dix's Ferry and would be in position to strike the rebels before they could cross the river.[23]

Greene's other option was to march to the Dan's lower crossings at Irwin's and Boyd's ferries (at today's South Boston, Virginia) in

Halifax County, close to 80 miles from Guilford Courthouse, and hope to outrun the British. Here Greene's skill and experience as the army's quartermaster general starting in 1778 provided invaluable foresight as he travelled to Charlotte upon taking command in December, and afterwards. Thinking of logistics, maneuvers, and defenses, he detailed several intrepid staff officers to scout river crossings in southern Virginia and North Carolina for their potential value in transporting supplies and to position his army. Moreover, these officers were to learn how many barges, flats, and batteaux (which Greene called "boats of a peculiar kind") were used on the rivers, and where they were located, including the Catawba, Dan, and Roanoke Rivers. This valuable staff work, particularly the "indefatigable industry" of Deputy Quartermaster General for the Southern Army, Col Edward Carrington of Virginia, and the Polish engineer Col Thaddeus Kościuszko, who had served so valuably in the Saratoga campaign, continued into February. Greene chose to attempt the crossings on the lower Dan, "which the great fall of rain rendered impassable without the assistance of boats," recalled Henry Lee, and ordered all available vessels collected at these ferries, although there were few actually available.[24]

And how to get to these crossings ahead of the enemy? In a daring plan made by Greene and his officers at Guilford, the Continentals and what few militia remained with them would divide into two elements. The main body of the army, including Huger's troops, the artillery, and wagons, would be under Greene's direct command. They left camp on February 10, headed for the lower crossings on the Dan River, where they would be met with any boats Col Carrington and others could collect. Greene then reorganized his mobile force of light troops previously led by Daniel Morgan, who left the field that day due to declining health after much hard service, into a fast-marching screening element that would operate in front of Cornwallis's oncoming column. Led by Maryland's Col Otho Holland Williams, this detachment of 700 troops consisted of "Light-Horse Harry" Lee's Legion, William Washington's light dragoons, several dozen mounted Virginia riflemen, and 280 Maryland, Delaware, and Virginia Continentals, commanded by veteran officer Lt Col John Eager

Howard, another Marylander. Williams was ordered to "keep as near the enemy as he could without exposing the party too much and retard their march all in his power."[25]

Since the war, historians and authors have offered differing interpretations of the so-called "Race to the Dan," particularly as to when it began.[26] This phrase has been popular with writers since Greene himself used the term "race" at the time. More than one modern study posits that the hurried trek to the Dan River began with Morgan's month-long movement to escape Cornwallis and his reinforced army in mid-January after the fight at Cowpens. Others conclude that the "race" began when the British burned their excess baggage at Ramsour's Mill near the Catawba River. Perhaps these interpretations of Greene's narrow escape to Virginia are meant to (over)dramatize Cornwallis's failed pursuit of the retreating rebels for the excitement of readers. Or, maybe to add to Greene's luster as a general, i.e. to "give" him an ironic victory in retreat, in the absence of battlefield success in the South from 1781 to 1783. The "race" can more accurately be seen as a prudent retreat in which Greene barely avoided being caught.

In truth, Morgan did not have the Dan River in mind after his Cowpens victory; rather he focused on getting over the swirling Catawba and sending the enemy prisoners safely into Virginia. When Greene arrived at the Catawba fords on January 30, he and Morgan had quickly concluded that the British could be delayed but not stopped from continuing their pursuit, and here Greene may have first considered retreating all the way to the Dan. As noted above, he had directed his staff and engineer officers to explore the Dan and locate boats in case of future need. But he had also assigned officers to assess other Piedmont rivers as well. In addition, Greene and Morgan seem to have initially considered defending points along the Yadkin River, at Salisbury. But the firm determination to retreat into Virginia really came when the army combined at Guilford Courthouse, where on February 9, the generals decided unanimously to retreat across the Dan. Thus the "race," though certainly heroic, lasted four days, not several weeks marching from Ramsour's Mill. As I have suggested elsewhere, "given the lack of newspapers and poor roads in the south, in addition to slow communications of the Revolutionary period, the vast majority of the public knew nothing of these events until long after the campaign was over."[27]

The mythology that has developed around this episode of the campaign notwithstanding, the events themselves were decidedly dramatic and heroic. According to the plan, Williams's light force made contact with the British, then led the enemy on a withdrawal toward Dix's Ferry, frequently skirmishing along the road, at times perilously close to the vanguard of the pursuing foe. Williams succeeded in duping Cornwallis into thinking the whole rebel army was bound for Dix's Ferry, rather than the downstream crossings, where Greene was heading on another nearby road. As Lee recalled years later, "the greater the distance between the main body and the light troops, the surer would be Greene's retreat."[28] Tarleton later wrote that "on the road many skirmishes took place between the British and the American light troops, without great loss to either party, or any impediment to the progress of [Greene's] main body."[29] One of the Virginians in the light corps reported that the Patriots were "employed night and day on the lines throwing every difficulty in their power in the way of the advancing enemy," often without "rest and sleep and every necessary comfort."[30]

As Greene's weary column trudged onward over the Haw River, with little support from area militia units, he received an urgent message from Williams on the night of February 13/14. The pursuing British enemy was closing in on his distressed light troops, and now threatened the main body. Williams even thought he might have to sacrifice his rear guard to ensure the other troops could escape. Greene therefore ordered Williams off the road to Dix's Ferry and to move east toward the lower ferries on the 14th, as he thought a combined force might deter the British more than two separate elements. By the time Williams' footsore men reached the rushing Dan River that night to cross at Irwin's Ferry on a few flats and batteaux after marching 40 miles that day, Greene's troops had already crossed the river there by 5:30pm. Lee's worn-out cavalrymen crossed at Boyd's shortly thereafter. The rearguard had made it safely to Halifax County and could now finally rest. With the available boats secured, and the American troops out of reach, all the exhausted British could do was peer across the swirling waters when they arrived at the ferries early on the 15th, several hours too late to catch their elusive quarry.

The campaigning of the two belligerents for the next four weeks of winter days prior to the decisive battle in Guilford County were complex and widespread in central North Carolina. However, the armies' maneuvers and skirmishes leading up to March 15, while often brutal and grueling in cold, rainy weather, can only be summarized in these pages. Details about the battle at the courthouse and its significance will be the focus of the last section of this chapter.

While today we may look at the situation on February 15 as a cause for the Patriot troops to celebrate their successful retrograde movement, at the time the British could also interpret the strategic situation in their favor. Cornwallis had driven the only significant Continental army in the South out of the Carolinas, and this success had largely dampened Patriot militia companies from mustering at towns and crossroads across most of the state. He could now try to restore royal government to the former colony, particularly the courts which were necessary to administer and record loyalty oaths. He also looked to the Loyalists for support in securing the province, turning out in arms, and crushing whatever resistance remained among the rebels.

Thwarted at the Dan River, on February 16 the British moved leisurely south toward Hillsborough, 50 miles away, which they reached four days later. At this key backcountry town, Cornwallis staged a public ceremony to "raise the King's colors," a call for all those loyal to the Crown to appear there and swear allegiance to George III. Few men joined the ranks, however, and many just wanted to see the regiments formed up and hear a salute of 21 guns. While at Hillsborough Cornwallis wrote to British officers at Charleston asking for reinforcements and provisions, especially shoes, for his lean, worn-down command.

Meanwhile, Greene implored North Carolina and Virginia officials for militia, arms, and supplies. "I have some expectation of collecting a force sufficient in this country to enable me to act offensively," he wrote optimistically, "and in turn race Lord Cornwallis as he has done me."[31] Greene moved his famished troops back into North Carolina beginning on February 19, in an attempt to prevent the British from "pillaging, plundering and getting provisions." As he advised Governor Jefferson, "It was necessary to convince the Carolinians that they were not conquered," though he had to be cautious of tangling with the superior enemy army.[32]

During the next several weeks between Hillsborough and the Yadkin River to the west, both armies maneuvered, skirmished, foraged, and tried to strengthen their ranks. Col Lee and militia commander Andrew Pickens of South Carolina devastated a Loyalist force under Loyalist Col John Pyle near Alamance Creek on February 25, in "a great slaughter" at what came to be known as "Pyle's Massacre."[33] These weeks were a "game of checkers" between the armies, wrote a Carolina militiaman, and British general Charles O'Hara recalled that "the two armies were never twenty miles asunder, they constantly avoiding a general action and we industriously seeking it. These operations obliged the two armies to make numberless moves, which it is impossible to detail." An observant Virginian in Greene's army also noted that "the movements of the army consisted of marching to and fro, sometimes hanging upon Cornwallis and at others flying from him." And a North Carolina soldier wrote that Greene "kept the Army in almost constant motion not suffering it to encamp on the same ground two nights in succession."[34]

On March 6, elements of the two armies clashed at Weitzel's Mill on Reedy Fork Creek in a sharp fight that one Virginian called "a severe battle with Cornwallis's army." There an alert Cornwallis tried to destroy part of the rebel army under Col Williams that was separated from the main force. Attacked by the redcoats, Williams managed to rejoin his soldiers with Greene, but the British did not pursue the Patriots. Greene moved his weary men north of the Haw River by March 10, which placed his force closer to the reinforcements he expected from Virginia and put the troops behind a river in an excellent defensive position. Still, to prevent surprise, he moved his army's camps every one or two days.[35]

In the sparsely settled Piedmont region of North Carolina, to obtain food and fodder for his army Cornwallis had to keep on the move. The British general therefore led his small army about 50 miles west of Hillsborough to the scattered settlements along the Deep River and halted there at a Quaker meeting house on March 13. During this time the ever-vigilant Greene designated Washington's Continental dragoons and Lee's mounted troops, supported by several hundred mounted riflemen, as "parties of observation" with the mission to observe the enemy's movements and screen the American troops. Additionally, the light infantrymen under Williams were ordered back to serve with their regular units.

Although militia companies continued to come and go from the army's camps along the Haw River, by March 10 Greene's ranks began to welcome significant reinforcements. Brig Gen Robert Lawson's Virginia militia arrived in the camps by the 11th, and a second, smaller Virginia brigade was also formed under the veteran Gen Stevens. Around 1,200 North Carolina militiamen led by respected generals John Butler and Thomas Eaton also marched into camp. More importantly Greene now had two regiments of Virginia Continentals led by Gen Huger. The 1st Virginia Regiment was commanded by the long-serving Col John Green, and the 2nd Virginia – all new recruits – was under Lt Col Samuel Hawes of Caroline County. Additionally, the reorganized 1st and 2nd Maryland Regiments were led by former minuteman Col John Gunby and Camden survivor Lt Col Benjamin Ford respectively, and while the former regiment was an experienced unit, Ford's battalion was made up of all new recruits. Other units in Greene's expanding host included two sections of Continental Artillery, two veteran companies of Delaware and North Carolina Continentals, three Virginia and Maryland light infantry companies, and two companies of militia dragoons. All told, Greene had about 4,400 men under arms.

On March 13, the footsore American army marched west from their Haw River lines toward Guilford Courthouse, about a dozen miles away, and arrived there early the next morning. Many modern studies of the battle assume that Greene's intention was to bring his troops to Guilford Courthouse, deploy there in defensive positions on the Great Salisbury Road, then wait to be attacked by the British. These accounts posit that in early February Greene had evaluated the courthouse area as a suitable place to await an eventual assault from Cornwallis's army, and that the Continental general maneuvered the redcoats into doing so after he recrossed the Dan River back into Virginia. This interpretation, however, is false.

Once Greene assembled his army with (barely) enough food and fodder to keep his men in the field for a short time, he knew he had a longed-for opportunity to strike the British army, also suffering from supply problems and now numbering about 2,300 troops. From contemporary accounts it is clear that Greene intended to operate offensively against the British until the very morning of battle on March 15. An optimistic Virginia officer with the army wrote at the time that "the troops at present indulge the most pleasing expectations, and anticipate the happiness they hope to enjoy by making the British shortly retreat before them with precipitation." And a militia officer wrote that the army marched toward Guilford Courthouse "to look for Cornwallis," and noted on the 14th that the American army was "marching to attack Cornwallis." The day before the battle Greene wrote to Col Lee that he planned to advance on the enemy at Deep River seeking an engagement, and even Cornwallis assumed that the American army "was marching to attack the British troops." Moreover in a letter to Congress after the battle, Greene wrote that on March 10, "I took the resolution of attacking the enemy without loss of time."[36]

But Greene did not get the chance to act offensively. In the pre-dawn hours of March 15, "Light-Horse Harry" Lee's alert advance scouts detected active movement in the British camp. When it became obvious that Cornwallis had begun to march his army back toward Guildford Courthouse, mounted rebels rushed back to alert the main army by 4am. Indeed, in the rainy darkness, the British were moving steadily northeast on the Old Salisbury Road to the New Garden Meeting House, just five miles from Greene's position at Guilford Courthouse. Tarleton's dragoons cautiously led the way forward on the narrow road. Between the Quakers' meeting house and Greene's waiting lines, the road was known as New Garden Road. Along this section of the muddy trail a series of sharp, bloody engagements occurred for two hours between Lee's advance element and Tarleton's tough horsemen, supported by deadly musket volleys of the 23rd Regiment's veteran fusiliers. Lee's troops "behaved with the most undaunted bravery and maintained himself against the most formidable opposition," wrote an impressed redcoat in the close-in fighting,[37] but once "Light-Horse Harry" glimpsed hundreds of British soldiers coming up behind Tarleton's screening force, he prudently withdrew to the courthouse area.

As soon as Greene received word that the enemy was hastening toward his army, he and his officers placed his mixed force of Continentals and militia in defensive positions around the little courthouse. Greene deployed his regiments based on the lessons of Cowpens and the sage advice of Daniel Morgan, who offered it in a letter of February 20. "You'll have from what I see, a great number of militia – if they fight you'll beat Cornwallis[,] if not, he will beat you and perhaps cut your regulars to pieces, which will be losing all our hopes," the old Virginian surmised. Morgan also recommended placing "riflemen ... on the flanks under enterprising officers who [are] acquainted with that kind of fighting," and putting "some picked troops to [the militia's] rear with orders to shoot down the first man that runs."[38] Clearly, he was thinking of the Camden debacle.

Greene knew Cornwallis had to approach his position on the New Garden Road, for ease in moving his dragoons, wagons, and artillery, and to deploy his foot regiments close to the American lines prior to a frontal assault. The brush-choked forests of leafless trees all around, with occasional farm fields here and there, would restrict the dreaded British cavalry, limit artillery fire, and make maneuvering battalions effectively quite difficult. The Rhode Islander likely knew he outnumbered Cornwallis, and thus a defensive stand in the heavy woods was a prudent plan. The British, American officers knew, had not been resupplied in weeks, were a long way off from the nearest port they occupied (Wilmington), and were now woefully short of food, as both armies had picked clean the Piedmont region since the fall. The fact that Cornwallis elected not to retire down the Deep River from the Quaker settlements but rather turned to fight the rebels showed both confidence and desperation. Finally, Greene's longed-for moment for battle arrived: he knew just where the British would attack him. He correctly recognized that the stars had aligned to put more musket-wielding men in his ranks than he would ever likely lead again; and that making a firm stand on ground well-suited for what modern soldiers would term a "defense in depth" offered a singular opportunity to defeat his exhausted foe.

The particulars of the seminal battle of Guilford Courthouse have been detailed in numerous general histories of the Revolutionary War in the South, the 1780–81 Carolinas Campaign, and a few recent monographs about the battle itself. As such, only a broad overview of the desperate encounter on March 15 will be provided in these pages, followed by an exploration of its bloody results, profound significance, and why it was one of the five most decisive turning points of the revolutionary struggle.

Greene deployed his troops that morning much as Morgan had at Cowpens two months earlier. His four Continental regiments and two of his field artillery pieces took up elevated ground overlooking Hunting Creek by the courthouse, with their left on the New Garden Road. The rough trace called the Reedy Fork Road ran north from the courthouse just to their rear, a handy path to move troops and guns around behind the rearmost line. This narrow road led north about a dozen miles to Speedwell Iron Works on Troublesome Creek, which had been designated as the entire army's rallying point in case of retreat.

About 500 yards to the Continental regiments' front was the army's second line consisting of the two Virginia militia brigades. They were placed in brushy woods on ground that straddled the New Garden Road. Many of these men were former Continentals or had seen prior service in recent militia tours, led by competent officers. Still, Stevens placed trusted men behind this line to shoot down any militiamen who ran away from the enemy. Having seen hundreds of his men at Camden flee combat like scared rabbits, he was not about to allow such desertions again.

The Americans' first line, 300 yards in front of the Virginians, was on a low ridge. The men were on the edge of heavy woods, behind a rail fence overlooking a muddy, plowed field, along the New Garden Road. This advanced position was defended by the North Carolina militia companies, taking up positions on both sides of the main road, "that being a position ... thought most advantageous for raw troops who were unaccustomed to stand the shock of battle," recalled a militiaman who survived the fighting.[39] As at Cowpens, these inexperienced men had orders to fire two close-range volleys at the enemy as they advanced across the muddy stubble fields, then to fall back to the Virginians' line to the rear. Following Morgan's advice, Greene posted veteran troops on each flank of this line, including frontier Virginia riflemen, dragoons, Capt Robert Kirkland's Delaware company, and steady Continentals led by colonels Washington and Lee. On the road itself, two six-pounder field guns stood ready to hit the enemy's advance with deadly blasts.

Greene's deployment, partly based on the learned advice of Daniel Morgan, Otho Holland Williams, Edward Stevens, John Eagar Howard, and other experienced officers who had fought at Camden, Cowpens, or both, was aimed at blunting the powerful attack of some 2,000 tired and hungry British fusiliers, guards, grenadiers, Highlanders, Hessians, cannoneers, and Loyalist dragoons. None of the American officers doubted the striking power of Cornwallis's veterans, nor did they think the battle would be won on the first line. The Continental commander instead expected the first two lines of militia to retreat once pressed by the enemy's levelled bayonets, but hoped his stalwart rear line of Virginia and Maryland Continentals would stop the onslaught at the little rustic courthouse.

Cornwallis advanced along the main road as expected, and that morning deployed his unfed regiments in open ground on both sides of it. On his left he placed Lt Col James Webster's brigade, made up of the 23rd and 33rd Regiments, the grenadiers and light infantry of the British Guards, and a company of Hessian Jaegers. On the right was Leslie's brigade, including the 71st Regiment, blue-coated Hessians of the Regiment von Bose, and in their immediate rear two battalions of the Guards infantry. In the center on the road were three Royal Artillery field guns, and champing at the bit in reserve were Tarleton's dragoons, set to exploit any favorable opportunity the unpredictable battle offered. By 1pm, "an engagement now became inevitable," Tarleton later recalled.[40]

Cornwallis quickly attacked the rebels' first line on both sides of the road. At first the North Carolinians delivered some effective fire but after the redcoats fixed bayonets and charged the fence line "with steadiness and composure," the militia panicked and ran for the rear.

As one account of the fighting later stated, "the King's troops threw in their fire, and charged rapidly with their bayonets. The shock was not waited for by the militia, who retreated behind their second line." Many frightened militiamen left the field entirely, having failed to fire a single shot. Greene soon reported to Congress that "a considerable part [of the militia] left the ground without firing at all; some fired once, and some twice, and none more" than that. He complained that "neither the advantages of position nor any other consideration could induce them to stay. They left the ground and many of them threw away their arms" as they sprinted to the rear.⁴¹ With other officers, Col Lee "joined in the attempt to rally the fugitives, threatening to fall upon them with his cavalry. All was vain, so thoroughly confounded were these unhappy men, that, throwing away arms, knapsacks, and even canteens, they rushed like a torrent headlong through the woods."⁴² One prominent officer on the field that day blamed the leaders, writing that the Carolina militia "never were so wretchedly officered as they were that day."⁴³

Col Lee's small force on the American left was attacked by Hessians and Highlanders after the militia fled, and in hand to hand fighting his men eventually got shoved back south of the New Garden Road and away from the main battle. There, Tarleton's cavalry "charged with considerable effect. The [American] enemy gave way on all sides, and were routed." However, many of the Virginia riflemen held firm, fired telling shots from behind trees, and "did great execution in the ranks of the [British] enemy." On the rebels' right flank, Washington's defenders were similarly pushed back by the onrushing 33rd Regiment once the militia bolted for safety.⁴⁴

The center of the oncoming British line moved forward into the dense woods and soon struck the Virginians of the second line. There the close-range fighting was intense and bloody, among fallen trees, entangling brush, and gun smoke that made maneuver difficult. The 1,000 Virginians on this line put up a stout defense in what a militia soldier called "a most desperate engagement." Volleys were fired from mere yards away, and some soldiers fired as many as 20 rounds. Greene boasted that "the Virginia militia gave the enemy a warm reception and kept up a heavy fire for a long time" in the thick forest. The Virginians never shy to give his unsolicited advice, raised concerns about the timing of the (ultimately successful) Rhode Island operations. Sir Henry's warning to Howe – who had grown tired of his irksome subordinate – about his overextended line of posts was unwisely ignored.[22]

At the far western end of the overstretched line of British cantonments, Howe placed several regiments of Hessians at Trenton, Bordentown, and Burlington, under the overall command of Col Carl von Donop of Hesse-Kassel.[23] Trenton was garrisoned by a Hessian brigade led by the veteran Col Johann Rall, whose troops had fought so well in storming Fort Washington in November. He was an experienced combat veteran and well-liked by his soldiers. The brigade consisted of Rall's own regiment augmented by the von Lossberg and von Knyphausen Hessian battalions, in addition to a company of jaeger riflemen, several British dragoons, and six pieces of field artillery. Rall's brigade numbered about 1,400 men at the time of Washington's attack on Trenton on December 26.

Hessian troops who served in America during the Revolutionary War were feared by Patriot soldiers and civilians as unlucky brutes forced into military service and prone to rape and plunder as they marched and camped in military campaigns beginning in 1776. As these German troops sailed for America in the summer of 1776, the Declaration of Independence condemned King George III for recruiting "large Armies of foreign Mercenaries to compleat the works of death, desolation and tyranny, already begun with circumstances of Cruelty & perfidy scarcely paralleled in the most barbarous ages." Then in December 1776, Congress issued a fiery proclamation decrying these "foreign mercenaries, who, without feeling, indulge themselves in rapine and bloodshed."[24] Gen Greene provided a vivid description of Hessian depredations to his wife in December. He observed bitterly that New Jersey Loyalists

lead the relentless foreigners to the houses of their neighbors and strip the poor women and children of everything they have to eat or wear; and after plundering them in this sort, the brutes often ravish the mothers and their daughters, and compel the fathers and sons to behold their brutality; many have fallen sacrifices in this way.[25]

The truth about the hired German auxiliary troops during the Revolutionary War is more complex, and recent scholarship has revised previous assumptions about these soldiers and the families that often accompanied them. Over 30,000 German soldiers were transported to England and America during the war years. One recent scholar notes that by the last two years of the war, more than one third of the British army in North America consisted of German auxiliaries. Historian Friederike Baer finds that the British decision to hire auxiliaries came down to numbers. "Britain believed it did not have enough troops to put down the rebellion," she writes, "while the German states had plenty of soldiers available for hire. The German rulers offered a reliable, well regarded, existing military force that could be assembled, outfitted, and dispatched to America in a relatively short time."[26] Although the Crown's hiring of foreign troops provoked outrage in American *and* Great Britain, German troops were "needed, the terms under which they had been procured were advantageous, and they would allow Britain to force the colonies into submission quickly." These were some of the foreign troops in Trenton in late December 1776, whom Washington decided to attack in one of his boldest decisions of the war.

Once across the Delaware in eastern Pennsylvania, the looming threat of a British attack against Washington's army was no longer imminent. But this did not mean that Patriot leaders' worries disappeared. The American army's strength on December 7 was down to "less than 3,000 men fit for duty owing to the Dissolution of our Force by short Inlistments." Washington recognized that the army was the visible, physical symbol of the Revolution's viability and of the American quest for liberty. But as the amateur army slowly dissolved through desertion and expired terms of military service, the spirits of the people and their attachment to the Revolutionary cause diminished.[27] "Fortune seems to frown upon the cause of freedom," wrote Gen Greene on December 16, "a combination of evils are pressing in on us from all sides."[28] Five days later he summarized the "critical situation" America and its army were in.

The enemy in the Heart of our Country; the disaffected dayly increasing; the Continental Money loosing its currency; very few enlisted upon the New Establishment; the Tide of publick "gave the enemy so warm a reception, and continued their opposition with such firmness ... that the fate of the day was dubious for a long time," wrote Col Williams, the Maryland brigade's commander.[45] British general O'Hara was wounded in the thigh during this confusing combat, as were several other officers in red coats. Eventually determined British bayonet charges pushed the militia back, and while some fled, several hundred of them managed to withdraw to the courthouse area at Greene's third line. "We were compelled to retreat at the top of our speed," recalled one Virginian.[46]

By this time, the oncoming British formations were not all in line with each other, due to the confusing terrain and the varied resistance they encountered as they fought against the southern rebel militia. The king's struggling troops had been bloodied and disorganized in the smoky woodland battle, and now they faced some of Greene's best troops posted on high ground, who had not yet been engaged in the terrible fighting. In front of the Continentals was a low, open marshy area crossed by a small creek that the British would have to traverse to make an attack – in the face of four field guns.

In a series of uncoordinated attacks, the fighting initially went well for Greene's Continentals. "At this juncture the battle became bloody, each party making an obstinate stand," wrote a Virginia regular.[47] Then on the American left flank, anchored on the New Garden Road at the courthouse, O'Hara's 2nd Battalion of Guards rushed the 2nd Maryland and routed this inexperienced regiment – and captured two of the rebels' guns near the courthouse. The Guards' advance put them behind the 1st Maryland, which smartly turned around and delivered "some well directed fires" at the redcoats. During this close quarters fighting, a sudden mounted attack by Washington's surging Continental Light Dragoons on the unsuspecting Guards from their rear allowed the 1st Maryland to recapture the lost guns. "Colonel Washington charged them so furiously that they either killed or wounded almost every man," wrote a Delaware Continental. But subsequent British artillery cannonading from the far side of the open ground hit the Marylanders and Washington's cavalry, preventing them from advancing.[48]

At this point most of Cornwallis's troops were opposite Greene's final line. Seeing this, the Rhode Island general decided that with most of the militia gone, one of his Maryland regiments routed, and ammunition low, it was unwise to remain near the courthouse to oppose the British regulars, now girding for a final bayonet assault. Moreover, it appeared to Greene that Webster's brigade was threatening to turn the American right flank. Rather than risk his best troops, he chose prudence. At about 3:30pm he ordered a retreat northeast on the Reedy Fork Road to Speedwell Iron Works. He could not risk a catastrophic defeat, and likely he reasoned that it would be better to still have the core of an army intact in the field, even if defeated, than have his command scattered and thrashed.

Although the withdrawal was for the most part made in good order, the British held the field and could claim a hard-won victory. They also captured all four of the rebels' field pieces on the third line in the bitter struggle. Maj Charles Magill, a Virginia officer at the battle, wrote that "never was ground contested for with greater obstinacy, and never were troops drawn off in better order."[49] Some redcoats followed the retreating rebels for a time, but gave up the chase when soundly repulsed where the road crossed Reedy Fork.

It was soon apparent after the battle, which in Tarleton's words was "one of the most hazardous, as well as severe, battles that occurred during the war," that Cornwallis's triumph was extremely costly. The two hours of fighting was "long, bloody and severe," Greene described to his wife soon afterwards.[50] American losses were 79 killed, 184 wounded, and 1,046 missing, almost all the latter likely those of the Virginia and Carolina militia who ran from the field. But British army losses included 93 killed, 413 wounded, and 26 missing, a staggering casualty rate of about 25 percent. The dead and pitiable wounded lay mingled throughout the woods and fields, suffering even more when a cold rain began to fall that afternoon. Moreover, dozens of the British wounded had to be left behind when the army marched away, too injured to move. Indeed, "the slaughter was prodigious" among the British troops, "Light-Horse Harry" Lee later recalled in his memoirs.[51] The British buried their dead hastily on the battlefield but left the rebel bodies untouched on the ground. Too weak to attack Greene again, on the 18th Cornwallis ordered the depleted regiments to march south away from Guilford Courthouse to Bell's Mill on the Deep River. Provisions were still scarce and no Loyalist support materialized, so he sought "some place of rest and refinement." Cornwallis then headed south to Cross Creek, a Loyalist stronghold on the Cape Fear River, pursued by Greene's army. Cornwallis soon afterwards learned that his troops could not effectively be supplied by water from British-occupied Wilmington, so he pressed on to that port town and arrived on April 7, "tired of marching about the country in search of adventures," he wrote.[52]

A little over two weeks after arriving at Wilmington to refit and rest, Cornwallis and his troops marched north toward Virginia. The British commander concluded that the Old Dominion had to be "subdued" to cut off reinforcements and logistical support going to the Carolinas. He must have been encouraged by the success of Crown forces raiding along the James River in April and May, led by Maj Gen William Phillips and Brig Gen Benedict Arnold, the traitor now in a new British uniform. Cornwallis's hardy veterans left Wilmington on April 24 to join forces with Phillips somewhere in Virginia's Tidewater, depending on the military situation upon their arrival. This fateful move eventually ended at Yorktown, the crucial campaign that is the subject of the next chapter.

Greene, however, had already moved in the opposite direction. Violating another maxim likely found in any military manual of the time, from Ramsey's Mill on the Deep River he marched into South Carolina in mid-April, angling for Camden and its garrison. This dangerous maneuver left Cornwallis at his back, but Greene gambled that after the arduous campaigning in North Carolina the armies had endured, the enemy would not chase him. He hoped to "draw the war out of [North Carolina] and give it an opportunity to raise its proportion of men," and saw no benefit to staying there. Instead, he would operate against the British and Loyalist outposts and "share" the enemy's much-needed supplies. In this decision he was ultimately correct, and as the cagey belligerents set out on their separate ways, the narrative of the battle of Guilford Courthouse can be concluded.[53]

One of the remarkable facets of the violent clash in North Carolina's Piedmont region was that it was immediately seen as a Pyrrhic Crown victory by those who fought it, and soon thereafter by those learning of the bloody engagement. Greene wrote the day after the battle that the British "have met with a defeat in a victory." When Cornwallis failed to pursue the Americans to Speedwell Iron Works, and soon limped off to the Deep River to head south, the Rhode Island general boasted that "the enemy have been so soundly beaten that they dare not move toward us since the action."[54] Word eventually arrived in Congress of the bloody engagement far to the south, a battle "dearly purchased owing to wholly superior discipline. One or two more such victories would ruin his Lordship," wrote a pithy New Jersey congressman.[55] "Cornwallis undoubtedly gained a dear bought victory" wrote Maj St George Tucker of the Virginia militia while recovering from a bayonet wound he received fighting on the second line.[56] Colonel Otho Williams concurred, writing "I have no doubt but the enemy won [the battle] at so great an expense of blood, that the consequences would prove to him equal to a defeat."[57] And "Light-Horse Harry" Lee guessed at Cornwallis's sensations after the battle: "nearly a third of his force slaughtered; many of his best officers killed or wounded; and that victory for which he had so long toiled and at length gained, bringing in its train not one solitary benefit." Indeed, Lee concluded years later that only the "name of victory" belonged to the decimated British ranks, but "the substance belonged to the vanquished."[58]

On the victors' side, news of the battle evoked outrage once it reached the British Isles. "Another such victory would ruin the British Army," said Charles James Fox, a British member of Parliament and prominent opponent of the war. Likewise, English politician and writer Horace Walpole observed wryly that "Lord Cornwallis has conquered his troops out of shoes and provisions and himself out of troops." This ironic result was not what King George III, Lord Germain, and Gen Clinton expected of Cornwallis's campaign to conquer North Carolina. "Alas! That victory had every consequence of a defeat," Clinton wrote several years after the war ended.[59]

The "long, obstinate, and bloody" battle of March 15, 1781, was *the* decisive turning point of the Carolinas Campaign of 1780–81, and profoundly changed the course of the war toward ultimate American victory. It was not, however, the only important engagement of the campaign. The battles of Kings Mountain and Cowpens in South the campaign. Although Germain neglected to send Howe a copy of these orders, he did instruct Carleton to communicate the contents to Howe. However, Germain sent no direct orders to Howe to confirm his role in the campaign.[8]

On April 2, Burgoyne sailed back to Canada with Germain's orders for Carleton. That same day Howe once again revised his proposal to attack Philadelphia in a letter to Germain. He would leave an adequate garrison to protect New York City and transport most of his troops by sea to attack Philadelphia and Washington's army. Complaining that he would not get the 15,000 reinforcements for his 1777 operations that he requested and that the war could not be won that year, he also wrote that he did *not* anticipate being able to cooperate with Burgoyne. Three days later Howe wrote to Carleton, reporting his doubts that he could cooperate with any force coming south from Canada with his army operating near Philadelphia, but the 7,000 troops designated to remain as a garrison for New York would (he claimed) support operations launched from Canada. It should be noted that Burgoyne read this letter after he arrived at Quebec on May 6, and *before* setting out in late June on his waterborne, wilderness campaign. Thus, he already knew Howe was not planning to join forces with him somewhere along the Hudson River.

On May 18, Germain responded to Howe's April 2 letter. The secretary wrote to the general that no matter the status of his operations against Philadelphia and Washington's army, he had to allow time and opportunity to coordinate with Burgoyne's campaign from Canada. Howe received this letter on August 16, while already at sea with the expedition to take Philadelphia. At the end of August Howe wrote Germain after landing his forces at Head of Elk, Maryland, reiterating that he would be unable to support operations along the Hudson.

Back on July 5, prior to Howe sailing off on June 23 to approach Philadelphia Gen Clinton arrived at New York after months spent in London, quite familiar with Germain's expectation of Gen Howe cooperating with the expedition to take Albany. Quickly realizing that Howe's focus was on Philadelphia and not on supporting Burgoyne, Clinton grew alarmed. He then spent three weeks badgering the commanding general to give up his questionable decision to move by with his whole Force to the Southward." However, nowhere in this plan was Howe *required* to make a junction with Burgoyne's troops, or to reach Albany himself. Moreover, none of the British leaders, Germain included, ever specified what Burgoyne's troops would do once they arrived at Albany.[7]

While Burgoyne travelled by sea to England, Howe was still in New York considering his plans for the next year. Before his two November letters were received in Germain's office (they arrived on December 30), he sent a revised proposal to the ministry on December 20, which now made no mention of marching his troops from New York toward Albany to support the Canada army, or any operations against New England. In Howe's new suggestion, he would attack Philadelphia in an overland campaign from New York to capture the rebels' capital and force Washington to defend the city in a pitched battle, in which superior British arms were likely to prevail. This plan was approved by King George III and Lord Germain. Of great importance, Burgoyne was aware of the details of Howe's revised intentions to focus on Philadelphia *before* the former left London to return to America in April.

On January 20, 1777, Howe revised his campaign plan yet again in a letter to Germain. Because of Washington's two winter victories in New Jersey, his sole objective was now Philadelphia, where he thought there would be significant loyalist support. He planned his operations against the city to be both overland and seaborne. Again, he did not mention moving north up the Hudson River to support the movements of Burgoyne. This new proposal arrived in London in late February, just as Burgoyne submitted his own written plan for summer operations. Germain wrote to Howe on March 3, informing the general that the king approved his new plan.

With Burgoyne preparing to set sail for Quebec in early April, Germain penned two letters to Carleton on March 26, providing guidance and outlining Burgoyne's campaign objectives. Sent with Burgoyne, the letters included unambiguous wording about Burgoyne cooperating with Howe on the Hudson. In fact, Germain advised both Burgoyne and St Leger that they "must never lose View of their intended junction with Sir William Howe as their principal objects" of

Carolina, as noted above, were clear Patriot victories that shaped the campaign in their favor and influenced British operations in North Carolina from October 1780 to March 1781. Over the years much attention to these two seminal battles has been paid by historians and the public stressing their importance. Even 200 years ago, Thomas Jefferson considered Kings Mountain to be "that turn of the tide of success by which terminated the Revolutionary War, with the seal of our independence."[60] Likewise British general Sir Henry Clinton similarly thought that Kings Mountain "unhappily proved the first link in a chain of evils that followed each other in regular succession until they at last ended in the total loss of America."[61]

Modern students of the battle of Kings Mountain often concur with this assessment, giving the clash an exalted importance. For instance, a 1995 National Park Service Historic Resource Study of Kings Mountain National Military Park echoed Sir Henry Clinton in finding that the battle "was the first in a string of British defeats that culminated in the October, 1781, surrender of Lieutenant General Charles Cornwallis at Yorktown, Virginia."[62] The US Army's 2020 *Staff Ride Handbook for The Battle for Kings Mountain, 7 October 1780* also concludes that "the Patriot victory at Kings Mountain ... fundamentally changed the course of the war in the South." Its author also finds that "the unexpected Patriot success" at Kings Mountain "halted the string of British victories in the south and raised morale after a summer of depressing reversals."[63] Recent studies also consider the backcountry battle to have been salient. Historian John Ferling concludes that Kings Mountain (as well as Cowpens and Guilford Courthouse) "set Cornwallis ... on the road to Virginia, and perdition," meaning his surrender at Yorktown.[64] Author Bob Thompson, in his delightfully unconventional and thoroughly enjoyable book *Revolutionary Roads: Searching for the War That Made America Independent... and All the Places It Could Have Gone Terribly Wrong*, finds that "Jefferson was right to declare Kings Mountain a turning point," which it certainly was in the fall of 1780. And the National Park Service is correct to describe the engagement as "an important American victory during the Revolutionary War." The popularity of and emphasis on the Kings Mountain mêlée is perhaps due to a popular affiliation with the idea of the rustic homespun, rifle-toting frontiersmen who left their hardscrabble backwoods farms and rude cabins to thrash a haughty aristocratic officer threatening their individualism and liberties. Or perhaps the interested public likes to root for the underdog, even the 18th-century variety.[65]

Cowpens seems to attract even more attention than the mountain-top battle nearby in a variety of sources, not all of them scholarly. Typical of numerous online popular accounts is an article in the US Army's *NCO Journal*, which rightly finds "the battle of Cowpens changed the course of the war and ... [it] was a surprising victory and a turning point that changed the psychology of the entire war." But the author goes on to claim implausibly that the victory "allowed Brigadier General Daniel Morgan to secure the south" and averted "a different outcome to the American Revolution."[66]

Exaggerated claims like this are not hard to find online. Most historians, however, offer more serious although varied assessments of what Cowpens meant. The battle's preeminent authority, Lawrence E. Babits, writes that "the battle marked a turning point in American fortunes. The road through the American position led symbolically, if not quite literally, to Yorktown and British surrender."[67] Noted Daniel Morgan biographer and scholar of the Revolution Don Higginbotham finds the battle was "one of the tactical masterpieces of the war."[68] Historian Mark Boatner tempers his assessment of the victory. It was a "substantial but not fatal British tactical reverse," he finds.[69] But author Henry Lumpkin concludes that the battle "may well have been the real turning point of the American Revolution," not just the 1780–81 campaign.[70]

It should be clear from the preceding paragraphs that interpretations of Cowpens vary widely. Perhaps, though, military historian and battlefield guide John Moncure's conclusions in *The Cowpens Staff Ride and Battlefield Tour* come closer to the truth. He finds that Morgan "had won a decisive tactical victory," which "may be one of the most important battles ever fought on American soil". But strategically, "the battle had little effect on the war," as it "did not alter the outcome of the war or even the course of the campaign in the south."[71]

As earlier noted, decisive turning points in this book's context are those that substantially alter the trajectory of the war toward ultimate American victory. The battle of Guilford Courthouse was one such event, even though the British won the contest, at least by 18th-century military conventions. The consequences of the battle – not which side retreated that chilly winter day – were substantial, the most momentous of any contest fought in the South except the siege of Yorktown six months later. Why the battle was so important to American independence is explored in the remainder of this chapter.

Looking broadly at the trajectory of the military events in the Carolinas in 1780 and 1781, and painting with broad strokes, a pattern emerges that clearly shows the Guilford battle's significance and prominence on the road to victory. After Charleston's garrison surrendered in May 1780, the British advanced into the interior of South Carolina to occupy the province and establish the king's authority. Three months later, Cornwallis won an overwhelming victory at Camden, scattering Gates's army of regulars and militia, then advanced to Charlotte by late September. On October 7, Patriot militia won a complete victory at Kings Mountain, which caused Cornwallis to fall back to Winnsboro later that month. This set-back, however, was only temporary, as the British again surged north toward Charlotte in mid-January. While paused near the North Carolina border, Tarleton's detachment was virtually wiped out at Cowpens off to the west. But this time Cornwallis did not fall back; rather, he continued his advance into North Carolina, the invasion of which was his primary objective. From January 17 to March 15, nothing the rebels managed to throw in their way prevented the British from moving across the state, pushing back the Patriot forces across the Catawba, Yadkin, Haw, and Dan rivers. At that point, February 14, the British had scattered the backcountry and Piedmont militia, discouraged more from joining, and most importantly pushed Greene's Continental force out of North Carolina. Cornwallis had achieved his objective and rid the state of almost all its armed forces, and he set up a post at Hillsborough.

The British trajectory from Charleston to Hillsborough was a successful campaign in which they advanced toward their objective immediately after each battle, with the exception of Kings Mountain, which caused a temporary delay, *not* a retreat, a point that must be emphasized. "The Kings Mountain affair ... had only postponed the occupation of North Carolina" until the British could be reinforced, notes Henry P. Johnston accurately in his early Yorktown campaign study.[72] And Cowpens, while an undeniable defeat and a costly loss of a thousand troops, certainly did *not* result in a British retreat. "This event did not deter me from the original plan," Cornwallis plainly stated in a letter to Germain. Nor did Davidson's brave defense of the Catawba crossings at Cowan's Ford stop or even delay the redcoats. Morgan's quickness and a rain-flooded river prevented the British from crossing the Yadkin near Salisbury, but did not stymie their advance, for they forded upstream and swiftly marched to Salem, within striking distance of Greene's army. And while the fleetfooted Americans could not be caught prior to crossing the flooded Dan River, they were in fact forced out of North Carolina.[73] Yet none of these battles and maneuvers decisively changed the trajectory of the war toward American victory. Cornwallis had rid North Carolina of its defenders, wreaked havoc on the state's logistical capabilities, and claimed his military operations a success. However, the only engagement that completely reversed British fortunes and ultimately drove the redcoat invaders out of the state, apart from a small garrison at Wilmington, was the pivotal battle of Guilford Courthouse.

As we have seen, Cornwallis's costly March 15 victory reduced his already depleted army by about 25 percent. The battle did not crush Greene's army because the worn-out British were unable to pursue at the end of the fighting. Their momentum was stopped, their heavy losses were shocking, and so for the first time in their long march from Charleston, the redcoats had to retreat. The British made a wearisome trek to Wilmington near the coast, soon leaving there for Virginia, effectively abandoning North Carolina for the rest of the war. The British made no other major offensive campaigns in the Carolinas or Georgia afterwards. And symbolizing the British reverse, Greene then advanced into South Carolina to threaten enemy outposts across the backcountry.

What also made the battle of Guilford Courthouse a salient turning point of the entire war was the maturity of Greene's decision to retreat when his Continentals along the third line became hard pressed by the onrushing redcoats. The decision saved the American army – the only one then in the South, and the symbol of the Patriots' cause. Generals then and now do not want to retreat from a battlefield, especially when victory and glory still hung in the balance. For most of the war glory was about all American officers could expect as a reward for their service. When Greene was with Washington's army, he often supported bold offensive plans in war councils, seeking battle and decision. But like Washington, he learned to be cautious, aware that risk could mean a costly defeat, which American arms could not afford militarily and politically. Not that Greene avoided all risks – he divided his army in the face of a superior foe at Charlotte upon assuming command, played a tactical trick on Cornwallis to reach the Dan safely, then finally offered battle at Guilford Courthouse. And he later turned his back on Cornwallis by marching into South Carolina in April 1781, hoping to lure him into pursuit.

Greene's mature thoughts on the army's basic need for caution can be seen in his earlier letter of January 19 to Daniel Morgan, in which he advised him to "put nothing to the hazard, a retreat may be disagreeable but not disgracefully ... it is not our business to risk too much, our affairs are in a critical situation, and require time and nursing to give them a better tone."[74] Similarly, to the often uncooperative Brig Gen Thomas Sumter in South Carolina he reported in early February "if I should risque a General action [i.e., a battle] in our present situation, we stand ten chances to one of getting defeated, & if defeated all the Southern States must fall. I shall avoid it if possible; but I am afraid it will be out of my power."[75] In pleading for troops, supplies, and provisions from Governor Jefferson a month before the clash at Guilford, he astutely reminded the erudite Virginian that "the army is all that the states have to depend upon for their political existence." At the same time, he also lectured North Carolina militia commander Richard Caswell that "while there is an army kept in the field, the hopes of the people are kept alive."[76]

As Greene rode along the ranks of the Continentals during the cauldron of fighting at Guilford Courthouse and saw the 2nd Maryland routed, his frightened militia almost all gone off, and most of the enemy's bayonet wielding redcoats now preparing to assault his last line, he understood that he need not risk his command like a desperate gambler. Although writing in a Civil War history context, historian Don H. Doyle's recent observations certainly capture what General Greene knew in 1781: "rebels need not fully triumph on the field of battle so long as they can continue to field an army, wear down the enemy, and hope for international intervention of some sort. Davids often triumph over Goliaths in such struggles…"[77] Greene saved his army, wore down the enemy, and ultimately triumphed over the British in 1783, in part because he prudently retreated from the hotly contested battleground in the backcountry of Guilford County, North Carolina.

The Definitive Capitulation: The Yorktown Campaign, 1781

In October 1981, at the end of America's 200th anniversary of independence festivities, the Yorktown Bicentennial Celebration welcomed visitors from all over the world to the quaint Virginia river town to commemorate the historic Patriot victory with the surrender of Lord Cornwallis and the British army he commanded there during the Revolutionary War. Thousands of tourists on a fall weekend visited the $4.2 million Yorktown Victory Center near the battlefield, opened six years earlier by the Commonwealth of Virginia to herald the events of October 1781. From October 16–19, there were reenactments, parades, a living history military encampment, and the Colonial Heritage Festival "with 16 acres of exhibits and entertainments." And of course, there were fireworks.

The nearby National Park Service Visitor Center, perched on the riverside bluff on the actual battlefield, offered a "separate museum, well worth seeing," including displays of Washington's marquee tent and "bus tours to the redoubts and surrender field." The Bicentennial Committee offered bronze souvenir medals engraved with John Turnbull's famous painting "The Surrender of Lord Cornwallis at Yorktown." Of course, the French were involved too, with a ceremony to highlight the decisive naval battle off the Virginia Capes on September 5, but so too were the British, who staged a military tattoo (a performance of martial music and marching) featuring the Coldstream Guards and the Royal Scots

Dragoon Guards at nearby Hampton Coliseum.[1] Royal Marines and the Royal Welsh Fusiliers band marched smartly in a parade in Colonial Williamsburg, where US President Ronald W. Reagan hosted a dinner at the Governor's Mansion for French President François Mitterrand. Also in attendance were Lord Hailsham, the Speaker of the House of Lords, and Sir Nicholas Henderson, Britain's ambassador to the United States. About one thousand journalists, reporters, and cameramen descended on the area that weekend to capture the events.[2]

On the cool afternoon of October 19, 1981, President Reagan delivered a brief address at the culmination of the Yorktown commemoration. "This field, this ceremony, and this day hold a special meaning for people the world over," he said, and he called it "an extraordinary moment in history." In a reflection of the Cold War's prominent shadow of the time, and with Reagan in office just nine months, he added that at Yorktown "the beacon of freedom shines here for all who will see, inspiring free men and captives alike, and no wall, no curtain, nor totalitarian state can shut it out."[3] During the long weekend over 200,000 tourists and visitors attended bicentennial events.

The victory at Yorktown "retained" a "cherished place in American folklore," a *Washington Post* article in the fall of 1981 noted, while another article in that newspaper proclaimed that while America was born in 1776, "it was baptized in blood at Yorktown in 1781. That is when the Revolution finally was won."[4] Just after these celebrations were over, the Virginia Independence Bicentennial Commission concluded in a report to the state assembly that in 1781 "on that cold October [19th] afternoon, the American Republic was born."[5] And the US Army designated "The Army at Yorktown-Spirit of Victory" as its theme for Fiscal Year 1981.[6] It seems evident that Yorktown's birthday was widely publicized that year.

The 1981 celebrations were certainly not the first occasion Washington's grand victory had been celebrated in or near Yorktown. One hundred years earlier, the centennial of the surrender was remembered by a slew of events and activities, including a visit of "200 congressmen, governors and descendants of revolutionary generals from Washington to Yorktown"; a concert with John Phillip Sousa as guest conductor of the Marine Band that played the "Marseillaise" and "Hail,

Columbia"; a procession of two thousand Masons; and remarks given by President Chester A. Arthur (only a month in office after James Garfield died from an assassin's bullet), Marquis de Rochambeau, and Baron von Steuben – the last two descendants of the originals. Even in 1931, Yorktown's sesquicentennial year, there occurred the dedication of the Virginia state memorial, the "unveiling of the Comte De Grasse Tablet, dedications of tablets for Thomas Nelson, William Gooch and French soldiers," and an address by President Herbert Hoover.[7]

The decisive importance of the Yorktown campaign has been recognized since the British surrendered there on October 19, 1781, through today. One of the first modern historians of the campaign whose 1881 study is still considered reliable was Henry P. Johnson, author of *The Yorktown Campaign and the Surrender of Cornwallis*. He saw the siege along the York River as a "signal victory," where "the independence of the United States may be said to have been then and there assured beyond question." Washington's triumph was the "death knell of British domination in America," after which undoubtedly "the Revolution [was] accomplished." Johnson held that Yorktown was the end of a series of battles, not all of which were Patriot victories. Rather, the final campaign was "the last and most brilliant of a series of blows delivered in spite of a series of defeats sustained."[8] Fifty years later, US Army historian H.L. Landers wrote in his detailed campaign study that "it was at Yorktown that the nascent nationalism of each of the thirteen States of America was assured of eventual coalescence into a single nationalism, and where an endless fraternalism between the peoples of the United States and France was sealed." With bounding enthusiasm Landers held that the name Yorktown was "indicative of achievement ... expressive of greatness ... and significant of independence." The victory meant that the "independence of the United States was now assured."[9]

More recent scholars are not hesitant to confirm Yorktown's decisive role in the winning of American independence. Historian John Ferling, for instance, writes that the Yorktown campaign and the resultant surrender of Cornwallis's army in Tidewater Virginia was "the war's pivotal engagement that at last secured American independence."[10] And author Robert Tonsetic concludes that the campaign "was a stunning turn of events."[11]

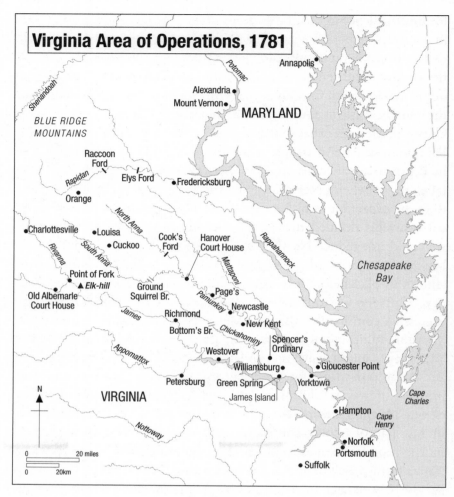

Virginia Area of Operations, 1781

Annapolis

Potomac

Alexandria
Mount Vernon

MARYLAND

Shenandoah

BLUE RIDGE
MOUNTAINS

Raccoon
Ford

Rapidan

Elys Ford

Fredericksburg

Orange

North Anna

Charlottesville Louisa

Cuckoo

Cook's
Ford

Hanover
Court House

Rappahannock

Chesapeake
Bay

Rivanna

South Anna

Point of Fork

▲ Elk-hill

Ground
Squirrel Br.

Mattaponi

Page's

Pamunkey

Newcastle

Old Albemarle
Court House

James

Richmond

Bottom's Br.

New Kent

Chickahominy

Spencer's
Ordinary

Appomattox

Westover

Williamsburg

Gloucester Point

N

Petersburg

Green Spring

Yorktown

VIRGINIA

James Island

Cape
Charles

Nottoway

Hampton

Cape
Henry

Norfolk
Portsmouth

0   20 miles

0   20km

Suffolk

MAP 5

Likewise, former National Park Service historian at Yorktown Jerome Greene finds that these momentous operations constituted the "pivotal event in American history."[12] Greene is correct to point out the lack of full-length studies of the siege and the complex, far reaching operations from France and Great Britain to North America and the West Indies that led up to it, considering how impactful the result was. Although the war did not officially end for another two years, the Franco-American victory at Yorktown was the final blow to the British military efforts to end the War for Independence in their favor, and a decisive culminating turning point in the Allies' favor.

The triumphant results along the York River were a long time in the making. The genesis of the decisive campaign may be said to have originated in North Carolina. As described in the previous chapter, after the bloody clash at Guilford Courthouse on March 15, 1781, Lord Cornwallis led his exhausted troops down the tidal Cape Fear River to Wilmington. After a couple of restful weeks refitting his small army, he began to advance his 1,450 soldiers northward to Virginia. Having failed to overwhelm North Carolina and secure South Carolina – which were the expectations of his superior in New York, Sir Henry Clinton – Cornwallis decided that "until Virginia was to a degree subjected we could not reduce North Carolina or have any certain hold of the back country of South Carolina."[13] Although he wrote Clinton of his ambitious plan before leaving Wilmington, Cornwallis set out on his new campaign without waiting for his superior's response. A far more aggressive commander than Clinton, Cornwallis wrote to Maj Gen William Phillips, then operating along the James River in Virginia, that "if we mean an offensive war in America, we must abandon New York, and bring our whole force into Virginia …"[14] There was one major problem, however: Clinton did not support an effort to shift the "seat of war" to the Chesapeake. He was not opposed to active operations there as part of an overall offensive campaign to end the rebellion in the southern provinces and to establish a defensible naval base in Virginia waters from which to attack the French possessions in the West Indies. But he saw danger in making the Chesapeake the primary focus of campaigning, noting that a British army or garrison there could be cut off and destroyed by a French fleet. Moreover, Clinton and Cornwallis had not been in touch with each other for months until the latter reached Wilmington, which added to the disjointed nature of the conduct of the campaign in the South.

Clinton thought that operations in Virginia could be of two types: either to employ a major force there "with a fighting army," or to launch "desultory expeditions" from a secure post such as Portsmouth, to interdict the logistical efforts of the Americans.[15] He had previously ordered several destructive raids of the Chesapeake region with strong naval support to destroy enemy tobacco, ships, provisions, and other military stores. The first, in 1779, known as the Mathew-Collier expedition, in which Commodore Sir George Collier of the Royal Navy described the purpose of the raid (and for those to come in the next two years). It was "... the most feasible way of ending the rebellion ... by cutting off the resources by which the enemy could continue war, these being principally drawn from Virginia." He surmised that "an attack and the putting up and shutting up of the navigation of the Chesapeake would probably answer very considerable purposes and if not of itself sufficient to end the war," it would at least "drive the Rebels to infinite inconvenience and difficulty especially as [their] army was constantly supplied by provisions sent by water through the Chesapeake."[16] That was Cornwallis's intent too, and was a plan favored by Lord Germain in London as well. Indeed, the secretary wrote in May 1781 that "the reduction of the Southern provinces must give the death-wound to the rebellion," even with the French on their side.[17]

Marching out of Wilmington on April 25, Cornwallis's objective was to join forces with those of Gen Phillips, operating since March 20 in the Virginia Tidewater along the James River with several thousand veteran troops burning numerous tobacco warehouses and military supplies, and whatever else could be used by the rebels. Phillips joined his expedition with the troops of Brig Gen Benedict Arnold, the notorious traitor, who began his own destructive Tidewater raids at the end of December 1780. In April and May, from his base at Portsmouth, Phillips continued to seek out and destroy Virginia's scattered supply caches along the James and inland, to cripple the state's ability to sustain Gen Greene's ongoing campaign in the Carolinas.

On April 25, the same day Cornwallis departed Wilmington, Phillips struck Petersburg on the south bank of the Appomattox River, a bustling commercial town where supplies and a large magazine were located. Although over 1,000 of Brig Gen John Peter Gabriel Muhlenberg's plucky Virginia militiamen fought stubbornly that day under the overall command of Baron von Steuben, the British defeated the Americans, who were forced to retreat in haste northward toward Richmond. Phillips' troops followed them, continuing to destroy tobacco, barns, and supplies between Petersburg and the James River, which they reached on April 29 at Manchester opposite Richmond, Virginia's new capital. From the south bank of the James, Phillips observed a force of a thousand Continental troops and a formation of militia companies occupying high ground, commanded (as he would soon find out) by the Marquis de Lafayette, whose footsore Continental light troops had arrived there just the day before.

Lafayette's timely arrival at Richmond was part of a series of efforts by American and French military leaders in early 1781 to thwart the destructive British raids in Virginia and to capture and hang the traitor, Arnold. Ordered by Washington, the marquis's expedition to the Old Dominion began in February, when his light infantry detachment began its long trek south from the Hudson River. This small force was organized into three battalions, commanded by Col Joseph Vose of Massachusetts; Lt Col Jean-Joseph Sourbader de Gimat, who had accompanied Lafayette from France; and Lt Col Francis Barber of New Jersey. To support Lafayette's expedition, the French sent a small naval squadron from their anchorage in Rhode Island led by Vice Adm Armand Legardeur de Tilly, but it amounted to nothing. A second, larger naval expedition from Rhode Island under Vice Adm Charles-Rene-Dominique Gochet, Chevalier Destouches with over a thousand French troops set sail from Rhode Island for the Chesapeake Bay. But at the same time the British Navy dispatched a flotilla from New York commanded by the sluggish Vice Adm Marriot Arbuthnot, which led to a brief sea battle on March 16, 1781, off Virginia's Capes Henry and Charles at the mouth of the Chesapeake. After the broadsides were over the French sailed back to their Rhode Island anchorage at Narragansett Bay, while the British stood fast to maintain control of the bay's entrance. This action would not be the last naval battle off the coast of the Old Dominion that year between France and Great Britain.

Because Destouches's ships were prevented from attacking the British base at Portsmouth, Lafayette started his column back northward to the Hudson River camps. But at Annapolis, he received orders from Washington to return to the James River to counter Phillips' unchecked threat. Lafayette's command of 1,200 men from New Jersey and the New England states also expected to be joined by a supporting contingent of a thousand Pennsylvania troops led by Brig Gen Anthony Wayne. After a grueling march with several stops and starts, Lafayette's soldiers eventually reached Annapolis, then moved into Virginia across the Potomac River to Alexandria on April 21, where they rested and tried to refit. Trudging farther south along the King's Highway through Fredericksburg and Hanover, the light troops reached Richmond late on April 28, where they faced Phillips's redcoats on the James River the following day.

As the river was too deep to wade there and the precise rebel strength was hard to determine, Phillips wisely decided to march his 3,500 troops back to Petersburg. There he suddenly contracted a raging fever and died on May 13, which left the turncoat Arnold in command. Then a week later Cornwallis and his weary soldiers arrived at Petersburg. After allowing the tired troops only a few days to rest, Cornwallis marched them east, and from May 24 to 26, the British troops, wagons, and artillery crossed by boat to the north side of the James River to the stately Georgian plantation called Westover, owned by the wealthy Byrd family, to whom Benedict Arnold was related by marriage to Margaret "Peggy" Shippen of Philadelphia. At Westover, Lord Cornwallis was met by 2,000 Hessian and British reinforcements sent up the James from the British base at Portsmouth. Reorganizing his command, Cornwallis detailed three of his regiments back to Portsmouth with generals Leslie and Arnold, and on the 27th began to move north with his main force of about 5,000 or so veteran troops. His objective now was to destroy supplies, munitions, ironworks, and tobacco in central Virginia, and to crush the young Lafayette's small command of ill-fed, unpaid, poorly clothed soldiers. "I shall now proceed to dislodge La Fayette from Richmond and with my light troops to destroy any magazines or stores in the neighborhood which may have been collected for his use or for General Greene's army," Cornwallis advised Clinton from the army's shaded riverside camps at Westover.[18]

Although just 23 years old, the ambitious Lafayette was experienced enough to recognize that his meager force was far too small to confront the powerful British host in a pitched battle, much less meaningfully impede their progress. The Frenchman wrote "was I to fight a battle I'll be cut to pieces, the militia dispersed, and the arms lost. Was I to decline fighting the country would think herself given up. I am therefore determined to scarmish, but not to engage too far … I am not strong enough even to get beaten."[19] Prudently he hurried his soldiers away from his position near Richmond – about 20 miles from Westover – to escape being flanked by the fast-moving redcoats to his left. The British indeed advanced quickly by way of Malvern Hill, Newcastle, and Hanover Court House until they halted on the high banks of the North Anna River at Cook's Ford on June 1. Lafayette avoided getting too close to the enemy's superior force as they advanced northward unimpeded, making sure to put a water barrier between him and the British at each step, including the Chickahominy, South Anna, North Anna, and Rapidan rivers in central Virginia.

From Cook's Ford, Cornwallis originally intended to press northward to Fredericksburg where a large state and Continental supply cache and ironworks were located by the rocky falls of the Rappahannock River. But as Lafayette shifted farther northwest to meet the expected Continental regiments under Gen Wayne marching southward from Pennsylvania, Cornwallis decided to realign his raid to concentrate on rebel depots dozens of miles off to the west at Charlottesville, Seven Islands, and Point of Fork, which were now weakly guarded as the marquis still avoided being too close to the redcoats. Moreover, Virginia's uprooted legislative assembly was also meeting at the small courthouse town of Charlottesville, having scurried away from Richmond in early May. Cornwallis hoped to capture them with a swift-moving cavalry strike – along with Governor Thomas Jefferson, who was in residence at his lofty home nearby called Monticello.

Early on the rainy morning of June 3, a mounted force led by Col Tarleton left the British camp at Cook's Ford toward Charlottesville in distant Albemarle County, about 60 miles away. Although the hard-riding British did not capture the governor – who "provided for his liberty by a precipitate retreat," according to Tarleton[20] – or most of the assemblymen, on the 4th they did destroy a thousand muskets, several hundred barrels of gunpowder, and other military equipment in the town and forced the delegates to flee west to Staunton across the Blue Ridge Mountains. A second strike from Cook's Ford led by Lt Col John Graves Simcoe "with great zeal and indefatigable attention" attacked the supply collection and recruiting camp commanded by Baron von Steuben at Point of Fork, at the confluence of the James and Rivanna Rivers. Simcoe succeeded in destroying the depot and forcing hundreds of Continental recruits to flee south across the James. Cornwallis, with thousands of troops in the main body, followed Simcoe to the Point of Fork area, camping for several days at Elk-hill, a Jefferson-owned property on the James River in western Goochland County, a few miles east of the Point of Fork.

At the same time, having spent anxious weeks avoiding the onrushing redcoat colossus, Lafayette was finally joined by Wayne's longed-for Pennsylvania brigade in the rolling hills of Orange County on June 10. The marquis speedily moved the combined troops to a bridge on Mechunk Creek ten miles east of the courthouse town to block Charlottesville from further enemy attacks, where the main road crossed the small meandering stream. By this time, Cornwallis recognized that he was far away from any source of resupply and faced growing enemy forces in the Virginia Piedmont. He now marched back through Goochland County on the River Road to Richmond by June 16, where the troops burned more tobacco, and then occupied the old colonial capital at Williamsburg on the 25th. Lafayette's troops followed the enemy at a safe distance, as the marquis was still wary of the powerful British army.

Then on June 26, an emboldened Lafayette risked an engagement at a hamlet called Spencer's Ordinary, a crossroads with a tavern about six miles west of Williamsburg. There an advanced American detachment attacked an incautious British foraging expedition led by Simcoe. Although in effect this large skirmish was a draw, the British withdrew after several hours of fighting. Several days later in scorching hot weather on July 6 near Green Spring plantation by the James River a detachment under Gen Wayne boldly struck what Lafayette mistakenly assumed was the British army's rear guard as they crossed the river headed for Portsmouth. But Cornwallis deceived Lafayette, as most of the British battalions were concealed still north of the river, poised to strike. "The Marquis intended to attack our rear guard and luckily stumbled on our army," a witty Cornwallis soon reported. In a close run, bloody engagement, Wayne barely got his hard-pressed troops off the field and avoided a disaster. The redcoats continued their crossing the next day. Cornwallis rightly called the engagement a "smart action," and concluded that if there had been just a half hour more of daylight, the British force would have bagged almost all the brazen rebel troops. Still the British general must have taken note of Lafayette's new willingness to come to blows with the king's troops.[21]

Once the British had crossed the James, their operations took on a defensive nature as Cornwallis looked for a suitable base. Shortly before the bloody scrape at Green Spring, Cornwallis read a dispatch from Clinton that recommended the troops in Virginia "take a defensive station, in any healthy situation you choose," preferably Old Point Comfort (Hampton), Williamsburg, or Yorktown. Sir Henry also ordered Cornwallis to send 3,000 of his troops back to New York City, where he anxiously expected an attack on his lines from the threatening French and Americans. The nettlesome Clinton remained unhappy about his second in command's decision to leave the Carolinas for new operations in Virginia. He wrote Cornwallis in late May that had he known of the latter's intent to march to Petersburg to join Phillips, "I should certainly have endeavored to have stopped you, as I did then, as well as now, consider such a move as likely to be dangerous to our interests in the southern colonies."[22] But by then it was far too late to change Cornwallis's plans.

After the fighting near the fields and forests of Green Spring, Lafayette repositioned his army west to the healthier climate of Malvern Hill, southeast of Richmond, to monitor Cornwallis in case he tried to return to the Carolinas and campaign against his old nemesis Nathanael Greene. However, Cornwallis had no intention of returning south. Instead, the British moved to their old fortifications at Portsmouth, and per Clinton's orders searched for a new defensible post suitable for large ships and as a proper base for future operations around the Chesapeake Bay. After his engineers explored several locations, Cornwallis settled on Yorktown, a small port on the York River about 13 miles east of Williamsburg. Established on bluffs overlooking the river in 1691, the tobacco shipping town was, in Cornwallis's words, "the only harbour in which we can hope to be able to give effectual protection to line of battle ships."[23] The British forces occupied the area around the village by August 2, and a detachment of 1,000 troops fortified Gloucester Point across the river about a thousand yards distant, where the York River narrowed significantly. Thus, about one quarter of the British forces in the thirteen rebellious colonies were now at Yorktown, poised for future operations.

Given that there were few American or French troops in Virginia, having so large a British force at Yorktown was a questionable decision, and worried Clinton in New York, where he faced thousands of enemy troops with a garrison he considered inadequate. In fact, while Cornwallis and his regiments were traipsing around the hills and woods of Virginia's Piedmont, New York remained the persistent focus of George Washington, whose forces had been humiliatingly ousted from the city in the late summer of 1776. The British continued to maintain their base there, and it served as the headquarters of Gen Clinton. For years Washington was fixated on attacking and capturing the city. He tried to persuade the 55-year-old commander of the French troops of the *Expédition Particulière*, Gen Comte de Rochambeau, to cooperate in striking New York with his four infantry regiments, artillery, and other troops that totaled about 5,500 men at arms. But the veteran Rochambeau, along with French navy commanders in New England and the West Indies, instead discerned a better opportunity in the Chesapeake Bay, where they hoped to trap Cornwallis's army by blocking the mouth of the bay and put the British general in a perilous position.

That spring, Washington was nearly disconsolate at the Continental Army's camps by the Hudson. Previous attempts at Franco-American coordination had ended only in frustration, including disappointments at Rhode Island in 1778, and Savannah, Georgia, in 1779. By early 1781, a successful joint campaign seemed doubtful. Some Americans wondered if the French would quit the war. The commanding general called his force "the remnant of an Army ... our Troops are approaching fast to nakedness & that we have nothing to cloathe them with." He was desperate for an immediate loan of money from France. In April Washington thought the military prospects for the American cause so poor that "it may be declared in a word, that we are at the end of our tether, & that now or never [our] deliverance must come."[24]

In late May Washington and Knox rode east from the army's Hudson River camps to Wethersfield, Connecticut, near Hartford to meet Rochambeau and confer on campaign plans for the summer. The persistent American general still pressed for an attack on New York, but the French cadre only offered lukewarm interest. More importantly, they knew something Washington did not. In a private letter Rochambeau had already recommended to French Vice Adm the Comte de Grasse that he bring his fleet launched from Brest to operate in the Chesapeake Bay region rather than around New York City. Rochambeau did not think the combined allied force was strong enough to attack New York's defenses successfully, and transporting over land or by sea the French heavy artillery located at Newport needed for a siege would take time and naval support that Rochambeau could not promise. Moreover, French ships of war were of greater draft than their British counterparts, which made passing over the bar at the mouth of New York Harbor problematic. Instead, Rochambeau favored operations in the South, which was also closer to the French's rich sugar islands, threatened by the British Royal Navy since 1778.

Earlier in May 1781, several French ships commanded by Vice Adm the Comte de Barras sailed into the harbor at Newport, Rhode Island. Barras had tremendous news that earlier in March a major French fleet commanded by de Grasse had left France from Brest, bound for the West Indies for operations against British possessions and battle ships that summer. More importantly, de Grasse planned to sail northward to coordinate operations with Barras and the Americans against the British forces at New York or the southern provinces until the fall. Barras kept this information private from Washington for the time as it was considered highly confidential by the French.

Although not yet aware of the possibilities de Grasse's fleet could provide for allied arms, Washington was pleased to see Rochambeau's French troops arriving near the Hudson River, which the latter had agreed to do at the Weathersfield meeting. By Dobbs Ferry in Westchester County, in early July Washington's 6,600 troops fit for duty were joined by the 5,300 French troops from Rhode Island, now situated in sprawling camps about 12 miles north of New York. They were a "very fine body of troops," Washington's impressed private secretary remarked when they arrived at White Plains. In contrast, French officers could hardly miss seeing the destitute condition of the American soldiers, most of whom were poorly clothed, hungry, and barefoot.[25] But a French nobleman, the Comte de Clermont-Crèvecoeur, while noting the rebels' obvious poor appearance, nevertheless added that "these are the élite of the country and are actually very good troops, well schooled in their profession."[26] Another French officer, Rochambeau's young aide de camp Baron Ludwig von Closen, pitied the American troops, "almost naked with only some trousers and little linen jackets ... but very cheerful and healthy in appearance." And like several French officers at the time, they noted that a quarter of the troops "were negroes, merry, confidant, and sturdy." There they faced 10,000 British and Hessian defenders fortified on Manhattan Island and its vicinity, making an attack risky, a frustrating situation for Washington, who sought a way to capture the city he lost in the fall of 1776. "The enterprise against New York ... has to be our principal object," the American commander wrote on July 19. A week later, after several thousand French and American troops made a reconnaissance in force of the British defenses on Manhattan Island, a disappointed Washington could only conclude that his forces were not strong enough to carry the enemy's artillery-studded works, and that French naval support would be crucial to the attack. By early August he began to consider southern operations more seriously, but the lack of information about de Grasse's intentions and location made planning for the crucial summer campaign all but impossible.[27]

Then the military situation suddenly changed. Exciting news was received at the allies' camps at Philipsburg, New York, about 25 miles north of the city, on August 14, one of the brightest days for Washington during the entire war. That day, a letter from de Grasse arrived that advised he was going to sail north to North American waters by August 5 from Santo Domingo on the island of Hispaniola with 29 battle ships and just over 3,000 French soldiers. He would also bring supplies and over 1,000,000 livres on loan from the Spanish at Havana in 15 cargo ships he arranged for with his own funds. Most importantly for the purposes of strategic planning, Rochambeau (who had previous word of de Grasse's plans) and Washington could count on the expected force to head for the Chesapeake Bay, not New York, and remain in Virginia waters through October 15 – just two months off. An elated Washington wrote that "matters having now come to a crisis and a decisive plan to be determined on – I was obliged, from the Shortness of Count de Grasse's promised stay on this Coast – the apparent disinclination in their [French] Naval Officers to force the harbour of New York and the feeble compliance of the States to my requisitions for Men, hitherto, & little prospect of greater exertion in the future, to give up all idea of attacking New York."[28] Washington soon wrote to de Grasse to confirm that "it has been judged expedient to give up for the present the enterprise against New York and to turn our attention towards the South." He would instead immediately dispatch the "French Troops & a detachment from the American Army to the Head of Elk [Maryland] to be transported to Virginia for the purpose of cooperating with the force from the West Indies against the marauding British troops in Virginia."[29] He was finally going to defend his home state six years after he left it. More importantly, the French might be able to reinforce de Grasse with Barras's ships and infantry regiments from Newport to gain superiority over the British navy in Virginia, and bag Cornwallis's stranded men in the process. But this campaign had to be executed this year – France had begun to grow weary of the long war now in her fourth year of costly involvement, and with the Americans obviously "at the end of their resources," in Rochambeau's words to de Grasse.[30]

Along the Hudson River, feverish planning and busy staff work dominated the next several days of the American and French officers and sergeants as the armies prepared to travel by foot and vessel the 400 miles or so south to the old town of Williamsburg. Elements of the main force began their move to eastern Virginia on August 17 under Washington's overall command, an arrangement that Rochambeau and his lieutenants strictly respected during the entire campaign. The Virginia general left about 2,500–3,000 troops north of New York City commanded by Brig Gen William Heath of Massachusetts to deceive Sir Henry of the true intentions of the allied commanders. Heath was to increase "the Uncertainty which the present Movement [to Yorktown] of the Army will probably Occasion with the Enemy," with "the Deception kept up as long as possible." These troops were also "to keep the Enemy at New York in Check, to prevent their detaching [troops] to reinforce their Southern Army, or to harass the Inhabitants on the Sea Coast."[31]

The rest of the Continentals – 2,500 strong – marched south with 4,200 of Rochambeau's smartly uniformed soldiers with their horses and wagons on a separate but nearby route "with all the Dispatch that our Circumstances will admit."[32] The allies spent several days moving around New York to mimic an impending attack or a long siege; even the soldiers were kept in the dark. But once Clinton learned that Washington's column in New Jersey had passed Staten Island, he discerned Washington's true intent. "I wished to deceive the Enemy with regard to our real object as long as possible," Washington wrote, "our movements have been calculated for that purpose."[33] As historian Robert Selig has written, "Clinton remained convinced that New York City was the Franco-American army's objective until it was too late for him to influence the campaign's outcome."[34] Congress was kept guessing too, as Washington wisely did not advise the delegates of his plan to "March with a very considerable Detachment of the American Army and the whole of the French Troops, for Virginia" until August 27.[35]

As the armies passed through New Jersey *en route* for Trenton and Philadelphia, Washington seemed to grow more confident and hopeful. To the new Virginia governor and state militia commanding general Thomas Nelson Jr, Washington wrote that with "the arrival of the Count De Grasse with a formidable Fleet and Corps of land forces in the Cheasapeak (which may every moment be expected) will I flatter myself (with proper exertions on our part) give a moral Certainty of succeeding in the great object now in contemplation." Certain of victory? This was not the Washington of five months earlier who thought American patriots were "at the end of our tether" that spring. Now he predicted "the greatest advantages will, in all human probability result, from the Vigor of our present exertions."[36]

The French ships that appeared in late August off the Virginia coast commanded by de Grasse had endured quite a journey. Having left Brest on March 22 and engaging in several actions and maneuvers in the West Indies along the way, by July 16 the large fleet arrived at Cap Français, a bustling colonial port town in what is now Haiti. At this landfall, de Grasse received the letters that Rochambeau and Washington had written him, and welcomed on board a number of skilled ship pilots familiar with Chesapeake Bay waters. Upon considering their urgent messages de Grasse decided to sail for the Chesapeake for offensive operations against the British there. After several hectic weeks refitting his ships, resting his weary crews, and taking on fresh water and supplies, he sailed north with his fleet of 28 ships of the line by way of the seldom-used Bahama Straits (also referred to as the Old Bahama Channel) to avoid prowling British ships farther east, with chests of borrowed Spanish coins for use by the American forces. This was a powerful naval force that threatened not only Cornwallis's troops at Gloucester and Yorktown, but the Royal Navy in North America as well.

In that decisive summer of 1781, the Royal Navy's Caribbean fleet was commanded by Vice Adm Sir George Brydges, Baron Rodney, who just months before had captured the major Dutch trade island of St Eustatius, a critical source of military supplies for the American war effort. It was "a nest of villains," according to Rodney.[37] Having looted the island's residents of both military and personal property, on August 1 the rapacious Rodney decided to take these valuable prizes and money home to England, in part to defend his financially questionable practices while a naval commander, and also claiming ill health. He ordered a small detachment to escort the prize vessels and cargo ships of confiscated goods consisting of four ships of the line taken from Rear Adm Sir Samuel Hood's squadron, seemingly unconcerned about de Grasse's whereabouts or intentions.[38]

The remainder of the fleet in the Caribbean sugar islands then sailed under Hood with just 14 ships of the line, a questionable decision given the powerful size of French battle fleets known to be in American and Caribbean waters. Hood left the West Indies from Antigua on August 10, and arrived off the entrance to the Chesapeake Bay on 25 August. He saw no French presence there, so he proceeded north to New York (after looking in at Delaware Bay too), where he arrived three days later. There, he conferred with Clinton and Rear Adm Sir Thomas Graves, who was now the overall commander of British naval forces in the North American theater. These seasoned officers instantly recognized the urgent need to sail south to the Chesapeake before de Grasse arrived there – and also worried that Barras would beat them there as well from Rhode Island. This combined naval force, now under Graves's authority, sailed past Sandy Hook, New Jersey, bound for Virginia on August 31. Graves's objective was to secure the vital entrance to the bay, protect Cornwallis's vulnerable Yorktown garrison, and otherwise oppose the French ships.

But on the same day, de Grasse and his imposing armada of 28 ships of the line and 6 frigates reached the Chesapeake and sheltered at Lynnhaven Roads, just inside the mouth of the bay – a mere six days after Hood had briefly been there and departed. Now de Grasse had beaten Graves to the bay, controlled its entrance, and could prevent the Royal Navy from supporting Cornwallis's army at Yorktown. Soon thereafter, several of the French ships ascended the wide James River where they landed 3,000 troops near Williamsburg, led by the Marquis de Saint-Simon-Montbléru. Meanwhile, Lafayette moved his burgeoning command of just over 5,000 Continentals and Virginia militiamen east from New Kent to Williamsburg from his encampment about 25 miles to the west, to prevent Cornwallis from escaping the closing trap in which he would soon find himself ensnared. An anxious Washington had written Lafayette the previous week from New York that "as it will be of great Importance towards the Success of our present Enterprize that the Enemy on the Arrival of the [French] Fleet, should not have it in their Power to effect their Retreat – I cannot omit to repeat to you my most earnest Wish, that the Land & Naval Force which you will have with you, may so combine their Operations, that the British Army may not be able to escape you."[39] Thus, even before Washington, Rochambeau, and their troops arrived, the allied forces were already beginning to concentrate a powerful host on Virginia's Lower Peninsula.

It is an ironic circumstance that the most decisive event in the entire Yorktown campaign was a sea battle that involved no American forces. British and French fleets off the coast of Virginia fought a decisive naval battle on September 5 that sealed the fate of Cornwallis's army

and directly led to the collapse of British military efforts to crush the American rebellion. The complex engagement and the wide-ranging scope of the naval operations leading up to it can be but briefly summarized in these pages, but their strategic importance was nonetheless particularly decisive.

Admiral Graves commanded 19 ships of the line upon reaching the waters off Virginia's Cape Charles and Cape Henry. Opposed to him were de Grasse's 24 ships (his remaining warships were securing the offloading of Saint-Simon's troops and stores on the James River, and blockading the mouth of the York River). Upon siting the British ships off the coast in the early afternoon of the 5th, the French admiral on board his massive 104-gun flagship *Ville de Paris* quickly ordered his ships to sail out of the bay in line of battle – so suddenly, in fact, that hundreds of his sailors on fatigue duty on shore had to be left behind. The opposing fleets positioned themselves within firing range just before 4pm. In the action that afternoon from his flagship *London*, Graves hoisted confusing signals at the beginning of the engagement, and Hood's insistence in adhering to them at the expense of closing with the French line made many of the British ships fail to engage in the fighting at all. With only one ship lost – a British vessel – the battle ended after 6:30pm, and for the next several days the fleets remained within sight of each other as they floated as far south as Cape Hatteras, North Carolina. Although Hood advocated vigorously for an attempt to return swiftly to the Chesapeake Bay ahead of the slower French ships in order to secure Cornwallis's garrisons on the York River, the more hesitant Graves opted against the suggestion, fearing that his ships could be bottled up and captured inside the bay by the numerically stronger French fleet.

While Graves dithered over his next course of action, on September 9 de Grasse sailed back to the Chesapeake Bay, which he entered on September 11, to a delightful sight: the eight ships of Barras's small fleet that had arrived from Rhode Island the previous day with more troops, these commanded by the veteran Brigadier General Claude Gabriel de Choisy, and an "immense" trove of siege artillery, "most amply furnished with ammunition." With 36 powerful ships of the line now floating just inside the capes, de Grasse's large fleet was an intimidating force

to Graves when, a few days later, the English seaman spied the French ships from outside the bay. The British naval commander, outnumbered with just 18 battle ships, sailed back north to New York on September 14 to regroup and restore his sailors and vessels.[40]

After Graves set off for the safety of New York's harbor, it became immediately obvious to the anxious British officers at Yorktown and the Franco-American commanders surrounding them that the massive French fleet at anchor in Lynnhaven Roads now tightly blocked Cornwallis's primary resupply route, and all but closed the door to getting reinforcements to the British garrison. In an unsettling letter just days after Graves's ships sailed off, Cornwallis wrote candidly to Clinton in New York of his now perilous situation. "I am of the opinion," the redcoat commander admitted, "that you can do me no effectual Service, but by coming directly to this place ... If you cannot relieve me very soon, you must be prepared to hear the Worst."[41] The Battle of the Chesapeake, also called the Battle of the Capes, was known – then and now – as the most telling moment of the Yorktown campaign. Congress would soon thank de Grasse "for the display of your skill and bravery in attacking and defeating the British Fleet off of the Chesapeake."[42] It also illuminates the most valuable assistance the French gave to the American cause: naval support, which in this remarkable instance came together with French troops, Washington's army, and British blunders to ensure a victorious campaign for America. Although some accounts of the Yorktown campaign claim that this ultimate victory was inevitable after the Battle of the Capes, such an interpretation fails to allow for the ever-present element of contingency in all military operations. The Franco-American army still had to successfully lay siege to Yorktown, prevent Cornwallis from escaping, and block any seaborne rescue effort from New York City or elsewhere to relieve the British garrison. All that notwithstanding, de Grasse's naval victory made a successful siege far more likely by the time Washington and Rochambeau rode into Williamsburg on September 14, having spent four days at Mount Vernon *en route*. This visit was the first time the American general had returned home to his Potomac River plantation – "an elegant seat," according to one of his aides – since 1775. Three days later, these officers sailed out to the *Ville de Paris* off Cape Henry for a consultation with

the admiral, at which point the deferential French navy commander agreed to stay in the Tidewater region until 1 November, now that the prospects for victory seemed so promising.

To the north, the French and American armies continued their overland march to the Chesapeake Bay, where by September 9 they boarded ships in Maryland at Head of Elk, Baltimore, and Annapolis. Washington, who on September 5 had received confirmation that de Grasse and his fleet had arrived at the Chesapeake, borrowed money from the French to distribute to his soldiers one month's pay in specie – a rare event – prior to embarking for the Virginia Tidewater. From September 9 to 26, most of the troops were shipped to the James River, came ashore at College Creek Landing, and encamped near Williamsburg. It was an "arduous and very hazardous undertaking," a Pennsylvania officer noted.[43] The French cavalry, some of the army's wagons, and their cattle continued to travel by land by way of Alexandria, Fredericksburg, and King and Queen County to reach the former Virginia capital and college town.

By September 26 the allied army concentrated at Williamsburg consisted of 19,000 troops, of which 11,000 were Continentals and militiamen. They faced about 8,000 men in Cornwallis's army dug in around Yorktown and at Gloucester Point, across the James. Supply problems still nagged the American army's logisticians, and of course the soldiers even more. To Governor Thomas Sims Lee of Maryland, Washington advised "on my Arrival at Williamsburg … the Supplies for the Army here, are not in that desirable Train, that could be wished – they [the troops] have already experienced a Want of Provisions – and are greatly apprehensive for the Prospect in future, particularly in the Article of Bread … An Army cannot be kept together without Supplies – if these fail us, our Operations must cease, & all our high Hopes will banish into Disappointment & Disgrace."[44] And to Congress he reported he was "distressed to find the supply of the Army collecting here, on too precarious a footing. Already they have experienced a want of provisions."[45] Arms, gunpowder, and cartridges were scarce too, as were uniforms. The general wrote on September 16 that "upon viewing the troops of the Virginia Line this morning I find that they are almost totally destitute of Cloathing that is even necessary for the present season in consequence of which upwards of one third of them are rendered at present unfit for service."[46] Still Washington was guardedly optimistic about the state of affairs. "Our Prospects are at present fair & promising," he wrote on September 24, "we anticipate the Reduction of Ld Cornwallis with his Army with much Satisfaction."[47]

With the soldiers assembled with the army's wagons and artillery, "we commenced our March for the Investiture of the Enemy at York," about 13 miles away, on September 28, the commander recorded. Now close to the enemy, "all the Troops – Officers & Men – lay upon their arms during the Night."[48] On the following day the troops moved into their semi-circular lines to besiege Yorktown, with the French on the left and the Americans on the right. Washington deployed his divisions carefully. Lincoln's two infantry brigades of New York, New Jersey, and Rhode Island troops occupied the American far right flank, while Lafayette's two light brigades were posted in the center. Von Steuben's Pennsylvania and Maryland regiments were on the left. All told about 8,000 Continentals manned the American positions in the fields outside Yorktown, one of the largest forces of regulars Washington was able to collect in the entire war. And to support them, there were thousands of Virginia militiamen in three brigades (one of which was at Gloucester), a detachment of riflemen, and a state regiment all commanded by Virginia's Governor Nelson, whose stately brick home was in Yorktown.

The left section of the Allies' lines was manned by French troops of Rochambeau's *Expédition Particulière* and those of Gen Saint-Simon, whose three regiments had been transported by de Grasse's ships from Saint-Domingue to Virginia. Additionally, the invaluable French cavalry was led by the Duc de Lauzun, whose legion had led the advance party on the march from the Hudson to Williamsburg. This combined French force numbered about 8,000 men, in addition to their siege artillery of heavy cannons and mortars, which the Americans would never have been able to procure or transport to the Tidewater. And since de Grasse planned to stay in Chesapeake waters until November 1 to keep the British from supplying or rescuing their beleaguered garrisons hunkered down on the York River, Washington elected to conduct a formal siege of Cornwallis's defenses rather than storm his works with a potentially costly frontal attack. But he knew the invaluable French ships planned to leave the bay in just a month.

Inside the town, before the actual siege began, Lord Cornwallis observed the French and American operations with growing concern. At the end of September, he received a letter from Clinton at New York written on September 24, in which the latter advised Cornwallis that he was preparing a relief expedition to the Chesapeake in Cornwallis's favor consisting of "above five thousand men rank and file," which he expected to launch on October 5.[49] This news led Cornwallis to advise his commander that "your letter of the 24th ... has given me the greatest satisfaction. I shall retire this night within my works ..."[50] The British general hoped "by the labor and firmness of the soldiers to protract the defence" of the town until Clinton's relief force arrived. This message meant that upon news of Clinton to his rescue, Cornwallis decided to abandon his soon-to-be exposed forward positions outside the main defenses close to the town, except for the Fusiliers' Redoubt on the British right and Redoubts 9 and 10 on his left. Once Cornwallis pulled his troops in closer to the port, the allies quickly occupied the evacuated fieldworks and converted them into fighting positions for their own troops when they arrived on September 29.[51]

Across the river from Yorktown were the British defenses of Gloucester Point, less than half a mile distant. All told, the defenders numbered about 1,000 men, under the command of Tarleton. In addition to its value as an artillery position to engage French ships in the York River and as a base to procure supplies and food in the local area, Gloucester Point was also held by the British as a possible escape route from Yorktown if Cornwallis needed to abandon the port village under heavy enemy pressure. Deployed north of the British fieldworks at the sandy point was a force of 3,000 allied troops commanded by French General Choisy including Lauzun's Legion, French marines, and a Virginia militia brigade led by Brig Gen George Weedon, a Fredericksburg native with prior Continental Army service. Their mission was "to prevent any incursions of the Enemy into the Country" looking for food and fodder.[52]

Soon after Choisy established his lines opposing the enemy at Gloucester, on October 3, his ranging troops detected and struck the rear of a large British foraging expedition led by Tarleton returning to the point with cattle and wagons. In the ensuing mounted fighting known as the Battle of the Hook (named for a peculiar road intersection nearby), almost a thousand cavalrymen fought the largest mounted engagement of the Revolutionary War. Although tactically indecisive, once Tarleton withdrew inside the British fieldworks, this small battle allowed the allies to tighten their siege of Gloucester Point and prevent additional foraging operations by the British north of the York River. Eventually fodder for the army's horses became so scarce Cornwallis had to order most of them killed.

The focus of the Franco-American army remained on the British force entrenched at Yorktown. At this point, the allies began their deliberate efforts to reduce the town's defensive works according to the customs of 18th-century siege operations. This methodical process entailed digging a series of extensive trenches (called "parallels") for artillery firing positions, each one closer to the enemy's works, so that fire from siege guns could be delivered at a devastatingly close range. Eventually the attacker would offer the defender an opportunity to surrender before a final attack. If rejected, the forces who made the final assault were not restricted from sacking the town and putting the garrison to the sword. This process was conducted expertly by the well trained, experienced French engineers of Rochambeau's army and those volunteers on Washington's staff, particularly Brig Gen Louis Lebègue Duportail, his chief engineer since July 1777.

During the night of October 6, American and French soldiers began to establish the first parallel, which included trenches, artillery batteries, and earthen redoubts. As recent rains had made the ground easy to dig, these positions were completed three days later and allowed the massive bombardment of Yorktown to begin. "The work was executed with so much secresy & dispatch that the enemy were, I believe, totally ignorant of our labor till the light of the Morning discovered it to them," Washington exulted. That evening, no doubt with great satisfaction Washington fired the first cannon shot from the American Grand Battery on the right end of the first parallel, directed at Cornwallis's headquarters. A Hessian officer later wrote that this shot killed a British commissary and badly wounded an officer while at dinner.[53] Henry Knox described the events

colorfully: "On the evening of the 6th we broke ground and began our first parrell[el] within 600 Yards of the Enemies Works undiscoverd. The first parrallel, some redouts and all our batteries [were] finished by the 9th at 2 oClock PM when we opened our batteries and kept them playing continualy."[54] Four days later, the French Grand Battery on high ground at Pigeon Quarter along the Hampton Road south of town opened fire on the Yorktown defenders as well. French artillery close to the York also managed set fire to several British vessels with heated shot, including the 44-gun HMS *Charon,* and forced others to seek shelter on the far side of the river.

French and American troops advanced to within 300 to 400 yards of Cornwallis's defenses with the completion of most of the second parallel on October 13, "undertaken so much sooner than the enemy expected." Lt Col Alexander Hamilton wrote optimistically "Thank heaven, our affairs seem to be approaching fast to a happy period,"[55] especially because the army could expect French naval support for just over two more weeks. But on the Americans' far right flank on high ground near the York River British and Hessian soldiers still occupied two enclosed earthen positions in advance of the redcoats' main lines. Called Redoubts 9 and 10 and situated about 250 yards from each other, these two forward positions had to be captured and occupied by the allies to complete the second parallel. Artillery fire against the two stubborn redoubts did not reduce them or drive off their steady defenders, so Washington ordered simultaneous infantry attacks on the advanced posts. The American commander was also acutely aware that November 1 was the looming date de Grasse had set for sailing away from the Chesapeake area for the West Indies, so the time for a decisive action had now arrived. The evening of October 14 was set for the assaults.

Per Washington's orders, the attack on Redoubt 10 was made by 400 light infantry troops against 70 redcoats and Hessians, who were unsupported by artillery. The American troops were led by Lt Col Alexander Hamilton, "whose well known talents and gallantry, were on this occasion most conspicuous and serviceable." To assault Redoubt 9, the general assigned 400 French grenadiers and light infantry chasseurs. Lafayette chose Lt Col Jean-Joseph Sourbader de Gimat, a volunteer

French officer serving in his light division, to command these troops in a rush against the field fort. About 140 British and Hessians manned Redoubt 9, supported by two light field guns. At 7pm, French artillery fired six guns in quick succession, the much-anticipated signal to begin the assaults soon after dark. Advancing silently with bayonets fixed on their unloaded muskets, the steady American troops stormed Redoubt 10, and captured it with only 40 casualties. One of the officers in the attack wrote "we had not gone far before we were discovered and now the enemy opened a fire of cannon, grape shot, shell and musketry upon us, but all to no effect." Col Hamilton reported that "the rapidity and immediate success of the assault are the best comment on the behaviour of the troops." The French faced stiffer resistance at Redoubt 9, and suffered almost a hundred losses but pushed the defenders out in half an hour. "The Assaults commenced almost at the same moment," a congressional report later noted, "and were conducted & executed with the true spirit & Judgment of Officers & Men who fought in the Cause of human nature." The British did deploy more artillery along their main line near the allied attacks but made no responsive attacks themselves. Knox thought that "this advantage was important and gave us an opportunity of perfecting our 2d parall into which we took the two redoubts." It was a decisive moment. "My situation now becomes very critical," Cornwallis wrote to Clinton the next day. Washington was thrilled by the success of the assaults. "The bravery exhibited by the attacking Troops was emulous and praiseworthy – few cases have exhibited stronger proofs of Intripidity coolness and firmness than were shown upon this occasion," he wrote in his diary.[56]

With the victorious storming of the two earthen redoubts, the French and American forward fieldworks were now only 300 or so yards away from Cornwallis's main defenses, a devastatingly close range for the allied artillery to batter the enemy in Yorktown. The besiegers' cannon fire soon became so heavy that the British earthworks began to crumble, and casualties mounted as well. Cornwallis wrote Clinton desperately on October 15 that his deteriorating situation was now "critical," and the intense bombardment his troops were enduring meant that the army "dare not shew a gun to their old batteries" now part of the allies' lines. The British defenses "do not

resist their [i.e., besiegers'] powerful artillery," and he expected a powerful allied assault against his "ruined works, in a bad position, and with weakened numbers." The British lieutenant general glumly advised Clinton that his army's battered position was "so precarious, that I cannot recommend that the fleet and army should run great risque in endeavouring to save us."[57] Clearly the brave assaults by the French and American light infantrymen on redoubts 9 and 10 had worsened British prospects considerably. And several American officers commented on how remarkably passive the British defenders had been as the allies feverishly constructed their siege lines and opened their artillery fire for days on end. This was quite uncharacteristic of Cornwallis, known for his bold attacks at Brandywine, Camden, and Guilford Courthouse.

The curious inactivity on the part of the besieged forces ended on October 16, when British troops made a sortie from their earthworks against the allies' second parallel. Such a forlorn effort had no chance of significant success, but it was a *pro forma* part of siege craft expected of 18th-century armies, and Cornwallis also knew it was all but required to uphold British honor. At 4am 350 British troops rushed forward from their lines and attacked the allied trenches where the American and French positions met. They spiked several cannons in the French and American sectors but were soon pushed out of the parallel by the bayonets of the French infantry, "the guards of the Trenches advancing quickly upon them," and the heavy siege guns were soon repaired in about six hours.[58] This venture "proved of little publick advantage," Cornwallis later noted with dry understatement.[59]

A more determined breakthrough effort was made later that night, which would have been more dangerous to Washington's army if successful. With the few boats at Yorktown that French artillery fire had not sunk or burned, Cornwallis's troops attempted to escape across the York River to Gloucester Point under cover of darkness. During this daring operation, however, and prior to many soldiers of the garrison leaving their lines, a powerful rainstorm blew in with high winds, which drove several of the small British boats into the French navy's picket line downstream and sank a few others. This disaster ended the desperate measure that proved to be Cornwallis's final attempt to avoid the ultimate military humiliation.

After consulting his senior officers on the 17th, Cornwallis concluded the time had come to enter a parley with Washington to discuss surrender terms. "About ten Oclock the Enemy beat a parley and Lord Cornwallis proposed a cessation of Hostilities for 24 hours, that Commissioners might meet at the house of a Mr. Moore (in the rear of our first parallel) to settle terms for the surrender of the Posts of York and Gloucester," Washington recorded in his diary.[60]

The details of the terse communications between Washington and Cornwallis and the subsequent strained negotiations of terms between junior officers at the nearby Augustine Moore House have been described in other works and need not be presented here. Part of the settlement, however, was remarkable and shows Washington's steadfast insistence that he be treated like a professional soldier and that his army must be respected as a victorious fighting force. During the negotiations on October 18, British representatives included in their proposed terms was that the British army would be granted the typical honors for the capitulation, which included allowing the redcoats and Hessians to march out from their lines to the surrender site with their regimental colors flying, while playing an American ditty in honor of their victory. Washington, however, rejected this suggestion since the British refused similar terms to Maj Gen Benjamin Lincoln when he surrendered the American garrison at Charleston, South Carolina, to Sir Henry Clinton in May 1780. Instead, one of the 14 Yorktown surrender articles stated that the enemy were to "march out ... with shouldered arms, colors cased, and drums beating a British or German march. They are then to ground their arms and return to their encampment, where they will remain until they are dispatched to the places of their destination ..." Cornwallis had no option other than to accept what he considered harsh terms, and many of his lieutenants were enraged.[61]

On the afternoon of the 19th, about 3,300 British, Hessian, and Loyalist troops marched out from their Yorktown defenses along the road to a field where they grounded their arms and returned to their squalid camps. In addition, 1,741 were too ill to leave the town to lay down their muskets, as disease and fever had swept through the ranks during the siege. Many of those who surrendered were surly and intoxicated, and some hurled their muskets to the ground. "About two hundred pieces of Cannon, nearly one half of which are brass, a great number of Arms Drums and Colours are among the trophies of this decisive stroke," wrote Henry Knox with pleasure.[62] A similar ceremony took place across the river at Gloucester an hour later, while 2,000 Royal Navy personnel entered captivity with the French fleet. By the 21st, the army prisoners began their long march to Winchester, Virginia, and Frederick, Maryland, where they would be held in rather austere conditions until the war's end.

Lord Cornwallis did not attend the surrender ceremony. No doubt humiliated by his defeat and the terms of the surrender agreement imposed upon his army, he used illness as an excuse for his absence. When his second in command, Gen O'Hara, brought forth Cornwallis's sword and presented it to Rochambeau, the French commander properly refused it in favor of Gen Washington, demonstrating again the deference he and his fellow allied officers strictly observed during the long campaign. But when O'Hara next offered the sword to the great Virginian, the Continental commander directed the British officer to the American army's second in command – and thus, O'Hara's equal – who was none other than Benjamin Lincoln. The surrender was a "joyful event," wrote artilleryman Henry Knox.[63] The tables had turned for the armies – and their nations – and Washington savored the finest moment of his military career.

Shortly after "the Definitive Capitulation" was effected, the American commander in chief advised Congress that very day of the momentous victory. "I have the Honor to inform Congress, that a Reduction of the British Army under the Command of Lord Cornwallis, is most happily effected," and went on to praise "the unremitting Ardor which actuated every Officer & Soldier in the combined Army on this Occasion." Washington added that "the singular Spirit of Emulation, which animated the whole Army from the first Commencement of our Operations, has filled my Mind with the highest pleasure & Satisfaction – and had given me the happiest presages of Success." He then granted one of his loyal aides, the long-serving Marylander Col

Tench Tilghman, "the Honor to deliver these dispatches" to Congress.[64] "The advantages which must result from the Capture of that Army are more than can be conceived," a happy congressman wrote upon receiving Tilghman's reports.[65]

As in every battle and campaign, there were might have beens. From New York with 7,000 troops on board Royal Navy ships, Clinton was finally able to launch his promised relief expedition – on October 19, the very day Cornwallis's army surrendered. His ships appeared off the Virginia capes five days later, where he got the disappointing news from a passing refugee ship that had left Hampton Roads for New York. And what if Cornwallis had been able to move his troops across the York and escape northward? More than a few historians and interpreters have posed this as a distinct possibility, but the chances that Cornwallis's worn-down, fever-reduced soldiers who were short of boats, food, horses, clothing, and shoes could have marched from Gloucester to either Philadelphia or New York and reached safety while American and French troops pursued them are simply implausible. The British troops along the York River had been bagged, and now they were bound for captivity for two years, defeated by their ancient enemy France and the long-suffering American army led by an erstwhile colonial militia colonel, George Washington.

Alexander Hamilton neatly summed up his take on the campaign in a letter weeks later to Lafayette's brother-in-law Louis-Marie, vicomte de Noailles, who had served at Yorktown. "I chuse ... to find the cause of our victory in the superior number of good and regular troops," he concluded, "in the uninterrupted harmony of the two nations, and their equal desire to be celebrated in the annals of history, for an ardent love of great and heroic actions."[66] And the commanding general must have been gratified by a congratulatory letter he received from Thomas Jefferson, writing from Monticello. The former Virginia governor was relieved that Cornwallis had surrendered, and that Virginia was now safe. "I hope it will not be unacceptable to your Excellency to receive the congratulations of a private individual on your return to your native country, & above all things on the important success which has attended it," he wrote. It was indeed an important success, a decisive turning point on the path to independence.[67]

A poignant message still survives that for a fleeting moment illuminates the importance of the Yorktown victory. In a long October 21 letter written by New Jersey Congressman Elias Boudinot while in Philadelphia to his wife Hannah, in a brief postscript he added the next day before mailing it to her, he reports that "at three oClock this morning, an Express arrived this morning with the glorious News of the Surrender of Lord Cornwallis with his whole army. God be praised." Here we get details that the initial news of the Yorktown triumph arrived from Governor Thomas Sim Lee of Maryland (who got the notice of Cornwallis's surrender by a fast ship dispatched to Annapolis by de Grasse) in the small hours of the morning, when at least a few of the delegates were awake to receive the news. It was, Boudinot wrote, "a day which here ever after be famous in the annals of American history."[68] Others in Philadelphia agreed. On the 22nd, Maryland Patriot Daniel of St Thomas Jenifer wrote back to Governor Lee that the Yorktown success was a "most important event much heightened by little or no loss to the American army."[69] Congressman John Hanson called the victory "a most Capitol Stroke and will tend more towards obtaining peace and to the security of our independence than the best managed negotiations."[70] Washington's official dispatches to Congress arrived in town on October 24, carried by Tilghman.

The immediate result of the Franco-American victory at Yorktown was the loss of Britain's second largest field force in America, and one quarter of all King George III's soldiers in the former seaboard colonies. These troops were now eliminated from all active service, and at this stage in the war, they were in effect irreplaceable. "This Blow, I think must be a decisive one," wrote Virginia Governor Nelson, "it being out of the Power of G.B. to replace such a number of good Troops."[71] Likewise, James Madison concluded that "it would seem as if Heaven had abandoned [Great Britain] to her folly and her fate."[72] Gen Clinton commanded just enough troops at New York to defend the city but had few to spare for even a minor offensive. Although de Grasse and his fleet sailed off from the Chesapeake on November 4, leaving four ships to guard the mouths of the James and York Rivers, the French infantry battalions who served at Yorktown remained in Virginia over the winter, which left a powerful force to confront the British through 1782.

After the surrender at Yorktown and the elimination of thousands of British soldiers in America – with several hundred Hessians as well – few of the British generals favored continuing the hostilities, which was a large factor in convincing the king and his ministers to end the war. They were also worried about French naval and army forces, not only in the West Indies but also at home, given the looming threat of a cross-Channel invasion with Spanish support. And those thoughtful officers who looked back carefully saw that there had been few battlefield successes for redcoat armies in America over the last few years. Resources spent in the American colonies in a now unwinnable war would be better spent elsewhere. With fewer troops and increased costly military obligations in the West Indies and Gibraltar, the British could now no longer conduct any large-scale offensive operations in the American colonies. Unless King George managed to enlist a powerful ally to fight the Americans, James Madison wrote just after the surrender, "it seems scarcely possible for them much longer to shut their ears against the voice of peace," or to "try the fortune of another campaign."[73] President of the Continental Congress Thomas McKean of Delaware held that "the power of Britain in these states is now broken. I trust it will soon be annihilated," and the Loyalists "are struck with horror and despair."[74]

A letter written from Philadelphia by North Carolina Congressman Benjamin Hawkins to his state's governor, Abner Nash, colorfully assessed the military state of affairs a month after Cornwallis's surrender. He suspected that "Britain is by this [defeat] seriously inclined to make peace, and from her situation will be compelled to make an equitable and honorable one for us." He pointed out that the British "efforts this year have been greater this year than ever before," in which they spent over £21,000,000, "notwithstand[ing] which her navy (the grand bulwark of the Nation) hath been disgraced in every quarter, and her armies in America and the two Indies sharing the same fate." Hawkins wrote that the British "troops at New York are much dispirited," and believed that if a general pardon were offered to the numerous Loyalist "refugees" there, "a large majority would return from the enemy."[75] Lafayette was more succinct: "The play, sir, is over, the fifth act has just been closed."[76]

There were political results from the Franco-American victory on the York River as well. As became obvious by early 1782, a growing number of Members of Parliament opposed a further prosecution of the war. Many of this body's members also called for an end to the costly conflict that disrupted trade with the colonies and raised land taxes in Britain. Lord North's ministry, which had hoped to continue the fight with France and America after Yorktown, fell in late February 1782, and Lord Germain stepped down at the same time. In April 1783 Washington signed an armistice agreement with Clinton's successor, Sir Guy Carleton, and the final peace treaty was signed in Paris on September 3, that year. The fighting was over, and independence of the United States was recognized by Great Britain. The long-sought-after goal of the war had finally been achieved, seven years after the signing of the Declaration of Independence. The treaty itself had significant results as well, which can be said to come from the Yorktown victory. The treaty set the new nation's western border at the Mississippi River north of Florida, which would allow for American western expansion, often at the expense of Native Americans. Another provision was that "the Navigation of the river Mississippi, from its source to the Ocean, shall forever remain free and open to the Subjects of Great Britain and the Citizens of the United States," although this right was blocked by the Spanish for a time after they took over the Floridas from the British after the signing.

George Washington also greatly benefitted politically. The victory at Yorktown was largely seen as his triumph, a campaign of American arms led by the Virginian with French assistance. Not for several years did the important roles of French commanders and their military assets in the successful operations become widely known in America, nor was the importance of the September 5 Battle of the Capes recognized as the key event of the campaign for quite some time. Instead, Americans hailed Washington as the victor of the last battle of the war that secured independence. "The events of the present campaign," wrote the new president of Congress, John Hanson, "will, no doubt, fill the most brilliant pages in the history of America."[77] It was his greatest victory as commander in chief, and how different the result than the dark days of Long Island, Harlem Heights, Fort Washington, Brandywine, and

Germantown. His almost universal fame and admiration translated into two presidential terms for the man who left an indelible mark on the new nation's character and development.

Historian Robert Selig writes in his overview of the campaign that the outcome of the Yorktown operations "had a resounding impact that eventually proved decisive."[78] This conclusion is inescapable. Looking again to the 1981 Bicentennial commemorations, President Reagan – known as "the Great Communicator" – delivered remarks that captured the spirit of the celebrations. "The promise made on July 4th was kept on October 19th," he said, "The dream described in that Pennsylvania hall was fulfilled on this Virginia field. Through courage, the support of our allies, and by the gracious hand of God, a revolution was won, a people were set free, and the world witnessed the most exciting adventure in the history of nations: the beginning of the United States of America."[79]

Conclusion

Not every military event can be described as decisive or as a salient turning point in a violent conflict. As noted in the introduction, this study defines turning points as battles, campaigns, sieges, and other military occurrences that result in significant changes that alter the trajectory of the conflict toward the war's outcome. The five military events detailed above fall within this definition, while others – including many well-known battles and campaigns – do not.

Not all authors and historians, past and present, and some quite well-known, have looked at decisive turning points accurately. Some show an inadequate familiarity with the depth of military history or the conflicts about which they write, leading to misinterpretations of the importance and consequences of wars and the significance of battles, campaigns, and other wartime events that constitute them. Several examples illustrate this tendency.

Pulitzer Prize-winning author, National Book Award winner, and academic historian Joseph J. Ellis writes about the events of 1776 leading up to and following the proclamation of the Declaration of Independence on July 4 in his 2013 book *Revolutionary Summer: The Birth of American Independence*. Curiously the military part of his story ends in mid-campaign, just after General Howe's contested amphibious landing at Pell's Point near Westchester, New York, on October 18, when Washington's army retreated to White Plains. Ellis then claims that "the battles of Long Island and Manhattan [were] where the British army and navy delivered a series of devastating defeats to an American army of amateurs, but missed whatever chance existed to end" the war.

He also adds that "hindsight does allow us to know that once the Howes missed the opportunity to destroy the Continental Army early in the war, it would never come again."¹ Ellis later writes that in the New York area battles, the Continental "army had managed to survive what proved to be the most vulnerable moment of the war," adding that "Washington, from lessons learned in New York, would never again allow the survival of the Continental Army to be put at risk."²

Ellis, however, ignores altogether the course of the Revolutionary War after the battle of White Plains (October 28, 1776). Proposing that after the Pell's Point landing the British had no more opportunities to destroy the American rebels ignores many other chances the rebellion could have been crushed, such as at Brunswick in early December 1776, where Cornwallis missed an opportunity to overtake and crush what was left of Washington's fleeing army. Another case is Second Princeton in January 1777, when Washington's own officers thought that the British would annihilate the army the next day, as did Cornwallis. Washington put his army at grave risk that day, as he also did that fall at Brandywine, where he made a stand with all his troops to defend Philadelphia in a stand-up fight against a superior foe. Moreover, Washington, and those with him along the icy Delaware River in late December of 1776, when the army was dissolving, soldiers refused to reenlist, and the British seemed poised to deal a death blow to the cause, might scoff at Ellis's odd claim that White Plains was "the most vulnerable moment of the war."³ Ellis's rigid concept of a "revolutionary summer" constricts his interpretation of the military struggle to a tidy six-month period early in the war, completely ignores the military history of war after October of 1776, and thus limits his idea of a turning point of the war, or any other "vulnerable moment of the war.⁴

Before Ellis, historian Page Smith, writing in *A New Age Now Begins: A People's History of the American Revolution* (1976), asserts that while the "consequences of Saratoga were of course considerable," the surrender "did not do what Americans hoped beyond hope it would:" convince Britain that victory was hopeless and to "seek an end to the conflict on terms acceptable to their American cousins." Is that actually what Americans were hoping? Smith also asserts that the Saratoga victory did not on its own persuade the French to ally with the United

States against Great Britain; rather it was Washington's "near-victory" at Germantown that impressed French ministers and King Louis XVI to sign a treaty with the Americans. "I am inclined to argue that the French military alliance was an actual disservice to the American cause." For Smith the victory in the Saratoga campaign was not responsible for securing French assistance, it was *solely* the defeat – not (in his words) a so-called "near victory" – at Germantown. Ignoring Saratoga's consequences is a questionable interpretation few historians espouse, and it is unsupported by the events. To contend that a defeat suffered by Washington's army was more consequential in French minds than Burgoyne's 1777 surrender is implausible.[5]

Revolutionary War scholar John Ferling also claims in a 2010 article that "protracted conflicts...are seldom defined by a single decisive event," and that "Saratoga was not the turning point of the war." With no other explanation, however, he instead goes on to describe "four other key moments [that] can be identified" as decisive events. Ferling's turning points are the "victories in the fighting along the Concord Road on April 19, 1775, and at Bunker Hill two months later;" the battles of Trenton and Princeton; "when Congress abandoned one-year enlistments and transformed the Continental Army into a standing army [of] long-term service;" and "the campaign that unfolded in the South during 1780 and 1781[,] the final turning point of the conflict."[6] Yet in Ferling's latest book written eleven years later, *Winning Independence: The Decisive Years of the Revolutionary War, 1778–1781*, he no longer includes Lexington, Concord, Bunker Hill, Trenton, and Princeton as decisive, and Saratoga is again ignored.

As these three historians demonstrate, the concept of decisive military turning points can be hard to pin down. Using my interpretive framework that looks at key events as those that markedly changed the direction of the war, many campaigns and battles, while important, were not decisive. A few examples will illustrate this point.

The battles on April 19, 1775, at Lexington Green, Concord, and on the British march back to Boston in essence began the war. Bunker (Breed's) Hill was a bloody battle that showed the British army the Americans' combat mettle. These early war engagements convinced many of the British generals that the rebels would fight, and the war would not be won in one campaign. The British remained in Boston, increased their armed forces in America, and planned for future campaigns undeterred. None of the three well-known engagements of 1775, however, altered the war's trajectory; the British were back with a vengeance the next year with far more troops and ships, although at New York.

General Howe's victory on Long Island in August 1776 was an undisputed tactical victory, where 20,000 troops routed the rebels and forced them to evacuate the island. But the battle was not a knockout blow: Washington's army survived and managed to regroup on Manhattan Island. Indeed, Howe's hesitancy to attack Washington's troops after his victory made it indecisive. Likewise, Howe's two subsequent victories over Washington in 1777 at Brandywine and Germantown led to the capture and eight-month occupation of Philadelphia but did not knock the American army out of the war, even with the loss of their capital and a harrowing winter encampment. And in 1778 at Monmouth Courthouse, although claimed as a victory by Washington, the result was that British general Clinton protected his long column of wagons and troops with a stout rear-guard action, then successfully made it to New York – his main objective. The fight did not alter the war's trajectory toward an ultimate American victory, as Clinton got his army to New York intact, where it remained for five more years. The American army's improved performance at Monmouth Courthouse was not a turning point; rather, the improved discipline and training learned at Valley Forge was instead. Monmouth "was a standoff that had no immediate impact on the course of the war," writes Ferling.[7] As explained above, a careful look at the Carolinas' Campaign of 1780–81 shows that the two Patriot victories in South Carolina at Kings Mountain and Cowpens were indeed important in that they both reduced British military strength and built up American morale. Other small actions in this campaign also produced telling results for the British army, such as Cowan's Ford, which allowed the British to cross the Catawba River, chase Morgan, and frighten Patriot Whigs from turning out for militia service. This affair did not, however, alter the ultimate outcome of the winter campaign. Only the costly redcoat victory at Guilford Courthouse eventually prevented

Lord Cornwallis from conquering North Carolina, and then led to his march north into Virginia.

Over the course of the Revolutionary War, numerous battles and campaigns were important and contributed to eventual American victory in 1783. Bunker Hill, Charleston (in 1776), Hubbardton, and Bennington showed the Crown forces early on that the upstart rebels could fight. Kings Mountain and Cowpens demonstrated that militiamen could help win important battles when appropriately engaged. And the campaigns of Washington and Greene in the war's last few years showed that caution, patience, and persistence could lead to victory. As Napoleon would later state, "victory belongs to the most persevering." But none of these altered the trajectory of war to a successful Patriot victory.

Studying the events of the Revolutionary War to determine which were decisive turning points is a subjective pursuit. But when looking at which events were crucial in leading to ultimate American victory and independence, the campaigns and battles of Trenton, Princeton, Saratoga, Guilford Courthouse, and Yorktown, along with the winter encampment at Valley Forge, must be counted as the most important. Without the small but crucial successes at Trenton and Princeton, Washington's army – and the cause – would have collapsed, as none other than Washington predicted. Burgoyne's disastrous Saratoga campaign not only wiped out an entire British field force but convinced France to become America's ally. Valley Forge changed the character and quality of the army, while establishing Washington as the indispensable commander (to paraphrase James Thomas Flexner). The bloodbath at Guilford Courthouse ended British success in the South, ended an invasion, and dealt a mortal blow to the region's only British field army. The surrender of a second army of redcoats at Yorktown was the final military and political blow to British arms and the country's will to keep fighting. And these four battles and an encampment show that Patrick Henry was prescient in 1775 when he proclaimed to the Virginia House of Burgesses inside Saint John's Church at Richmond, Virginia, that "the battle, sir, is not to the strong alone; it is to the vigilant, the active, the brave."[8]

Bibliography

Aaron, Larry. *The Race to the Dan: The Retreat That Rescued the American Revolution*. South Boston, VA: Halifax County Historical Society, 2007.

Atkinson, Rick. *The British Are Coming: The War for America, Lexington to Princeton, 1775–1777*. New York: Henry Holt and Company, 2019.

Babits, Lawrence E. *A Devil of a Whipping: The Battle of Cowpens*. Chapel Hill: University of North Carolina Press, 1998.

Babits, Lawrence E., and Joshua B. Howard. *Long, Obstinate, and Bloody: The Battle of Guilford Courthouse*. Chapel Hill: University of North Carolina Press, 2009.

Baer, Friederike. *Hessians: German Soldiers in the American Revolutionary War*. London: Oxford University Press, 2022.

Baker, Thomas E. *Another Such Victory*. Fort Washington, PA: Eastern Acorn Press, 1981,

Barbieri, Michael. "Brown's Raid on Ticonderoga and Mount Independence." *Journal of the American Revolution*, January 20, 2022, https://allthingsliberty.com/2022/01/browns-raid-on-ticonderoga-and-mount-independence/.

Barry, Quintin. *Crisis at the Chesapeake: The Royal Navy and the Struggle for America 1775–1783*. Warwick: Helion & Co, 2021.

Billias, George. "Horatio Gates, Professional Soldier" in George Billias, ed., *George Washington's Generals and Opponents*. New York: DeCapo Press, 1994.

Blythe, Robert W., Maureen A. Carroll, and Steven H. Moffson. "Kings Mountain National Military Park Historic Resource Study," US National Park Service, May 1995.

Boatner, Mark M. *Encyclopedia of the American Revolution*. 3rd ed. Mechanicsburg, PA: Stackpole Books, 1994.

Bodle, Wayne K. *The Valley Forge Winter: Civilians and Soldiers in War*. University Park, Pennsylvania State University Press, 2002.

Braisted, Todd W. "All London Was Afloat," in Edward G. Lengel, ed., *The 10 Key Campaigns of the American Revolution*. Washington, DC: Regnery Publishing, 2020, pp.45–64.

Brumwell, Stephen. *George Washington, Gentleman Warrior*. London: Quercus, 2013.

Buchanan, John. *The Road to Valley Forge: How Washington Built the Army that Won the Revolution*. Hoboken, NJ: John Wiley & Sons, 2004.

Buchanan, John. *Road to Guilford Courthouse: The American Revolution in the Carolinas*. Hoboken, NJ: John Wiley & Sons, 1997.

Carp, E. Wayne. *To Starve the Army with Pleasure: Continental Army Administration and American Political Culture, 1775–1783*. Chapel Hill: University of North Carolina Press, 1984.

Churchill, Winston. *Marlborough: His Life and Times*, 4 vols. London: Thornton Butterworth, 1933–38.

Clark, Harrison. *All Cloudless Glory: The Life of George Washington*. Washington, DC: Regnery, 1995.

Collins, Denis. "Governor Opens Celebration Of Yorktown Amid Pageantry." *The Washington Post*. October 16, 1981. https://www .washingtonpost.com/archive/local/1981/10/17/governor-opens -celebration-of-yorktown-amid-pageantry/01e00fe8-9b72-48a1-9b22 -17ac6427c172/

Collins, Denis. "Summer Soldiers, Spectators Rejoice at Yorktown Battle." *The Washington Post*. October 18, 1981. https://www.washingtonpost .com/archive/politics/1981/10/18/summer-soldiers-spectators-rejoice-at -yorktown-battle/a29c30f9-f633-4209-bb8a-90f0979aabf9/

Corbett, Theodore. *A Maritime History of the American Revolutionary War*. Havertown, PA: Pen and Sword Books, 2023.

Corbett, Theodore. *No Turning Point: The Saratoga Campaign in Perspective*. Norman: University of Oklahoma Press, 2012.

Creasy, Edward S. *The Fifteen Decisive Battles of the World: From Marathon to Waterloo*. New York: A. L. Burt, 1851.

Cubbison, Douglas. *Burgoyne and the Saratoga Campaign: His Papers*. Norman, OK: The Arthur H. Clark Company, 2012.

Curry, Anne. *Great Battles: Agincourt*. Oxford: Oxford University Press, 2015.

Dann, John C., ed. *The Revolution Remembered: Eyewitness Accounts of the War for Independence*. University of Chicago Press, 1980.

Davies, Huw J. *The Wandering Army: The Campaigns that Transformed the British Way of War*. New Haven, CT: Yale University Press, 2022.

Doyle, Don H., *The Cause of All Nations: An International History of the American Civil War*. New York: Basic Books, 2014.

Dunkerly, Robert. *Unhappy Catastrophes: The American Revolution in Central New Jersey, 1776–1782*. New York: Savas Beatie, 2022.

Dwyer, William. *The Day is Ours!: November 1776–January 1777: An Inside View of the Battles of Trenton and Princeton*. New York: Viking Press, 1983.

Ellis, Joseph J. *Revolutionary Summer: The Birth of American Independence*. New York: Alfred A. Knopf, 2013.

Fallaw, Robert, and Marion W. Stoer. "The Old Dominion Under Fire: The Chesapeake Invasions, 1779–1781," in Ernest M. Eller, ed., *Chesapeake Bay in the American Revolution*. Centreville, MD: Tidewater Publishers, 1981, pp. 432–74.

Fenster, Julie M. *Jefferson's America: The President, the Purchase, and the Explorers who Transformed a Nation*. New York: Crown Publishing, 2017.

Ferling, John. "Myths of the American Revolution." January 2010, *Smithsonian Magazine*, https://www.smithsonianmag.com/history/myths-of-the-american-revolution-10941835/.

Ferling, John. *Almost a Miracle: The American Victory in the War of Independence*. New York: Oxford University Press, 2009.

Ferling, John. *Winning Independence: The Decisive Years of the Revolutionary War, 1778–1781*. New York: Bloomsbury Publishing, 2021.

Ferreiro, Larrie. *Brothers at Arms: American Independence and the Men of France and Spain Who Saved It*. New York: Vintage Books, 2017.

Fischer, David Hackett. *Washington's Crossing*. New York: Oxford University Press, 2006.

Flavell, Julie. *The Howe Dynasty: The Untold Story of a Military Family and the Women Behind Britain's Wars for America*. New York: Liveright, 2021.

Forrest, Alan. *Great Battles: Waterloo*. Oxford: Oxford University Press, 2015.

Franklin, Ben A. "Even British Cheery At Fete Of Yorktown," *New York Times*, October 20, 1981.

Gabriel, Michael P. *The Battle of Bennington: Soldiers and Civilians*. Charleston, SC: The History Press, 2012.

Gaines, James R. *For Liberty and Glory: Washington, Lafayette, and their Revolutions*. New York: W. W. Norton, 2009.

Golway, Terry. *Washington's General: Nathanael Greene and the Triumph of the American Revolution*. New York: Henry Holt, 2006.

Greene, Jerome A. *The Guns of Independence: The Siege of Yorktown, 1781*. New York: Savas Beatie, 2009.

Greenwalt, Phillip S. *The Winter That Won the War: The Winter Encampment at Valley Forge, 1777–1778*. Havertown, PA: Savas Beatie, 2021.

Hagist, Don N., ed. *A British Soldier's Story: Roger Lamb's Narrative of the American Revolution*. Baraboo, WI: Ballindoch Press, 2004.

Hagist, Don N., ed. *Waging War in America, 1775–1783: Operational Challenges of Five Armies during the American Revolution*. Warwick, MASS: Helion and Co. Ltd, 2023.

Hanson, Victor Davis. *Ripples of Battle: How the Wars of the Past Still Determine How We Fight, How We Live, and How We Think*. New York: Doubleday, 2003.

Harari, Yuval Noah, "The Concept of 'Decisive Battles' in World History." *Journal of World History*, Vol. 18, No. 3 (Sep. 2007), pp. 251–66.

Hardyman, Christine O., ed. *Department of the Army Historical Summary, Fiscal Year 1981*. Washington, DC: US Army Center of Military History, 1988.

Harris, Michael C. "The Empire Strikes Back: The Campaign of 1777," in Edward Lengel, ed., *10 Key Campaigns of the American Revolution*. Washington, DC: Regnery Publishing, 2020, pp. 111–28.

Harris, Michael C., and Gary Ecelbarger. "Continental Army Numerical Strength at Valley Forge." *Journal of the American Revolution*, May 18, 2021, https://allthingsliberty.com/2021/05/a-reconsideration-of-continental-army-numerical-strength-at-valley-forge/.

Herrera, Ricardo A. "'Our Army will hut this Winter at Valley Forge': George Washington, Decision Making, and the Councils of War." *Army History*, Fall 2020.

Hererra, Ricardo A. *Feeding Washington's Army: Surviving the Valley Forge Winter of 1778*. Chapel Hill: The University of North Carolina Press, 2022.

Higginbotham, Don. *The War of American Independence: Military Attitudes, Policies, and Practice, 1763–1789*. Boston, MA: Northeastern University Press, 1983.

Idzerda, Stanley J. *Lafayette in the Age of the American Revolution: Selected Letters and Papers, 1776–1790*. 4 vols. Ithaca, NY: Cornell University Press, 1989.

Jackson, Donald, ed. *The Diaries of George Washington*. Charlottesville: University Press of Virginia, 1978.

Johnson, Henry P. *The Yorktown Campaign and the Surrender of Cornwallis*. New York: Harper and Brothers, 1881.

Kidder, William L. *Ten Crucial Days: Washington's Vision for Victory Unfolds*. Nashville, TN: Knox Press, 2019.

Kidder, William L. "The Times That Try Men's Souls," in Edward G. Lengel, ed., *The 10 Key Campaigns of the American Revolution*. Washington, DC: Regnery Publishing, 2020.

Kowner, Rotem. *Great Battles: Tsushima*. Oxford: Oxford University Press, 2022.

Landers, H.L. *The Virginia Campaign and the Blockade and Siege of Yorktown, 1781*. Washington, DC: US Government Printing Office, 1931.

Lee, Henry. *The Revolutionary War Memoirs of General Henry Lee*. New York: Da Capo Press, 1998.

Lefkowitz, Arthur. *George Washington's Revenge: The 1777 New Jersey Campaign*. New York: Stackpole Books, 2022.

Lefkowitz, Arthur. *Long Retreat: The Calamitous American Defense of New Jersey, 1776*. New Brunswick, NJ: Rutgers University Press, 1999.

Lender, Mark E. and Gary W. Stone. *Fatal Sunday: George Washington, the Monmouth Campaign, and the Politics of Battle*. Norman: University of Oklahoma Press, 2016.

Lender, Mark E. *Cabal!: The Plot against General Washington*. Yardley, PA: Westholme, 2019.

Lengel, Edward. *General George Washington: A Military Life*. New York: Random House, 2005.

Lockhart, Paul. *The Drillmaster of Valley Forge: The Baron de Steuben and the Making of the American Army*. New York: HarperCollins, 2008.

Lockhart, Paul. *The Whites of Their Eyes: Bunker Hill, the First American Army, and the Emergence of George Washington*. New York: Harper, 2011.

Long, Derrick. "The Fall of Fort Washington: The 'Bunker Hill Effect.'" *Journal of the American Revolution*, www.allthingsliberty.com (July 2020).

Lumpkin, Henry. *From Savannah to Yorktown: The American Revolution in the South*. New York: Paragon House Publishers, 1981.

Luzader, John. *Saratoga: A Military History of the Decisive Campaign of the American Revolution*. El Dorado Hills, CA: Savas Beatie, 2014.

Luzader, John. *Decision on the Hudson: The Battles of Saratoga*. Fort Washington, PA: Eastern National, 2002.

Maass, John R. "'Too Grievous for a People to Bear': Impressment and Conscription in Revolutionary North Carolina." *Journal of Military History*, 73 (October 2009), pp 1091–115.

Maass, John R. "From Cowpens to Guilford Courthouse," in Edward G. Lengel, ed., *The 10 Key Campaigns of the American Revolution*. Washington, DC: Regnery History, 2020.

Maass, John R. *The Battle of Guilford Courthouse: A Most Desperate Engagement*. Charleston, SC: The History Press, 2020, pp. 177–95.

Mack, Ebeneezer. *The Life of Gen. Gilbert Motier de Lafayette...* Utica, NY: G.G. Brooks, 1859.

Mackesy, Piers. *War for America, 1775–1783.* Lincoln: University of Nebraska Press, 1992.

MacLeod, D. Peter. *Northern Armageddon: The Plains of Abraham and the Making of the American Revolution.* New York: Alfred A. Knopf, 2016.

Maloy, Mark. *Victory or Death: The Battles of Trenton and Princeton, December 25, 1776–January 3, 1777.* El Dorado, CA: Savas Beatie, 2017.

Martin, James K., and David L. Preston. *Theaters of the American Revolution: Northern, Middle, Southern, Western, Naval.* Yardley, PA: Westholme Publishing, 2017.

Martin, James K., and Mark E. Lender. *A Respectable Army: The Military Origins of the Republic, 1763–1789.* Arlington Heights, IL: Harlan Davidson, 1982.

Meyers, William H., ed. "Diary of Captain James Duncan," *Pennsylvania Archives*, Second Series. Harrisburg: E.K. Myers, 1890.

Mandelbaum, Michael. "Decisive Battles, Past and Present." *American Purpose*, June 1, 2022, https://www.americanpurpose.com/articles/decisive-battles-past-and-present/.

McBurney, Christian. *George Washington's Nemesis: The Outrageous Treason and Unfair Court-martial of Major General Charles Lee during the American Revolution.* El Dorado, CA: Savas Beatie, 2019.

McNab, Chris. *The Improbable Victory: The Campaigns, Battles and Soldiers of the American Revolution, 1775–83* (Oxford: Osprey Publishing, 2017), p. 121.

Moncure, John. *The Cowpens Staff Ride and Battlefield Tour.* Fort Leavenworth, KS: Combat Studies Institute, 1996.

Murphy, Daniel. *William Washington: An American Light Dragoon.* Yardley, PA: Westholme Publishing, 2014.

Nelson, Craig. *Thomas Paine: Enlightenment, Revolution, and the Birth of Modern Nations.* New York: Penguin Books, 2007.

Nolan, Cathal J. *The Allure of Battle: A History of How Wars Have Been Won and Lost.* New York: Oxford University Press, 2017.

Nolan, Cathal J. "Wars are not Won by Military Genius or Decisive Battles." *Aeon*, May 5, 2017, https://aeon.co/ideas/wars-are-not-won-by-military-genius-or-decisive-battles.

O'Shaughnessy, Andrew Jackson. *The Men Who Lost America: British Leadership, the American Revolution, and the Fate of the Empire.* New Haven, CT: Yale University Press, 2013.

Overy, Richard. *A History of War in 100 Battles.* New York: Oxford University Press, 2014, pp. 54–78.

Pancake, John S. *This Destructive War: The British Campaign in the Carolinas, 1780–1782.* Tuscaloosa: University of Alabama Press, 2003.

Pell, John. "Phillip Schuyler: The General as Aristocrat," in George Billias, ed., *George Washington's Generals and Opponents.* New York: De Capo Press, 1994.

Philbrick, Nathaniel. *In the Hurricane's Eye: The Genius of George Washington and the Victory at Yorktown.* New York: Viking, 2018.

Pratt, Fletcher. *The Battles that Changed History.* New York: Dolphin, 1956.

Price, David. *The Road to Assunpink Creek: Liberty's Desperate Hour and the Ten Crucial Days of the American Revolution.* Nashville, TN: Knox Press, 2019.

Price, David. "Perspectives on the Ten Crucial Days of the Revolution." *Journal of the American Revolution,* March 2, 2023, https://allthingsliberty .com/2023/03/perspectives-on-the-ten-crucial-days-of-the-revolution/.

Reagan, Ronald W. "Remarks at the Bicentennial Observance of the Battle of Yorktown in Virginia." October 19, 1981, https://www.reaganlibrary .gov/archives/speech/remarks-bicentennial-observance-battle-yorktown -virginia.

"Report of the Virginia Independence Bicentennial Commission to the Governor and the General Assembly of Virginia," State Document No. 8, Richmond, VA, 1986.

Risch, Erna. *Supplying Washington's Army.* Washington, DC: US Army Center of Military History, 1981.

Rossie, Jonathan. *Politics of Command in the American Revolution.* Syracuse, NY: Syracuse University Press, 1975.

Royster, Charles. *A Revolutionary People at War: The Continental Army and American Character, 1775–1783.* Chapel Hill: University of North Carolina Press, 1986.

Ruddiman, John A. "'A Mere Youth': James Monroe's Revolutionary War." *Journal of the American Revolution,* August 12, 2021, https:// allthingsliberty.com/2021/08/a-mere-youth-james-monroes-revolutionary -war/.

Saberton, Ian. "Cornwallis and the Winter Campaign, January to April, 1781," *Journal of the American Revolution,* April 24, 2020, https:// allthingsliberty.com/2020/04/cornwallis-and-the-winter-campaign -january-to-april-1781.

Saberton, Ian. "Cornwallis and the Autumn Campaign of 1780." *Journal of the American Revolution,* July 18, 2017, https://allthingsliberty.com/2017 /07/cornwallis-autumn-campaign-1780-advance-camden-charlotte/.

Saberton, Ian, ed. *The Cornwallis Papers: The Campaigns of 1780 and 1781 in the Southern Theatre of the American Revolutionary War.* 6 vols. Uckfield: Naval & Military Press, Ltd, 2010.

Schnitzer, Eric, and Don Troiani. *Don Troiani's Campaign to Saratoga - 1777: The Turning Point of the Revolutionary War in Paintings, Artifacts, and Historical Narrative.* Guilford, CT: Stackpole Books, 2019.

Selig, Robert. *March to Victory: Washington, Rochambeau, and the Yorktown Campaign of 1781.* Washington, DC: US Army Center of Military History, 2007.

Seymour, William. *The Price of Folly: British Blunders in the War of American Independence.* London: Brassey's, 1995.

Shachtman, Tom. *How the French Saved America: Soldiers, Sailors, Diplomats, Louis XVI, and the Success of a Revolution.* New York: St Martin's Press, 2017.

Showman, Richard, and Dennis Conrad, eds. *The Papers of General Nathanael Greene,* 13 vols. Chapel Hill: University of North Carolina Press, 1976–2005.

Shy, John. "Charles Lee: The Soldier as Radical," in George Billias, ed., *George Washington's Generals and Opponents.* New York: Da Capo Press, 1994, pp. 22–53.

Simms, Brendan. *Three Victories and a Defeat: The Rise and Fall of the First British Empire.* New York: Basic Books, 2007.

Skinner, Harold Allen Jr. *The Staff Ride Handbook for The Battle for Kings Mountain, 7 October 1780.* Fort Leavenworth, KA: Combat Studies Institute Press, 2020.

Smith, Page. *A New Age Now Begins: A People's History of the American Revolution,* 2 vols. New York: McGraw-Hill, 1976.

Smith, Paul H. "Sir Guy Carleton, Soldier-Statesman" in George Billias, ed., *George Washington's Generals and Opponents.* New York: Da Capo Press, 1994, pp. 103–41.

Smith, Paul H., ed. *Letters of Delegates to Congress, 1774–1789.* 26 vols. Washington, DC: Library of Congress, 1976–2000.

Snow, Dean. *1777: Tipping Point at Saratoga.* New York: Oxford University Press, 2016.

Stevens, Benjamin F., ed. *The Campaign in Virginia, 1781: An Exact Reprint of Six Rare Pamphlets on the Clinton-Cornwallis Controversy.* 2 vols. British Library, Historical Print Editions (London: 1888).

Stewart, David O. *George Washington: The Political Rise of America's Founding Father.* New York: Dutton, 2021.

Tarleton, Banastre. *A History of the Campaigns of 1780 and 1781 in the Southern Provinces of North America.* London: T. Cadell, 1787.

Taylor, Alan. *American Revolutions: A Continental History.* New York: W.W. Norton & Company, 2017.

Thompson, Bob. *Revolutionary Roads: Searching for the War that Made America Independent ... and All the Places It Could Have Gone Terribly Wrong.* New York: Twelve, 2023.

Tonsetic, Robert L. *1781: The Decisive Year of the Revolutionary War.* Havertown, PA: Casemate Publishers, 2011.

Trussell, John. *Birthplace of an Army: A Study of the Valley Forge Encampment.* Harrisburg: Pennsylvania Historical and Museum Commission, 1976.

Tucker, St George. "The Southern Campaign, 1781: From Guilford Courthouse to the Siege of York...", *The Magazine of American History,* 7 (1881).

Vance, Sheilah. "Valley Forge's Threshold: The Encampment at Gulph Mills," *Journal of the American Revolution,* November 5, 2019, https://allthingsliberty.com/2019/11/valley-forges-threshold-the-encampment-at-gulph-mills/.

Ventura, Katelyn J., "The Battle of Cowpens: A Turning Point in the American Revolution," NCO Journal, August 28, 2020, https://www.armyupress.army.mil/Journals/NCO-Journal/Archives/2020/August/Battle-of-Cowpens/#.

Waters, Andrew. *To the End of the World: Nathanael Greene, Charles Cornwallis, and the Race to the Dan.* Yardley, PA: Westholme, 2020.

Weddle, Kevin J. *The Compleat Victory: Saratoga and the American Revolution.* New York: Oxford University Press, 2021.

Weddle, Kevin J. "A Change in Both Men and Measures: British Reassessment of Military Strategy after Saratoga, 1777–1778," *Journal of Military History,* 77 (July 2013): 837–65.

Weigley, Russell F. *The Age of Battles: The Quest for Decisive Warfare from Breitenfeld to Waterloo.* Bloomington: Indiana University Press, 1991.

Welsch, William M. "Christmas Night, 1776: How Did They Cross." *Journal of the American Revolution,* December 24, 2020, https://allthingsliberty.com/2020/12/christmas-night-1776-how-did-they-cross/.

Werther, Richard J. "Victory at Saratoga: Getting the Word Out," *Journal of the American Revolution,* April 20, 2023, https://allthingsliberty.com/2023/04/victory-at-saratoga-getting-the-word-out/.

Wickwire, Franklin and Mary. *Cornwallis: The American Adventure.* Boston, MA: Houghton Mifflin, 1970.

Willcox, William B. *Portrait of a General: Sir Henry Clinton and the War of Independence.* New York: Knopf, 1964.

Willcox, William B., ed. *The American Revolution: Sir Henry Clinton's Narrative of His Campaigns, 1775–1782*. New Haven, CT: Yale University Press, 1954.

Williams, Otho Holland. "A Narrative of the Campaign of 1780," in William Johnson, *Sketches of the Life and Correspondence of Nathanael Greene*. Charleston, SC: A. E. Miller, 1822.

Wood, Gordon S. *The American Revolution: A History*. New York: The Modern Library, 2002.

Wright, Sarah Bird. "The Victory of Yorktown: A Bicentennial Celebration." August 25, 1981, *The Christian Science Monitor*, https://www.csmonitor.com/1981/0825/082547.html.

Notes

INTRODUCTION

1 Allan Mallinson, *The Shape of Battle: The Art of War: From the Battle of Hastings to D-Day and Beyond* (New York: Pegasus Books, 2022), p. 4.

2 Patrick K. O'Donnell, *The Indispensables: The Diverse Soldier-Mariners Who Shaped the Country, Formed the Navy, and Rowed Washington Across Delaware* (New York: Atlantic Monthly Press, 2021); Patrick K. O'Donnell, *Washington's Immortals: The Untold Story of an Elite Regiment Who Changed the Course of the Revolution* (New York: Atlantic Monthly Press, 2016).

3 Jack Watkins, ed., *The Greatest Battles in History: An Encyclopedia of Classic Warfare from Megiddo to Waterloo* (London: Amber Books, 2019).

4 Charles Messenger, *Wars that Changed the World* (London: Quercus, 2019), p. 3; Jeremy Black, ed., *The Seventy Great Battles in History* (London: Thames and Hudson, 2005), p. 13; Richard Overy, *A History of War in 100 Battles* (New York: Oxford University Press, 2014), p. 8.

5 Edward S. Creasy, *The Fifteen Decisive Battles of the World: from Marathon to Waterloo* (New York: A. L. Burt, 1851), pp. xv–xviii.

6 Fletcher Pratt, *The Battles that Changed History* (New York: Dolphin, 1956), pp. 11–14.

7 Winston Churchill, *Marlborough: His Life and Times*, 4 vols. (London: Thornton Butterworth, 1933–38), 2:381. Conversely, author Peter MacLeod offers an incoherent argument that "battles are the wild cards of human history" that are "violent, haphazard, and chaotic," but "however complete a victory they may be, battles change very little." Yet he goes on to write that a few battles "generate military results ... to produce a future that would have been different if that battle had gone the other way." D. Peter MacLeod, *Northern Armageddon: The Plains of*

Abraham and the Making of the American Revolution (New York: Alfred A. Knopf, 2016), pp. 303–04.

8 Michael Mandelbaum, "Decisive Battles, Past and Present," *American Purpose*, June 1, 2022, https://www.americanpurpose.com/articles/decisive-battles-past-and-present/.

9 Cathal J. Nolan, *The Allure of Battle: A History of How Wars Have Been Won and Lost* (New York: Oxford University Press, 2017), pp. 1–3.

10 Nolan, *Allure*, pp. 18–37.

11 Cathal Nolan, "Wars are not Won by Military Genius or Decisive Battles," *Aeon*, May 5, 2017, https://aeon.co/ideas/wars-are-not-won-by-military-genius-or-decisive-battles.

12 Anne Curry, *Great Battles: Agincourt* (Oxford: Oxford University Press, 2015), pp. viii–ix.

13 National Army Museum, "Battle of the Boyne," https://www.nam.ac.uk/explore/battle-boyne.

14 Yuval Noah Harari, "The Concept of 'Decisive Battles' in World History," *Journal of World History*, Vol. 18, No. 3 (Sep. 2007), pp. 251–66.

15 Nolan, *Allure*, pp. 3–4.

16 Curry, *Agincourt*, pp. 36–39, 214.

17 Alan Forrest, *Great Battles: Waterloo* (Oxford: Oxford University Press, 2015), pp. xi–1 [xi–xii].

18 Forrest, *Waterloo*, pp. 3–4.

19 Forrest, *Waterloo*, pp. 28, 66.

20 Rotem Kowner, *Great Battles: Tsushima* (Oxford: Oxford University Press, 2022), p. xiv.

21 Victor Davis Hanson, *Ripples of Battle: How the Wars of the Past Still Determine How We Fight, How We Live, and How We Think* (New York: Doubleday, 2003), pp. 16–17.

22 Forest, *Waterloo*, p. xi.

CHAPTER I

1 David Hackett Fischer, *Washington's Crossing* (New York: Oxford University Press, 2006), pp. 66–73; Andrew Jackson O'Shaughnessy, *The Men Who Lost America: British Leadership, the American Revolution, and the Fate of the Empire* (New Haven, CT: Yale University Press, 2013), p. 89.

2 George Washington to Jonathan Trumbull Sr, April 26, 1776, *Founders Online,* National Archives, https://founders.archives.gov/documents/Washington/03-04-02-0113.

3 Todd W. Braisted, "All London Was Afloat," in Edward G. Lengel, ed., *The 10 Key Campaigns of the American Revolution* (Washington, DC: Regnery Publishing, 2020), pp. 45-64.

4 George Washington to John Hancock, September 25, 1776, *Founders Online,* National Archives, https://founders.archives.gov/documents/Washington/03-06-02-0305.

5 Arthur Lefkowitz, *Long Retreat: The Calamitous American Defense of New Jersey, 1776* (New Brunswick, NJ: Rutgers University Press, 1999), p. 54; John Ferling, *Almost a Miracle: The American Victory in the War of Independence* (New York: Oxford University Press, 2009), p. 164; Nathanael Greene to Nicholas Cooke, December 4, 1776, *The Papers of General Nathanael Greene*, Richard Showman, Dennis Conrad, et. al., eds., 13 vols. (Chapel Hill: University of North Carolina Press, 1976–2005), 1:362 (hereafter cited as *Greene Papers*); Arthur Lefkowitz, *George Washington's Revenge: The 1777 New Jersey Campaign* (New York: Stackpole Books, 2022), p. 6; Nathanael Greene to Christopher Greene, January 20, 1777, *Greene Papers*, 2:8; William Dwyer, *The Day is Ours!: November 1776–January 1777: An Inside View of the Battles of Trenton and Princeton*, New York: Viking Press, 1983), pp. 35, 47–48, 94–100.

6 Robert Dunkerly, *Unhappy Catastrophes: The American Revolution in Central New Jersey, 1776–1782*. (New York: Savas Beatie, 2022), p. 7; Dwyer, *The Day is Ours!*, p. 41.

7 George Washington to John Hancock, November 30, 1776, *Founders Online,* National Archives, https://founders.archives.gov/documents/Washington/03-07-02-0168

8 George Washington to John Hancock, December 1, 1776, *Founders Online,* National Archives, https://founders.archives.gov/documents/Washington/03-07-02-0175.

9 Nathanael Greene to Nicholas Cooke, December 4, 1776, *Greene Papers*, 1:362.

10 Nathanael Greene to Nicholas Cooke, December 4, 1776, *Greene Papers*, 1:362.

11 O'Shaughnessy, *Men Who Lost America*, p. 100.

12 O'Shaughnessy, *Men Who Lost America*, pp. 96–98, 100.

13 Lefkowitz, *Retreat*, p. 148; Fischer, *Crossing*, p. 99; Julie Flavell, *The Howe Dynasty: The Untold Story of a Military Family and the Women Behind Britain's Wars for America* (New York: Liveright, 2021), pp. 166–68; Derrick Long, "The Fall of Fort Washington: The 'Bunker Hill Effect,'" *Journal of the American Revolution*, www.allthingsliberty

.com; Paul Lockhart, *The Whites of Their Eyes: Bunker Hill, the First American Army, and the Emergence of George Washington* (New York: Harper, 2011), p. 311, 376; Huw J. Davies, *The Wandering Army: The Campaigns that Transformed the British Way of War* (New Haven, CT: Yale University Press, 2022), p. 120. Flavell's assertion that most historians dismiss the suggestion of the effect on Howe ignores much quality scholarship.

14 David Smith, *Whispers Across the Atlantick: General William Howe and the American Revolution* (London: Osprey, 2017), pp. 157–58.

15 William M. Welsch, "Christmas Night, 1776: How Did They Cross," *Journal of the American Revolution*, December 24, 2020, https://allthingsliberty.com/2020/12/christmas-night-1776-how-did-they-cross/.

16 Lefkowitz, *Retreat*, pp. 120–21; Edward Lengel, *General George Washington: A Military Life* (New York: Random House, 2005), p. 171; William Seymour, *The Price of Folly: British Blunders in the War of American Independence* (London: Brassey's, 1995), p. 77; Dwyer, *The Day is Ours!*, pp. 107–09.

17 Craig Nelson, *Thomas Paine: Enlightenment, Revolution, and the Birth of Modern Nations* (New York: Penguin Books, 2007), pp. 107–09.

18 Dwyer, *The Day is Ours!*, p. 107; O'Shaughnessy, *Men Who Lost America*, p. 96.

19 Washington's Orders to Brigadier General James Ewing, December 12, 1776, *Founders Online,* National Archives, https://founders.archives.gov/documents/Washington/03-07-02-0242.

20 John Shy, "Charles Lee: The Soldier as Radical," in George Billias, ed., *George Washington's Generals and Opponents* (New York: DeCapo Press, 1994), pp. 22–53; Christian McBurney, *George Washington's Nemesis: The Outrageous Treason and Unfair Court-martial of Major General Charles Lee during the American Revolution* (El Dorado, CA: Savas Beatie, 2019), pp. 31–40.

21 Harrison Clark, *All Cloudless Glory: The Life of George Washington* (Washington, DC: Regnery, 1995), pp. 294–301, 303; McBurney, *Washington's Nemesis*, pp. 45–48; Shy, "Charles Lee," pp. 22–53; John Sullivan to George Washington, December 13, 1776, *Founders Online,* National Archives, https://founders.archives.gov/documents/Washington/03-07-02-0261.

22 Seymour, *Folly*, p. 75; William B. Willcox, *Portrait of a General: Sir Henry Clinton and the War of Independence* (New York: Knopf, 1964), pp. 118–20.

23 These hired troops came from several German states but since most of them were hired from Hesse-Kassel, they were all commonly referred to as "Hessians."

24 O'Shaughnessy, *Men Who Lost America*, p. 115; Lengel, *General*, p. 175.

25 Nathanael Greene to Catherine Greene, December 16, 1776, *Greene Papers*, 1:368.

26 Friederike Baer, *Hessians: German Soldiers in the American Revolutionary War* (London: Oxford University Press, 2022), pp. 6, 21.

27 George Washington to Samuel Washington, December 18, 1776, *Founders Online*, National Archives, https://founders.archives.gov /documents/Washington/03-07-02-0299.

28 Nathanael Greene to Catherine Greene, December 16, 1776, *Greene Papers*, 1:368.

29 Nathanael Greene to John Hancock, December 21, 1776, *Greene Papers*, 1:370.

30 Lefkowitz, *Retreat*, p. 123.

31 George Washington to Samuel Washington, December 18, 1776, *Founders Online*, National Archives, https://founders.archives.gov /documents/Washington/03-07-02-0299.

32 Clark, *All Cloudless Glory*, p. 301.

33 James K. Martin and David L. Preston, *Theaters of the American Revolution: Northern, Middle, Southern, Western, Naval* (Yardley, PA: Westholme Publishing, 2017), p. 64.

34 Don Higginbotham, *The War of American Independence: Military Attitudes, Policies, and Practice, 1763–1789* (Boston: Northeastern University Press, 1983), p. 166.

35 George Washington to Samuel Washington, December 18, 1776, *Founders Online*, National Archives, https://founders.archives.gov /documents/Washington/03-07-02-0299.

36 Stephen Brumwell, *George Washington, Gentleman Warrior* (London: Quercus, 2013), p. 270.

37 Lengel, *General George Washington*, p. 178; Brumwell, *Gentleman Warrior*, pp. 274–75.

38 George Washington to Joseph Reed, December 23, 1776, *Founders Online*, National Archives, https://founders.archives.gov/documents/ Washington/03-07-02-0329.

39 George Washington to Joseph Reed, December 23, 1776, *Founders Online*, National Archives, https://founders.archives.gov/documents/ Washington/03-07-02-0329; George Washington to John Cadwalader,

December 24, 1776, *Founders Online*, National Archives, https://
founders.archives.gov/documents/Washington/03-07-02-0332.

40 William L. Kidder, *Ten Crucial Days: Washington's Vision for Victory
Unfolds* (Nashville, TN: Knox Press, 2019), pp. 84–100; Mark Malloy,
*Victory or Death: The Battles of Trenton and Princeton, December
25, 1776–January 3, 1777* (El Dorado, CA, Savas Beatie, 2017),
pp. 30–31; Brumwell, *Gentleman Warrior*, pp. 274–77; Thomas Paine,
The American Crisis, December 1776, Library of Congress Prints and
Photographs Division, https://www.loc.gov/resource/cph.3b06889/.

41 Dwyer, *The Day Is Ours!*, p. 227.

42 Nathanael Greene to Nicholas Cooke, January 10, 1777, *Greene Papers*,
2:4.

43 Kidder, *Ten Crucial Days*, pp. 93, 105–06; Malloy, *Victory*, p. 39.

44 North Callahan, "Henry Knox: American Artillerist," in George Billias,
ed., *George Washington's Generals and Opponents* (New York: DeCapo
Press, 1994), p. 246; Dwyer, *The Day Is Ours!*, p. 232.

45 Dwyer, *The Day Is Ours!*, p. 238.

46 George Washington to John Hancock, 27 December 1776, *Founders
Online*, National Archives, https://founders.archives.gov/documents/
Washington/03-07-02-0355.

47 Kidder, *Ten Crucial Days*, pp. 121, 124.

48 Malloy, *Victory*, pp. 37–38; Lefkowitz, *Washington's Revenge*, pp. 57–58;
William L. Kidder, "The Times That Try Men's Souls," in Edward
G. Lengel, ed., *The 10 Key Campaigns of the American Revolution*,
(Washington, DC: Regnery Publishing, 2020), pp. 69, 72.

49 Fischer, *Crossing*, pp. 234–46, 254; Dwyer, *The Day is Ours!*, p. 252;
George Washington to John Hancock, December 27, 1776, *Founders
Online*, National Archives, https://founders.archives.gov/documents/
Washington/03-07-02-0355.

50 John A. Ruddiman, "'A Mere Youth': James Monroe's Revolutionary
War, *Journal of the American Revolution*, August 12, 2021, https://
allthingsliberty.com/2021/08/a-mere-youth-james-monroes
-revolutionary-war/; Dwyer, *The Day is Ours!*, p. 255.

51 Dwyer, *The Day is Ours!*, p. 263.

52 General Orders, December 27, 1776, *Founders Online*, National
Archives, https://founders.archives.gov/documents/Washington/03-07
-02-0351.

53 George Washington to William Maxwell, December 28, 1776, *Founders
Online*, National Archives, https://founders.archives.gov/documents/
Washington/03-07-02-0367.

54 George Washington to John Cadwalader, December 27, 1776, *Founders Online,* National Archives, https://founders.archives.gov/documents/Washington/03-07-02-0352.

55 George Washington to John Cadwalader, December 27, 1776, *Founders Online,* National Archives, https://founders.archives.gov/documents/Washington/03-07-02-0352.

56 Ferling, *Miracle*, p. 179; John Cadwalader to George Washington, December 27, 1776, *Founders Online,* National Archives, https://founders.archives.gov/documents/Washington/03-07-02-0353.

57 George Washington to Robert Morris, December 31, 1776, *Founders Online,* National Archives, https://founders.archives.gov/documents/Washington/03-07-02-0389.

58 George Washington to the Executive Committee of the Continental Congress, January 1, 1777, *Founders Online,* National Archives, https://founders.archives.gov/documents/Washington/03-07-02-0395.

59 George Washington to John Hancock, January 1, 1777, *Founders Online,* National Archives, https://founders.archives.gov/documents/Washington/03-07-02-0398.

60 George Washington to John Hancock, January 5, 1777, *Founders Online,* National Archives, https://founders.archives.gov/documents/Washington/03-07-02-0411; Terry Golway, *Washington's General: Nathanael Greene and the Triumph of the American Revolution* (New York: Henry Holt, 2006), p. 115.

61 Malloy, *Victory*, p. 102.

62 George Washington to John Hancock, January 5, 1777, *Founders Online,* National Archives, https://founders.archives.gov/documents/Washington/03-07-02-0411.

63 David Price, *The Road to Assunpink Creek: Liberty's Desperate Hour and the Ten Crucial Days of the American Revolution* (Nashville, TN: Knox Press, 2019), p. 124.

64 George Washington to John Hancock, January 5, 1777, *Founders Online,* National Archives, https://founders.archives.gov/documents/Washington/03-07-02-0411; George Washington to the Executive Committee of the Continental Congress, January 1, 1777, *Founders Online,* National Archives, https://founders.archives.gov/documents/Washington/03-07-02-0395.

65 Nathanael Greene to Nicholas Cooke, January 10, 1777, *Greene Papers,* 2:4.

66 George Washington to the New York Committee of Safety, January 5, 1777, *Founders Online,* National Archives, https://founders.archives

.gov/documents/Washington/03-07-02-0414; Lengel, *General George Washington*, pp. 204-05.

67 Kidder, *Ten Crucial Days*, p. 321.

68 George Washington to John Hancock, January 7, 1777, *Founders Online,* National Archives, https://founders.archives.gov/documents/Washington/03-08-02-0008; Lengel, *General George Washington,* pp. 206-08; George Washington to William Heath, January 5, 1777, *Founders Online,* National Archives, https://founders.archives.gov/documents/Washington/03-07-02-0412. Washington briefly considered an immediate attack upon Brunswick but, concluding his troops were thoroughly worn out, abandoned this possibility.

69 George Washington to Israel Putnam, January 5, 1777, *Founders Online,* National Archives, https://founders.archives.gov/documents/Washington/03-07-02-0416.

70 George Washington to Nicholas Cooke, January 20, 1777, *Founders Online,* National Archives, https://founders.archives.gov/documents/Washington/03-08-02-0121.

71 George Washington to Nicholas Cooke, 20 January 1777, *Founders Online,* National Archives, https://founders.archives.gov/documents/Washington/03-08-02-0121.

72 Malloy, *Victory*, p. 150.

73 Price, *Assunpink Creek,* pp. 8, 49, 165.

74 Lengel, *Washington*, p. 209.

75 Fischer, *Crossing*, pp. 263, 346–67.

76 James Kirby Martin and Mark E. Lender, *A Respectable Army: The Military Origins of the Republic, 1763–1789* (Arlington Heights, IL: Harlan Davidson, 1982), p. 60.

77 Brumwell, *Gentleman Warrior*, p. 283; Malloy, *Victory*, p. 143; Price, *Assunpink Creek,* p. 169; Fischer, *Crossing*, p. 360.

78 Lengel, *Washington*, p. 210.

79 Lengel, *Washington*, p. 210.

80 Rick Atkinson, *The British Are Coming: The War for America, Lexington to Princeton, 1775–1777* (New York: Henry Holt and Company, 2019), p. 551.

81 Malloy, *Victory*, p. 144.

82 Ferling, *Miracle*, p. 178.

83 David Price, "Perspectives on the Ten Crucial Days of the Revolution," *Journal of the American Revolution*, March 2, 2023, https://allthingsliberty.com/2023/03/perspectives-on-the-ten-crucial-days-of-the-revolution/.

84 Kidder, *Ten Crucial Days*, p. 334; Julie M. Fenster, *Jefferson's America: The President, the Purchase, and the Explorers who Transformed a Nation* (New York: Crown Publishing, 2017), p. 138.

85 Price, "Perspectives," *Journal of the American Revolution*, March 2, 2023, https://allthingsliberty.com/2023/03/perspectives-on-the-ten-crucial-days-of-the-revolution/; Fischer, *Crossing*, 346-67; Malloy, *Victory*, p. 146.

86 Lengel, *Washington*, p. 209.

87 Brumwell, *Gentleman Warrior*, p. 294–95.

88 Ferling, *Miracle*, p. 180.

89 Atkinson, *British Are Coming*, p. 560.

90 Smith, *Whispers*, p. 184.

91 Lefkowitz, *Revenge*, p.131.

92 Kidder, *Ten Crucial Days*, p. 336.

93 Martin and Lender, *A Respectable Army*, p. 62.

94 Thomas Paine, "The American Crisis," *Writings of Thomas Paine*, Number V, Vol. I, March 21, 1778, Project Gutenberg, https://www.gutenberg.org/files/3741/3741-h/3741-h.htm#link2H_4_0009.

95 Maloy, *Victory or Death*, p. 51.

96 David Price, "Perspectives," *Journal of the American Revolution*, March 2, 2023, https://allthingsliberty.com/2023/03/perspectives-on-the-ten-crucial-days-of-the-revolution/

97 George Washington to Nicholas Cooke, January 20, 1777, *Founders Online*, National Archives, https://founders.archives.gov/documents/Washington/03-08-02-0121.

CHAPTER 2

1 Alan Taylor, *American Revolutions: A Continental History* (New York: W.W. Norton & Company, 2017), p. 178.

2 George Billias, "Horatio Gates, Professional Soldier," in Billias, *Generals and Opponents*, I, pp. 79–108.

3 John Pell, "Phillip Schuyler: The General as Aristocrat," in Billias, *Generals and Opponents*, I, p. 63; John Luzader, *Saratoga: A Military History of the Decisive Campaign of the American Revolution* (El Dorado Hills, CA: Savas Beatie, 2014), pp. 142–43, 154–57; Jonathan Rossie, *Politics of Command in the American Revolution* (Syracuse, NY: Syracuse University Press, 1975), p. x.

4 Anthony Wayne to Benjamin Franklin, November 15, 1776, *Founders Online*, National Archives, https://founders.archives.gov/documents/Franklin/01-23-02-0004.

5   Kevin J. Weddle, *The Compleat Victory: Saratoga and the American Revolution* (New York: Oxford University Press, 2021), pp. 51–52.

6   Schnitzer and Troiani, *Saratoga*, pp. 14–17; Douglas Cubbison, *Burgoyne and the Saratoga Campaign: His Papers* (Norman, OK: The Arthur H. Clark Company, 2012), pp. 179–80, 183–86.

7   Cubbison, *Burgoyne*, p. 184; Schnitzer and Troiani, *Saratoga*, p. 16.

8   Willcox, *Clinton*, p. 144; Cubbison, *Burgoyne*, pp. 36–37.

9   Cubbison, *Burgoyne*, pp. 265–74.

10 Four other British foot regiments remained in Canada during the Saratoga Campaign under Carleton's command.

11 Cubbison, *Burgoyne*, p. 205.

12 Philip Schuyler to George Washington, June 28, 1777, *Founders Online*, National Archives, https://founders.archives.gov/documents/Washington/03-10-02-0141.

13 Schnitzer and Troiani, *Saratoga*, p. 44; John Burgoyne to Lord Germain, July 11, 1777; Cubbison, *Burgoyne*, p. 267.

14 Schnitzer and Troiani, *Saratoga*, pp. 46–48; Luzader, *Saratoga*, pp. 47–48, 55–56; Philip Schuyler to George Washington, July 14, 1777, *Founders Online*, National Archives, https://founders.archives.gov/documents/Washington/03-10-02-0273.

15 Schnitzer and Troiani, *Saratoga*, pp. 52–58; Luzader, *Saratoga*, pp. 60–67.

16 Philip Schuyler to George Washington, July 9, 1777, *Founders Online*, National Archives, https://founders.archives.gov/documents/Washington/03-10-02-0226.

17 Philip Schuyler to George Washington, July 9, 1777, *Founders Online*, National Archives, https://founders.archives.gov/documents/Washington/03-10-02-0226; Philip Schuyler to George Washington, July 26–27, 1777; *Founders Online*, National Archives, https://founders.archives.gov/documents/Washington/03-10-02-0422.

18 Philip Schuyler to George Washington, July 14, 1777, *Founders Online*, National Archives, https://founders.archives.gov/documents/Washington/03-10-02-0273.

19 Cubbison, *Burgoyne*, pp. 219–21.

20 Philip Schuyler to George Washington, July 9, 1777, *Founders Online*, National Archives, https://founders.archives.gov/documents/Washington/03-10-02-0226.

21 Philip Schuyler to John Jay, July 27, 1777, *Founders Online*, National Archives, https://founders.archives.gov/documents/Jay/01-01-02-0264; John Burgoyne to Lord Germain, July 30, 1777, Cubbison, *Burgoyne*, pp. 275–76.

22 George Washington to Philip Schuyler, August 10, 1777, *Founders Online*, National Archives, https://founders.archives.gov/documents/Washington/03-10-02-0570; Philip Schuyler to John Jay, July 27, 1777, *Founders Online*, National Archives, https://founders.archives.gov/documents/Jay/01-01-02-0264; Philip Schuyler to George Washington, July 28, 1777, *Founders Online*, National Archives, https://founders.archives.gov/documents/Washington/03-10-02-0445.

23 Schnitzer and Troiani, *Saratoga*, p. 113.

24 Burgoyne's orders for Baum instructed him to bring the captured supplies, horses and vehicles to Albany, where he would meet the main army, which indicates the level of confidence Burgoyne still maintained at this point.

25 Michael P. Gabriel, *The Battle of Bennington: Soldiers and Civilians* (Charleston, SC: The History Press, 2012), pp. 18–20.

26 Schnitzer and Troiani, *Saratoga*, pp. 90, 93, 118–37; Gabriel, *Bennington*, pp. 26–28; Philip Schuyler to George Washington, August 19, 1777, *Founders Online*, National Archives, https://founders.archives.gov/documents/Washington/03-11-02-0008.

27 John Burgoyne to Lord Germain, August 20, 1777; Cubbison, *Burgoyne*, p. 302.

28 John Burgoyne to Lord Germain, July 30, 1777; Cubbison, *Burgoyne*, p. 275.

29 John Butler to Guy Carleton, August 15, 1777; Cubbison, *Burgoyne*, p. 285.

30 Schnitzer and Troiani, *Saratoga*, p. 146; Ludzader, *Saratoga*, p. 133; George Clinton to George Washington, August 13, 1777, *Founders Online*, National Archives, https://founders.archives.gov/documents/Washington/03-10-02-0592.

31 Schnitzer and Troiani, *Saratoga*, p. 149; Michael Barbieri, "Brown's Raid on Ticonderoga and Mount Independence," *Journal of the American Revolution*, January 20, 2022, https://allthingsliberty.com/2022/01/browns-raid-on-ticonderoga-and-mount-independence/.

32 Luzader, *Saratoga*, p. 249.

33 Schnitzer and Troiani, *Saratoga*, p. 187.

34 Schnitzer and Troiani, *Saratoga*, pp. 189–93; Weddle, *Compleat Victory*, pp. 282–85; John Luzader, *Decision on the Hudson: The Battles of Saratoga* (Fort Washington, PA: Eastern National, 2002), p. 43.

35 Schnitzer and Troiani, *Saratoga*, p. 190; Weddle, *Compleat Victory*, p. 284.

36 Schnitzer and Troiani, *Saratoga*, p. 204.

37 Horatio Gates to George Washington, October 5, 1777, *Founders Online,* National Archives, https://founders.archives.gov/documents/Washington/03-11-02-0418.

38 Cubbison, *Saratoga,* p. 315; Theodore Corbett, *No Turning Point: The Saratoga Campaign in Perspective* (Norman: University of Oklahoma Press, 2012), p. 221.

39 Michael C. Harris, "The Empire Strikes Back: The Philadelphia Campaign 1777," in Edward Lengel, ed., *10 Key Campaigns of the American Revolution* (Washington, DC: Regnery Publishing, 2020), pp. 111–128.

40 Schnitzer and Troiani, *Saratoga,* pp. 212, 221; Dean Snow, *1777: Tipping Point at Saratoga* (New York: Oxford University Press, 2016), p. 287.

41 Schnitzer and Troiani, *Saratoga,* pp. 199–204, 215.

42 Schnitzer and Troiani, *Saratoga,* p. 227; Weddle, *Compleat Victory,* pp. 308–09, 318–19.

43 Horatio Gates to George Washington, October 5, 1777, *Founders Online,* National Archives, https://founders.archives.gov/documents/Washington/03-11-02-0418.

44 Schnitzer and Troiani, *Saratoga,* pp. 232–33.

45 Horatio Gates to John Hancock, October 12, 1777, Digital Public Library of America, https://dp.la/primary-source-sets/revolutionary-war-turning-points-saratoga-and-valley-forge/sources/1371.

46 Schnitzer and Troiani, *Saratoga,* p. 224; Corbett, *No Turning Point,* pp. 237–42; Weddle, *Compleat Victory,* pp. 302–04. The opposing commanders signed a "convention," not a capitulation, which stipulated that Burgoyne's army would be shipped to Great Britain with the promise that these troops would not serve again in America. However, it did not bar the British from using these soldiers to replace garrisons in Europe, which could then in turn be sent to America. Congress later balked at these terms and eventually found excuses not to honor these unusual conditions. See also Richard J. Werther, "Victory at Saratoga: Getting the Word Out," *Journal of the American Revolution,* April 20, 2023, https://allthingsliberty.com/2023/04/victory-at-saratoga-getting-the-word-out/.

47 James Wilkinson to George Washington, October 24, 1777, *Founders Online,* National Archives, https://founders.archives.gov/documents/Washington/03-11-02-0618.

48 Gates's letter to Hancock is reported in Charles Thomson to George Washington, October 31, 1777, *Founders Online,* National Archives, https://founders.archives.gov/documents/Washington/03-12-02 -0066.

49 Gordon S. Wood, *The American Revolution: A History* (New York: The Modern Library, 2002), p. 81.

50 Ferling, *Miracle,* p. 259; Kevin J. Weddle, "A Change in Both Men and Measures: British Reassessment of Military Strategy after Saratoga, 1777–1778," *Journal of Military History* 77 (July 2013): 837–65.

51 Tom Shachtman, *How the French Saved America: Soldiers, Sailors, Diplomats, Louis XVI, and the Success of a Revolution* (New York: St Martin's Press, 2017), p. 114; Brendan Simms, *Three Victories and a Defeat: The Rise and Fall of the First British Empire* (New York: Basic Books, 2007), pp. 610–11; John Ferling, *Winning Independence: The Decisive Years of the Revolutionary War, 1778–1781* (New York: Bloomsbury Publishing, 2021), p. 53.

52 Piers Mackesy, *The War for America, 1775–1783* (Lincoln: University of Nebraska Press, 1992 repr.), pp. 154–56.

53 Weddle, "Men and Measures," p. 845.

54 Mackesy, *War for America,* pp. 157–59.

55 Mackesy, *War for America,* p. 141; Ferling, *Miracle,* p. 260; Shachtman, *French,* p. 115; Larrie Ferreiro, *Brothers in Arms: American Independence and the Men of France and Spain Who Saved It* (New York: Vintage Books, 2017), p. 96; The American Commissioners: A Public Announcement, December 4, 1777, *Founders Online,* National Archives, https://founders.archives.gov/documents/Franklin/01-25-02 -0166.

56 Ferreiro, *Brothers in Arms,* pp. 89–91.

57 O'Shaughnessy, *The Men Who Lost America,* p. 14.

58 Weddle, *Compleat Victory,* pp. 354–58.

59 Wayne K. Bodle, *The Valley Forge Winter: Civilians and Soldiers in War* (University Park, PA: Pennsylvania State University Press, 2002), p. 96.

60 Quintin Barry, *Crisis at the Chesapeake: The Royal Navy and the Struggle for America 1775–1783* (Warwick, UK: Helion & Co, 2021), p. 44.

61 Barry, *Crisis at the Chesapeake,* p. 44.

62 Ferriero, *Brothers in Arms,* p. 171.

63 Mackesy, *War for America,* p. 141, 147.

64 Ferreiro, *Brothers in Arms*, p. 101.

65 "A Long-Lost Letter Penned by George Washington During the Revolutionary War Hits the Market for $275,000," *Artnet News*, October 2, 2023, https://news.artnet.com/market/george-washington -revolutionary-war-letter-for-sale-2369895/amp-page; George Washington to Landon Carter, October 27, 1777, *Founders Online,* National Archives, https://founders.archives.gov/documents/Washington/03-12-02-0018.

CHAPTER 3

1 George Washington to the Convention of New Hampshire, December 29, 1777, the Gilder Lehrman Institute of American History, https:// www.gilderlehrman.org/news/george-washington-writes-valley-forge -day-december-29-1777.

2 Ricardo A. Herrera, Feeding Washington's Army: Surviving the Valley Forge Winter of 1778 (Chapel Hill: University of North Carolina Press, 2022), p. I.; John Laurens, *The Army Correspondence of Colonel John Laurens in the Years 1777–8* (New York: The Bradford Club, 1867), pp. 93–94.

3 Ricardo A. Herrera, "'Our Army will Hut this Winter at Valley Forge': George Washington, Decision Making, and the Councils of War," *Army History*, Fall 2020, pp. 6–26; Lengel, *Washington*, p. 266.

4 Nathanael Greene to George Washington, December 3, 1777, *Greene Papers*, 2:231.

5 Herrera, "'Our Army,'" pp. 6–26.

6 John Laurens, *The Army Correspondence of Colonel John Laurens in the Years 1777–8* (New York: The Bradford Club, 1867), pp. 93–94; General Orders, December 17, 1777, *Founders Online,* National Archives, https://founders.archives.gov/documents/Washington/03-12 -02-0566; Sheilah Vance, "Valley Forge's Threshold: The Encampment at Gulph Mills," *Journal of the American Revolution*, November 5, 2019, https://allthingsliberty.com/2019/11/valley-forges-threshold-the -encampment-at-gulph-mills/.

7 Greenwalt, *Valley Forge*, p. 24. The figure of 11,000 and 14,000 is commonly given by authors for the number of troops that entered the winter encampment at Valley Forge. A recent assessment, however, puts the figure at "roughly 19,000 soldiers." Michael C. Harris and Gary Ecelbarger, "Continental Army Numerical Strength at Valley Forge," *Journal of the American Revolution*, May 18, 2021, https:// allthingsliberty.com/2021/05/a-reconsideration-of-continental-army -numerical-strength-at-valley-forge/.

8 Greenwalt, *Valley Forge*, p. 28.

9 Greenwalt, *Valley Forge*, p. 31; Martin and Lender, *Respectable Army*, p. 100; Bodle, *Valley Forge Winter*, p. 103.

10 General Orders, December 18, 1777, *Founders Online,* National Archives, https://founders.archives.gov/documents/Washington/03-12-02-0573.

11 General Orders, December 18, 1777, *Founders Online,* National Archives, https://founders.archives.gov/documents/Washington/03-12-02-0573.

12 John Trussell, *Birthplace of an Army: A Study of the Valley Forge Encampment* (Harrisburg: Pennsylvania Historical and Museum Commission, 1976), p. 18.

13 Trussell, *Birthplace*, p. 20–21.

14 Trussell, *Birthplace*, p. 38; John Buchanan, *The Road to Valley Forge: How Washington Built the Army that Won the Revolution* (Hoboken, NJ: John Wiley & Sons, 2004), p. 286.

15 Greenwalt, *Valley Forge*, p. 36.

16 George Washington to Patrick Henry, December 19, 1777, *Founders Online,* National Archives, https://founders.archives.gov/documents/Washington/03-12-02-0579.

17 George Washington to Patrick Henry, December 27, 1777, *Founders Online,* National Archives, https://founders.archives.gov/documents/Washington/03-13-02-0015.

18 Nathanael Greene to Nicholas Cooke, January 13, 1778, *Greene Papers*, 2:255.

19 Nathanael Greene to Nicholas Cooke, January 13, 1778, *Greene Papers*, 2:255.

20 George Washington to Thomas Wharton, Jr., February 10, 1778, Founders Online, National Archives, https://founders.archives.gov/documents/Washington/03-13-02-0423.

21 Trussell, *Birthplace*, p. 27.

22 Trussell, *Birthplace*, p. 30.

23 Nathanael Greene to Alexander McDougall, January 25, 1778, *Greene Papers*, 2:261.

24 Trussell, *Birthplace*, p. 23, 32; Buchanan, *Valley Forge*, p. 287; George Washington to Israel Putnam, February 6, 1778, *Founders Online,* National Archives, https://founders.archives.gov/documents/Washington/03-13-02-0382.

25 George Washington to William Buchanan, February 7, 1778, *Founders Online,* National Archives, https://founders.archives.gov/documents/Washington/03-13-02-0385.

26 James Varnum to Nathanael Greene, February 12, 1778, Richard K, Showman, et.al., eds., *The Papers of General Nathanael*

Greene, 13 vols. (Chapel Hill: University of North Carolina Press, 1976–2005) 2:280.

27 Herrera, Feeding Washington's Army, p. 75.

28 George Washington to Jonathan Trumble, Sr, February 6, 1777, *Founders Online,* National Archives, https://founders.archives.gov /documents/Washington/03-13-02-0383.

29 George Washington to George Clinton, February 16, 1778, *Founders Online,* National Archives, https://founders.archives.gov/documents/ Washington/03-13-02-0466.

30 George Washington to Patrick Henry, February 19, 1778, *Founders Online,* National Archives, https://founders.archives.gov/documents/ Washington/03-13-02-0503.

31 John R. Maass, "'Too Grievous for a People to Bear': Impressment and Conscription in Revolutionary North Carolina," *Journal of Military History,* 73 (October 2009): 1091–115.

32 Nathanael Greene to Nicholas Cooke, July 10/11, 1777, *Greene Papers,* 2:118.

33 Nathanael Greene to Alexander McDougall, January 25, 1778, *Greene Papers,* 2:261; Tench Tilghman to Clement Biddle, March 5, 1778, *Writings from the Valley Forge Encampment of the Continental Army,* 6 vols. (Berwyn Heights, MD: Heritage Books, 2000-7), 4:75; Chris McNab, *The Improbable Victory: The Campaigns, Battles and Soldiers of the American Revolution, 1775–83* (Oxford: Osprey Publishing, 2017), p. 121.

34 Washington's General Orders, 8 February 1778, *Founders Online,* National Archives, https://founders.archives.gov/documents/ Washington/03-13-02-0392.

35 George Washington to Nathanael Greene, February 12, 1778, *Greene Papers,* 2:281.

36 Buchanan, *Valley Forge,* pp. 287–88.

37 Nathanael Greene to George Washington, February 15, 1778, *Greene Papers,* 2:285.

38 Nathanael Greene to Henry Knox, February 26, 1778, *Greene Papers,* 2:293.

39 Trussell, *Birthplace,* p. 33; Risch, *Washington's Army,* p. 7, 123.

40 Ebeneezer Mack, *The Life of Gen. Gilbert Motier de Lafayette...* (Utica, NY: G.G. Brooks, 1859), p. 59.

41 Martin and Lender, *Respectable Army,* pp. 103–06.

42 Nathanael Greene to Jacob Greene, March 17, 1778, *Greene Papers,* 2:318; Nathanael Greene to Henry Laurens, January 12, 1778, *Greene Papers,* 2:252.

43 Martin and Lender, *Respectable Army*, pp. 107–110.

44 Charles Royster, *A Revolutionary People at War: The Continental Army and American Character, 1775–1783* (Chapel Hill: University of North Carolina Press, 1986), p. 186.

45 Risch, *Washington's Army*, pp. 24, 207.

46 E. Wayne Carp, *To Starve the Army with Pleasure: Continental Army Administration and American Political Culture, 1775–1783* (Chapel Hill: University of North Carolina Press, 1984), p. 43.

47 William Buchanan to George Washington, July 19, 1794, *Founders Online,* National Archives, https://founders.archives.gov/documents /Washington/05-16-02-0295; David O. Stewart, *George Washington: The Political Rise of America's Founding Father* (New York: Dutton, 2021), p. 227.

48 Risch, *Washington's Army*, p. 45.

49 George Washington to Patrick Henry, December 27, 1777, *Founders Online,* National Archives, https://founders.archives.gov/documents/ Washington/03-13-02-0015.

50 George Washington to Henry Laurens, December 22, 1777, *Founders Online,* National Archives, https://founders.archives.gov/documents/ Washington/03-12-02-0611.

51 George Washington to Jonathan Trumbull, Sr, February 6, 1778, *Founders Online,* National Archives, https://founders.archives.gov /documents/Washington/03-13-02-0383.

52 George Washington to Henry Laurens, December 23, 1777, *Founders Online,* National Archives, https://founders.archives.gov/documents/ Washington/03-12-02-0628.

53 Stewart, *Washington*, pp. 244–45; Bodle, *Winter*, p. 145.

54 Nathanael Greene to Henry Knox, February 26, 1778, *Greene Papers*, 2:293; Wright, *Continental Army*, pp. 125.

55 Nathanael Greene to William Greene, March 7, 1778, *Greene Papers*, 2:301.

56 Carp, *To Starve the Army*, p. 45; Risch, *Washington's Army*, p. 42.

57 Greenwalt, *Valley Forge*, pp. 62–65.

58 Carp, *To Starve the Army*, p. 49.

59 Mark E. Lender, *Cabal!: The Plot Against General Washington* (Yardley, PA: Westholme, 2019), pp. 109–10; James R. Gaines, *For Liberty and Glory: Washington, Lafayette, and their Revolutions* (New York, W. W. Norton 2009), p. 78; Stewart, *Washington*, p. 233.

60 Lender, *Fatal Sunday*, pp. 34–39; George Washington to Horatio Gates, February 9, 1778, *Founders Online,* National

Archives, https://founders.archives.gov/documents/Washington/03
-13-02-0404.

61 Bernhard Knollenberg, *Washington and the Revolution, a Reappraisal: Gates, Conway, and the Continental Congress* (New York: Macmillan, 1940), passim; https://founders.archives.gov/documents/Washington/03-15-02-0278.

62 Lender, *Cabal!*, pp. xvii, 109, 138.

63 Trussell, *Birthplace*, pp. 101–02.

64 Nathanael Greene to Alexander McDougall, January 25, 1778, *Greene Papers*, 2:260.

65 Nathanael Greene to Jacob Greene, February 7, 1778, *Greene Papers*, 2:277.

66 Kenneth Schaffel, "The American Board of War, 1776–1781," *Military Affairs*, Vol. 50, No. 4 (October 1986), pp. 185–89. George Washington to Landon Carter, May 30, 1778, *Founders Online*, National Archives, https://founders.archives.gov/documents/Washington/03-15-02-0278.

67 Paul Lockhart, *The Drillmaster of Valley Forge: The Baron de Steuben and the Making of the American Army* (New York: Harper Collins, 2008), p. 88.

68 Martin and Lender, *Respectable Army*, p. 114.

69 Martin and Lender, *Respectable Army*, p. 114.

70 Trussell, *Birthplace*, p. 61.

71 Lockhart, *Drillmaster*, pp. 97, 106.

72 Lockhart, *Drillmaster*, pp. 72, 110.

73 George Washington to von Steuben, February 26, 1779, The American Revolution Institute, https://www.americanrevolutioninstitute.org/steubens-blue-book-manual/.

74 George Washington to von Steuben, February 26, 1779, The American Revolution Institute.

75 Royster, *Revolutionary People*, p. 218.

76 Royster, *Revolutionary People*, p. 214.

77 George Washington to Baron von Steuben, December 23, 1783, *Founders Online*, National Archives, https://founders.archives.gov/documents/Washington/99-01-02-12226.

78 George Washington to Thomas Johnson, May 17, 1778, *Founders Online*, National Archives, https://founders.archives.gov/documents/Washington/03-15-02-0139.

79 George Washington to Benjamin Franklin, 28 December 1778, *Founders Online*, National Archives, https://founders.archives.gov/documents/Washington/03-18-02-0584.

80 Lockhart, *Drillmaster*, p. 125.

81 Lengel, *General George Washington*, pp. 285, 291; Mark E. Lender and Gary W. Stone, *Fatal Sunday: George Washington, the Monmouth Campaign, and the Politics of Battle* (Norman: University of Oklahoma Press, 2016) p. 441.

82 George Washington to William Maxwell, May 25, 1778, *Founders Online,* National Archives, https://founders.archives.gov/documents/Washington/03-15-02-0222.

83 George Washington to Henry Laurens, June 28, 1778, *Founders Online,* National Archives, https://founders.archives.gov/documents/Washington/03-15-02-0620: George Washington to Horatio Gates, June 28, 1778, *Founders Online,* National Archives, https://founders.archives.gov/documents/Washington/03-15-02-0619; Nathanael Greene to Jacob Greene, July 2, 1778, *Greene Papers,* 2:450; George Washington to Horatio Gates, June 29, 1778, *Founders Online,* National Archives, https://founders.archives.gov/documents/Washington/03-15-02-0636.

84 Lengel, *General George Washington*, p. 304.

85 NPS "What Happened at Valley Forge," https://www.nps.gov/vafo/learn/historyculture/valley-forge-history-and-significance.htm.

86 Bodle, *Winter*, p. 253; Greenwalt, *Valley Forge*, pp. 115–16; Trussell, *Birthplace*, 115.

87 Lockhart, *Drillmaster*, p. 166.

88 Lender and Stone, *Fatal Sunday*, pp. 272, 406–07.

89 Lender and Stone, *Fatal Sunday*, pp. 272, 406–07.

90 General Orders, June 29, 1778, *Founders Online,* National Archives, https://founders.archives.gov/documents/Washington/03-15-02-0632.

91 Lockhart, *Drillmaster*, p. 166.

92 Lender and Stone, *Fatal Sunday*, p. 375.

93 Martin and Lender, *Respectable Army*, p. 113.

94 Greenwalt, *Valley Forge*, pp. 114–15.

95 George Washington to Patrick Henry, February 19, 1778, *Founders Online,* National Archives, https://founders.archives.gov/documents/Washington/03-13-02-0503; Harris and Ecelbarger, "Continental Army Numerical Strength at Valley Forge," https://allthingsliberty.com/2021/05/a-reconsideration-of-continental-army-numerical-strength-at-valley-forge/. About 3,600 sick men were left at Valley Forge in June 1778. Thomas Buchanan Read, "Head-Quarters," in *Wagoner of the Alleghenies: A Poem of the Days of Seventy-Six* (Philadelphia, PA: J.B. Lippincott, 1863), pp. 164–65.

CHAPTER 4

1 George Washington to Samuel Huntington, May 31, 1780, *Founders Online*, National Archives, https://founders.archives.gov/documents/Washington/03-26-02-0178.

2 Richard Caswell to Horatio Gates, July 30, 1780, in Walter Clark, ed., *The Colonial and State Records of North Carolina* (hereafter *CSRNC*), 26 vols (Raleigh, NC: Gale, Making of Modern Law, 1895–1907), 14:515–16.

3 Otho Holland Williams, "A Narrative of the Campaign of 1780," in William Johnson, *Sketches of the Life and Correspondence of Nathanael Greene* (Charleston, SC: A. E. Miller, 1822), 1:485–510.

4 Charles Magill to Magill (his father), August 1780, *CSRNC*, 14:584–85.

5 Lord Cornwallis to Henry Clinton, August 23, 1780, *CSRNC*, 15:273–76.

6 Lord Cornwallis to Lord Germain, Sept 19, 1780, *CSRNC*, 15:278–82; Benjamin F. Stevens, *The Campaign in Virginia, 1781: An Exact Reprint of Six Rare Pamphlets on the Clinton-Cornwallis Controversy*, 2 vols. (London: British Library, Historical Print Editions, 1888), 1:65; Ferling, *Winning Independence*, p. 322.

7 Ian Saberton, "Cornwallis and the Autumn Campaign of 1780," July 18, 2017, *Journal of the American Revolution*, https://allthingsliberty.com/2017/07/cornwallis-autumn-campaign-1780-advance-camden-charlotte/.

8 John S. Pancake, *This Destructive War: The British Campaign in the Carolinas, 1780–1782* (Tuscaloosa: University of Alabama Press, 2003), pp. 117–18.

9 William Campbell to Arthur Campbell, October 20, 1780, in Lyman C. Draper, *King's Mountain and its Heroes* (Cincinnati, OH: P.G. Thompson, 1881), p. 526.

10 John Buchanan, *Road to Guilford Courthouse: The American Revolution in the Carolinas* (Hoboken, NJ: John Wiley & Sons, 1997), p. 235.

11 John R. Maass, "From Cowpens to Guilford Courthouse," in Edward G. Lengel, ed., *The 10 Key Campaigns of the American Revolution* (Washington, DC: Regnery History, 2020), pp. 177–78.

12 Nathanael Greene to William H. Harrington, December 4, 1780, *Greene Papers*, 6:519.

13 Nathanael Greene to Abner Nash, December 6, 1780, *Greene Papers*, 6:533–34; Nathanael Greene to Henry Knox, December 7, 1780, *Greene Papers*, 6:547.

14 Nathanael Greene to Thomas Jefferson, December 6, 1780, *Founders Online,* National Archives, https://founders.archives.gov/documents/Jefferson/01-04-02-0222.

15 Nathanael Greene to Thomas Sumter, January 15, 1781, *Greene Papers,* 7:125.

16 Abner Nash to Samuel Huntington, October 6, 1780, *CSRNC,* 15:98–99.

17 Daniel Morgan to Nathanael Greene, January 19, 1781, *Greene Papers,* 7:152–55.

18 Lord Cornwallis to Lord Rawdon, January 25, 1781, in Ian Saberton, ed., *The Cornwallis Papers: The Campaigns of 1780 and 1781 in the Southern Theatre of the American Revolutionary War,* 6 vols. (Uckfield, UK: Naval & Military Press, Ltd, 2010), 3:252; Lawrence E. Babits and Joshua B. Howard, *Long, Obstinate, and Bloody: The Battle of Guilford Courthouse* (Chapel Hill: University of North Carolina Press, 2009), pp. 15–16; Andrew Waters, *To the End of the World: Nathanael Greene, Charles Cornwallis, and the Race to the Dan* (Yardley, PA: Westholme, 2020), p. 122.

19 Nathanael Greene to Baron von Steuben, February 3, 1781, *Greene Papers,* 7:244n; Nathanael Greene to George Washington, February 9, 1781, *Greene Papers,* 7:267; Tarleton, *Campaigns,* pp. 225–26.

20 Nathanael Greene to Isaac Huger, January 30, 1781, *Greene Papers,* 7:219–20.

21 "Proceedings of a Council of War," February 9, 1781, *Greene Papers,* 7:261–62.

22 "Proceedings of a Council of War," February 9, 1781, *Greene Papers,* 7:261–62; Nathanael Greene to Abner Nash, February 9, 1781, *Greene Papers,* 7:263; Nathanael Greene to N.C. Board of War, December 7, 1780, *Greene Papers,* 6:548–49. The Dan River is a tributary of the Roanoke River.

23 Nathanael Greene to George Washington, February 9, 1781, *Greene Papers,* 7:267–69.

24 Henry Lee, *The Revolutionary War Memoirs of General Henry Lee* (New York: Da Capo Press, 1998), p. 236; Nathanael Greene to Edward Carrington, December 4, 1780, *Greene Papers,* 6:516.

25 Nathanael Greene to George Washington, February 15, 1781, *Greene Papers,* 7:293.

26 For examples of these interpretations, see Waters, *To the End of the World;* Larry Aaron, *The Race to the Dan: The Retreat That Rescued the American Revolution* (South Boston, VA.: Halifax County Historical Society, 2007); Nathaniel Philbrick, *In the Hurricane's Eye: The Genius*

of George Washington and the Victory at Yorktown (New York: Viking, 2018); and Babits and Howard, *Long, Obstinate and Bloody*, p. 13, in which the authors state improbably that "the 'Race to the Dan' began shortly after the battle of Cowpens ended."

27 John R. Maass, *The Battle of Guilford Courthouse: A Most Desperate Engagement* (Charleston, SC: The History Press, 2020), p. 199n.

28 Lee, *Memoirs*, p. 236–37.

29 Banastre Tarleton, *A History of the Campaigns of 1780 and 1781 in the Southern Provinces of North America.* (London: T. Cadell, 1787), p. 229.

30 Pension application of John Hewitt, Botetourt County, Virginia, W2618, www.southerncampaign.org.

31 Nathanael Greene to John Butler, February 17, 1781, *Greene Papers*, 7:299.

32 Nathanael Greene to Thomas Jefferson, March 10, 1781, *Greene Papers*, 7:419–20.

33 John C. Dann, ed., *The Revolution Remembered: Eyewitness Accounts of the War for Independence* (Chicago, IL: University of Chicago Press, 1980), p. 202.

34 Ian Saberton, "Cornwallis and the Winter Campaign, January to April, 1781," *Journal of the American Revolution*, April 24, 2020, https://allthingsliberty.com/2020/04/cornwallis-and-the-winter-campaign-january-to-april-1781/; Pension application of Phillip Russell W2575, www.southerncampaign.org; Pension application of William Lorance (Lowrance) S31217, www.southerncampaign.org

35 Daniel Murphy, *William Washington: An American Light Dragoon* (Yardley, PA: Westholme Publishing, 2014), pp. 101–03; Pension application of Robert Love S8858, www.southerncampaign.org.

36 Nathanael Greene to Isaac Huger, February 5, 1781, *Greene Papers*, 7:252; Nathanael Greene to Thomas Jefferson, March 16, 1781, *Greene Papers*, 7:441; St George Tucker, "The Southern Campaign, 1781: From Guilford Courthouse to the Siege of York…", *The Magazine of American History*, 7 (1881), 39; Nathanael Greene to Henry Lee, March 14, 1781, *Greene Papers*, 7:430; Babits and Howard, *Long, Obstinate, and Bloody*, p. 50; Lord Cornwallis to Lord Germain, March 17, 1781, *Cornwallis Papers*, 4:17; Nathanael Greene to Samuel Huntington, March 16, 1781, *Greene Papers*, 7:433.

37 Don N. Haigst, ed., *A British Soldier's Story: Roger Lamb's Narrative of the American Revolution* (Baraboo, WI: Ballindoch Press, 2004), p. 84.

38 Daniel Morgan to Nathanael Greene, February 20, 1781, *Greene Papers*, 7:324.

39 Pension application of Nathan Slade, W6071, www.southerncampaign.org.

40 Tarleton, *Campaigns*, p. 271.

41 Tarleton, *Campaigns*, p. 273; Nathanael Greene to Samuel Huntington, March 16, 1781, *Greene Papers*, 7:434.

42 Lee, *Memoirs*, p. 278.

43 See note 4 in Nathanael Greene to Jethro Sumner, February 18, 1781, *Greene Papers*, 7:312.

44 Tarleton, *Campaigns*, pp. 275–76.

45 Babits and Howard, *Long, Obstinate, and Bloody*, p. 119; Nathanael Greene to Samuel Huntington, March 16, 1781, *Greene Papers*, 7:435; Otho H. Williams to Josias Carveill, March 17, 1781, Guilford Courthouse National Military Park files.

46 Pension application of Joseph Dameron S8310, www .southerncampaign.org.

47 Pension application of Lewis Griffin, S21248, www.southerncampaign .org.

48 Nathanael Greene to Samuel Huntington, March 16, 1781, *Greene Papers*, 7:433–35; Babits and Howard, *Long*, pp. 142–69, 221; Murphy, *Washington*, p. 115.

49 Charles Magill to Thomas Jefferson, March 16, 1781, Julien P. Boyd, ed. *The Papers of Thomas Jefferson* (Princeton, NJ: Princeton University Press, 1950) 5:162–63.

50 Nathanael Greene to Catherine Greene, March 18, 1781, *Greene Papers*, 6:446.

51 Lee, *Memoirs*, pp. 284, 286.

52 Lord Cornwallis to Henry Clinton, April 10, 1781, *Cornwallis Papers*, 4:110.

53 Nathanael Greene to George Washington, March 29, 1781, *Greene Papers*, 7:481–82; Nathanael Greene to James Emmett, April 3, 1781, *Greene Papers*, 8:481.

54 Nathanael Greene to Samuel Huntington, March 16, 1781, *Greene Papers*, 7:433–35; Nathanael Greene to Samuel Huntington, March 30, 1781, *Greene Papers*, 8:7–9; Nathanael Greene to Thomas Sumter, March 16, 1781, *Greene Papers*, 7:442–43.

55 Abraham Clark to Elias Dayton, April 1, 1781, in Paul Smith, ed., *Letters of Delegates to Congress, 1774–1789*, 26 vols. (Washington, DC: Library of Congress, 1976–2000), 17:111.

56 Tucker, "Southern Campaign," pp. 40–42.

57 Otho H. Williams to Josias Carveill, March 17, 1781, Guilford Courthouse National Military Park files.

58 Lee, *Memoirs*, p. 286.
59 Thomas E. Baker, *Another Such Victory* (Fort Washington, PA: Eastern Acorn Press, 1981), p. 1; Henry Clinton, *Observations on Mr. Stedman's* History of the American War (London: J. Debrett, 1794), p. 17.
60 Babits and Howard, *Long, Obstinate and Bloody*, p. xiv; Thomas Jefferson to John Campbell, November 10, 1822, *Founders Online*, National Archives, https://founders.archives.gov/documents/Jefferson/98-01-02-3152.
61 William Willcox, ed., *The American Revolution: Sir Henry Clinton's Narrative of His Campaigns, 1775–1782* (New Haven, CT: Yale University Press, 1954), p. 206.
62 Robert W. Blythe, Maureen A. Carroll, and Steven H. Moffson, "Kings Mountain National Military Park Historic Resource Study," May 1995, National Park Service, p. 1.
63 Harold Allen Skinner Jr, *The Staff Ride Handbook for The Battle for Kings Mountain, 7 October 1780* (Fort Leavenworth, KS: Combat Studies Institute Press, 2020), p. 1, 70.
64 Ferling, *Miracle*, p. 574.
65 Blythe, "Kings Mountain National Military Park Historic Resource Study," p. 1; Bob Thompson, *Revolutionary Roads: Searching for the War That Made America Independent... and All the Places It Could Have Gone Terribly Wrong* (New York: Twelve, 2023), p. 290.
66 Katelyn J. Ventura, "The Battle of Cowpens: A Turning Point in the American Revolution," August 28, 2020, *NCO Journal*, https://www.armyupress.army.mil/Journals/NCO-Journal/Archives/2020/August/Battle-of-Cowpens/#.
67 Babits, *A Devil of a Whipping*, p. xiii.
68 Don Higginbotham in Billias, *Washington's Generals*, pp. 291–315.
69 Mark M. Boatner, *Encyclopedia of the American Revolution*, 3rd ed. (Mechanicsburg, PA: Stackpole Books, 1994), p. 298.
70 Henry Lumpkin, *From Savannah to Yorktown: The American Revolution in the South* (New York: Paragon House Publishers 1981), p. 116.
71 John Moncure, *The Cowpens Staff Ride and Battlefield Tour* (Fort Leavenworth, KS: Combat Studies Institute, 1996), pp. 31, 43–44, 63.
72 Henry P. Johnston, *The Yorktown Campaign and the Surrender of Cornwallis* (New York: Harper and Brothers, 1881), p. 23.
73 Johnston, *Yorktown*, p. 24.
74 Nathanael Greene to Daniel Morgan, January 19, 1781, *Greene Papers*, 7:146–47.

75 Nathanael Greene to Thomas Sumter, February 9, 1781, *Greene Papers*, 7:266.

76 Nathanael Greene to Thomas Jefferson, February 15, 1781, *Greene Papers*, 7:291; Nathanael Greene to Richard Caswell, February 16, 1781, *Greene Papers*, 7:295.

77 Don H. Doyle, *The Cause of All Nations: An International History of the American Civil War* (New York: Basic Books, 2014), p. 28.

CHAPTER 5

1 Sarah Bird Wright, "The Victory of Yorktown: A Bicentennial Celebration, August 25, 1981," *The Christian Science Monitor*, https://www.csmonitor.com/1981/0825/082547.html.

2 Ben A. Franklin, "Even British Cheery At Fete Of Yorktown," *New York Times*, October 20, 1981, p. 7.

3 Ronald W. Reagan, "Remarks at the Bicentennial Observance of the Battle of Yorktown in Virginia," October 19, 1981, https://www.reaganlibrary.gov/archives/speech/remarks-bicentennial-observance-battle-yorktown-virginia.

4 Denis Collins, "Governor Opens Celebration Of Yorktown Amid Pageantry," *The Washington Post*, October 16, 1981, https://www.washingtonpost.com/archive/local/1981/10/17/governor-opens-celebration-of-yorktown-amid-pageantry/01e00fe8-9b72-48a1-9b22-17ac6427c172/; Denis Collins, "Summer Soldiers, Spectators Rejoice at Yorktown Battle," *The Washington Post*, October 18, 1981, https://www.washingtonpost.com/archive/politics/1981/10/18/summer-soldiers-spectators-rejoice-at-yorktown-battle/a29c30f9-f633-4209-bb8a-90f0979aabf9/;

5 "Report of the Virginia Independence Bicentennial Commission to the Governor and the General Assembly of Virginia," State Document No. 8 (Richmond, 1986), pp. 19–20.

6 Christine O. Hardyman, ed., "Department of the Army Historical Summary, Fiscal Year 1981" (Washington, DC: US Army Center of Military History, 1988), p. 3.

7 "Report of the Virginia Independence Bicentennial Commission," pp. 20–21.

8 Johnson, *Yorktown*, pp. 11–12.

9 H.L. Landers, *The Virginia Campaign and the Blockade and Siege of Yorktown, 1781* (Washington, DC: US Government Printing Office, 1931), p. 1.

10 Ferling, *Winning Independence*, p. xviii.

11 Robert L. Tonsetic, *1781: The Decisive Year of the Revolutionary War* (Havertown, PA: Casemate Publishers, 2011), p. 206.

12 Jerome Greene, *The Guns of Independence: The Siege of Yorktown, 1781* (New York: Savas Beatie, 2009), p. xi.

13 Lord Cornwallis to Henry Clinton, June 30, 1781, *Cornwallis Papers*, 5:105.

14 Lord Cornwallis to William Phillips, April 10, 1781, *Cornwallis Papers*, 4:114–15.

15 Johnston, *Yorktown*, p. 23.

16 Robert Fallaw and Marion W. Stoer, "The Old Dominion Under Fire: The Chesapeake Invasions, 1779–1781," in Ernest M. Eller, ed., *Chesapeake Bay in the American Revolution* (Centreville, MD: Tidewater Publishers, 1981), p. 443. Thanks to Dr J. Britt McCarley for drawing Collier's quote to my attention.

17 Johnston, *Yorktown*, p. 19.

18 Lord Cornwallis to Henry Clinton, May 26, 1781, *Cornwallis Papers*, 5:89.

19 Marquis de Lafayette to Chevalier de laa Luzerne, May 22, 1781, in Stanley J. Idzerda, ed., *Lafayette in the Age of the American Revolution: Selected Letters and Papers, 1776–1790*, 4 vols. (Ithaca, NY: Cornell University Press, 1989), 4:120.

20 Tarleton, *Campaigns*, pp. 297–98.

21 Tarleton, *Campaigns*, p. 300; Lord Cornwallis to Henry Clinton, July 8, 1781, *Cornwallis Papers*, 5:117; Lord Cornwallis to Alexander Leslie, July 8, 1781, *Cornwallis Papers*, 5:179.

22 Henry Clinton to Lord Cornwallis, May 29, 1781, *Cornwallis Papers*, 5:118.

23 Lord Cornwallis to Henry Clinton, July 26, 1781, *Cornwallis Papers*, 6:15.

24 George Washington to John Laurens, April 9, 1781, *Founders Online*, National Archives, https://founders.archives.gov/documents/Washington/99-01-02-05346.

25 Robert Selig, *March to Victory: Washington, Rochambeau, and the Yorktown Campaign of 1781* (Washington, DC: US Army Center of Military History, 2007), pp. 13, 16–18.

26 Crèvecoeur quote is found at Diary entry: 8 July 1781, *Founders Online*, National Archives, https://founders.archives.gov/documents/Washington/01-03-02-0007-0003-0006.

27 Selig, *March to Victory*, pp. 20–21; Robert Selig, "L'expedition," in Don Hagist, ed., *Waging War in America, 1775–1783: Operational Challenges*

of Five Armies during the American Revolution (Warwick: Helion and Co, 2023), pp. 171–91.

28 *The Diaries of George Washington, 1 January 1771–5 November 1781*, ed. Donald Jackson (Charlottesville: University Press of Virginia, 1978), 3: 409–410.

29 George Washington to François-Joseph-Paul, Comte de Grasse-Tilly, August 17, 1781, *Founders Online,* National Archives, https://founders.archives.gov/documents/Washington/99-01-02-06712.

30 Barry, *Crisis in the Chesapeake*, p. 156.

31 George Washington to William Heath, August 19, 1781, *Founders Online,* National Archives, https://founders.archives.gov/documents/Washington/99-01-02-06729.

32 George Washington to Marquis de Lafayette, August 21, 1781, *Founders Online,* National Archives, https://founders.archives.gov/documents/Washington/99-01-02-06739.

33 George Washington to Samuel Miles, August 27, 1781, *Founders Online,* National Archives, https://founders.archives.gov/documents/Washington/99-01-02-0680.

34 Selig, *March to Victory*, pp. 23–24, 26–27.

35 George Washington to Thomas McKean, August 27, 1781, *Founders Online,* National Archives, https://founders.archives.gov/documents/Washington/99-01-02-06800.

36 George Washington to Thomas Nelson Jr, August 27, 1781, *Founders Online,* National Archives, https://founders.archives.gov/documents/Washington/99-01-02-06803.

37 Theodore Corbett, *A Maritime History of the American Revolutionary War* (Havertown, PA: Pen and Sword Books, 2023), p. 197.

38 Corbett, *A Maritime History*, p. 198.

39 George Washington to Marquis de Lafayette, August 21, 1781, *Founders Online,* National Archives, https://founders.archives.gov/documents/Washington/99-01-02-06739.

40 Lord Cornwallis to Henry Clinton, October 20, 1781, *Cornwallis Papers,* 6:128.

41 Lord Cornwallis to Henry Clinton, September 16, 1781, *Cornwallis Papers,* 6:35.

42 Thomas McKean to the Comte de Grasse, October 31, 1781, in Smith, *Letters of Delegates,* 18:173.

43 William H. Meyers, ed., "Diary of Captain James Duncan," *Pennsylvania Archives*, Second Series, (Harrisburg: E.K. Myers, 1890), 15:744–52.

44 George Washington to Thomas Sim Lee, September 15, 1781, *Founders Online,* National Archives, https://founders.archives.gov/documents/ Washington/99-01-02-06963.

45 George Washington to Thomas McKean, September 15, 1781, *Founders Online,* National Archives, https://founders.archives.gov/documents/ Washington/99-01-02-06965.

46 George Washington to William Davies, September 16, 1781, *Founders Online,* National Archives, https://founders.archives.gov/documents/ Washington/99-01-02-06973.

47 George Washington to Robert Howe, September 24, 1781, *Founders Online,* National Archives, https://founders.archives.gov/documents/ Washington/99-01-02-07011.

48 Diary entry: 28 September 1781, *Founders Online,* National Archives, https://founders.archives.gov/documents/Washington/01-03-02-0007 -0005-0007.

49 Henry Clinton to Lord Cornwallis, September 24, 1781, Number 157, in Stevens/Clinton, *Campaign in Virginia,* 2:160.

50 Lord Cornwallis to Henry Clinton, September 29, 1781, *Cornwallis Papers,* 6:36.

51 Lord Cornwallis to Henry Clinton, October 20, 1781, *Cornwallis Papers,* 6:126.

52 Henry Knox to John Adams, October 21, 1781, *Founders Online,* National Archives, https://founders.archives.gov/documents/ Adams/06-12-02-0020.

53 "October 1781," *Founders Online,* National Archives, https://founders .archives.gov/documents/Washington/01-03-02-0007-0006; Johann von Ewald, *Diary of the American War: A Hessian Journal,* trans. and ed. by Joseph P. Tustin (New Haven, CT: Yale University Press, 1979), p. 334.

54 Henry Knox to John Adams, October 21, 1781, *Founders Online,* National Archives, https://founders.archives.gov/documents/ Adams/06-12-02-0020.

55 Alexander Hamilton to Elizabeth Hamilton, October 12, 1781, *Founders Online,* National Archives, https://founders.archives.gov/ documents/Hamilton/01-02-02-1199.

56 Lord Cornwallis to Henry Clinton, October 15, 1781, *Cornwallis Papers,* 6:40; Myers, ed., "Diary of Captain James Duncan," p. 752; Elias Boudinot to Lewis Pintard, October 24, 1781, in Smith, *Letters of Delegates,* 18:164; Alexander Hamilton to Marquis de Lafayette, October 15, 1781, *Founders Online,* National Archives, https://founders.archives.gov/documents/Hamilton/01-02-02-1200

-0001; Marquis de Lafayette to George Washington, October 16, 1781, *Founders Online,* National Archives, https://founders.archives.gov/documents/Washington/99-01-02-07176; Henry Knox to John Adams, October 21, 1781, *Founders Online,* National Archives, https://founders.archives.gov/documents/Adams/06-12-02-0020.

57 Lord Cornwallis to Henry Clinton, October 15, 1781, *The London Chronicle,* November 29, 1781.

58 "October 1781," Washington Diary, *Founders Online,* National Archives, https://founders.archives.gov/documents/Washington/01-03-02-0007-0006.

59 Lord Cornwallis to Henry Clinton, October 20, 1781, *Cornwallis Papers,* 6:127.

60 Diary entry: 17 October 1781, *Founders Online,* National Archives, https://founders.archives.gov/documents/Washington/01-03-02-0007-0006-0011.

61 See transcript of the surrender articles at the Gilder Lehrman Institute of American History website, https://www.gilderlehrman.org/history-resources/spotlight-primary-source/surrender-british-general-cornwallis-americans-october.

62 Henry Knox to John Adams, October 21, 1781, *Founders Online,* National Archives, https://founders.archives.gov/documents/Adams/06-12-02-0020.

63 That evening Cornwallis declined an invitation for dinner at Washington's headquarters and sent O'Hara instead. Henry Knox to John Adams, October 21, 1781, *Founders Online,* National Archives, https://founders.archives.gov/documents/Adams/06-12-02-0020.

64 George Washington to Thomas McKean, October 19, 1781, *Founders Online,* National Archives, https://founders.archives.gov/documents/Washington/99-01-02-07206.

65 John Hanson to Philip Thomas, October 27, 1781, in Smith, *Letters of Delegates,* 18:166.

66 Alexander Hamilton to Vicomte de Noailles, November–December 1781, *Founders Online,* National Archives, https://founders.archives.gov/documents/Hamilton/01-26-02-0002-0072.

67 Thomas Jefferson to George Washington, October 28, 1781, *Founders Online,* National Archives, https://founders.archives.gov/documents/Washington/99-01-02-07308.

68 Elias Boudinot to Hannah Boudinot, October 21, 1781, in Smith, *Letters of Delegates,* 18:150–51.

69 Daniel of St Thomas Jenifer to Thomas Lee, October 22, 1781, in Smith, *Letters of Delegates,* 18:152.

70 John Hanson to Philip Thomas, October 23, 1781, in Smith, *Letters of Delegates*, 18:160.

71 Thomas Nelson Jr to Virginia Delegates, October 20, 1781, *Founders Online*, National Archives, https://founders.archives.gov/documents/Madison/01-03-02-0143.

72 James Madison to Edmund Pendleton, October 30, 1781, in Smith, *Letters of Delegates*, 18:168.

73 James Madison to Edmund Pendleton, October 30, 1781, in Smith, *Letters of Delegates*, 18:169.

74 Thomas McKean to William Heath, November 31, 1781, in Smith, *Letters of Delegates*, 18:177.

75 Benjamin Hawkins to Abner Nash, November 17, 1781, in Smith, *Letters of Delegates*, 18:203.

76 Greene, *Guns of Independence*, pp. 305–06.

77 John Hanson to George Washington, November 10, 1781, in Smith, *Letters of Delegates*, 18:190-91.

78 Robert Selig, *March to Victory*, p. 47.

79 Ronald W. Reagan, "Remarks at the Bicentennial Observance of the Battle of Yorktown in Virginia," October 19, 1981, https://www.reaganlibrary.gov/archives/speech/remarks-bicentennial-observance-battle-yorktown-virginia.

CONCLUSION

1 Joseph J. Ellis, *Revolutionary Summer: The Birth of American Independence* (New York: Alfred A. Knopf, 2013), pp. xvii, xx.

2 Ellis, *Summer*, p. 205.

3 Ellis, *Summer*, pp. 205, 209.

4 O'Shaughnessy, *The Men Who Lost America*, p. 97. Lefkowitz, in *Washington's Revenge* (p. 11), argues that December 1, 1776, was the closest the British came to winning the war as Cornwallis was only one mile away from Washington and significantly outnumbered him.

5 Page Smith, *A New Age Now Begins: A People's History of the American Revolution*, 2 vols. (New York: McGraw-Hill, 1976), 2:944.

6 John Ferling, "Myths of the American Revolution," January 2010, *Smithsonian Magazine*, https://www.smithsonianmag.com/history/myths-of-the-american-revolution-10941835/.

7 Ferling, *Winning Independence*, p. 95.

8 Patrick Henry oration at St John's Church, Richmond, VA, March 23, 1775, http://hrlibrary.umn.edu/education/libertyordeath.html.

Index